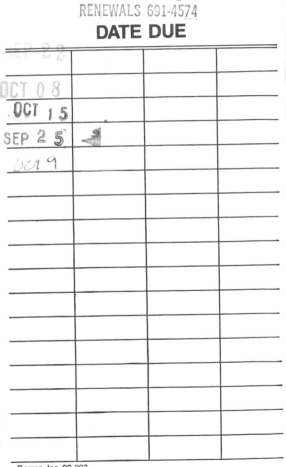

Klaus Fuchs, Atom Spy

Klaus Fuchs, Atom Spy

Robert Chadwell Williams

Harvard University Press
Cambridge, Massachusetts
and London, England   1987

Library of Congress Cataloging-in-Publication Data
Williams, Robert Chadwell, 1938–
  Klaus Fuchs, atom spy.

  Bibliography: p.
  Includes index.
  1. Fuchs, Klaus Emil Julius, 1911–   . 2. Spies—
Soviet Union—Biography. 3. Spies—Great Britain—
Biography. 4. Spies—United States—Biography.
5. Espionage—Great Britain—History—20th century.
6. Espionage—United States—History—20th century.
7. Nuclear weapons—Great Britain. 8. Nuclear weapons—
United States. I. Title.
UB271.R9F838   1987   327.1'2'0924 [B]   87-8672
ISBN 0-674-50507-7

Acknowledgments

In writing this book I depended heavily on the copious U.S. government archival materials obtained through the 1966 Freedom of Information Act, including the voluminous FBI file on the "Foocase" and on Klaus Fuchs's confessions. Numerous documents concerning Fuchs in Great Britain and Canada were not made available and are likely to remain closed. My key sources were people rather than archives, and I am grateful to the many who helped me understand the causes and effects of the Fuchs case. The conclusions, of course, are mine.

Many individuals assisted me in the preparation of this book, which could not have been completed without their time, effort, and memory. For archival assistance, I would like to thank Roger Anders, U.S. Department of Energy; Ian Carter, Science Museum Library, London; Susan K. Falb, Federal Bureau of Investigation; Allison Kerr, Los Alamos National Laboratory; Robert Lyon, Pendle Hill, Pennsylvania; Ronald Swerczek, U.S. National Archives; James M. Whalen, Public Archives of Canada; and Benedikt Zobrist, Harry S Truman Presidential Library.

Among those who helped by discussing aspects of the Fuchs case with me are, in the United States: Hans Bethe, Oscar Bunemann, Philip L. Cantelon, Mrs. John Cimperman, Lawrence Cranberg, Richard Feynman, Naomi French, John Kenneth Galbraith, Arthur Goldberg, Lindsay Helmholtz, Gregg Herken, Richard Hewlett, Jack Holl, Arnold Kramish, Robert Lamphere, David Lipkin, Kenneth Nichols, Sylvia O'Hickey, John Saxon, Martin J. Sherwin, Harold Shipton, Bradley F. Smith, Henry

Smyth, Edward Teller, Arthur Wahl, and Samuel Weissman; in Great Britain: Christopher Andrew, Mrs. Egon Bretscher, Lord Brian Flowers, Mrs. Otto Frisch, Martin Gilbert, Anthony Glees, Margaret Gowing, F. H. Hinsley, David Holloway, Percy Hoskins, R. V. Jones, Nicholas Kurti, A. S. Martin, Zhores Medvedev, Sir Nevill Mott, Sir Rudolf Peierls, Sir Michael Perrin, Max Perutz, Chapman Pincher, William J. Skardon, George R. Strauss, H. N. V. Temperley, Hugh Thomas, and Sir Dick White; in Germany, Jan Foitzik and Werner Roeder; and in Denmark, Aage Bohr.

I am especially indebted to my literary agent, Elizabeth Case, and my assistant, Venita Lake, for their constant attempts to improve my prose, and to Washington University in St. Louis for providing me with a creative environment for teaching and writing. The Alfred P. Sloan Foundation has also been generous in its support of my research and teaching in the field of nuclear energy history. Fellowship aid in 1985 enabled me to utilize the resources of the Hoover Presidential Library in West Branch, Iowa, and of St. Anthony's College, Oxford. Arthur Rosenthal and Howard Boyer of Harvard University Press were supportive and encouraging, and Peg Anderson significantly improved the organization and writing throughout.

Finally, my wife, Ann, and my children, Peter, Margaret, and Katharine, have been always tolerant of my bookish ways and my preoccupation with history as detective work. To them and to all my friends and colleagues I owe a debt of gratitude for supporting me in my attempt to understand what was once called, and may still be, "the crime of the century."

Contents

Illustrations

Following Page 104

Klaus Fuchs in 1933, twenty-two years old

Jurgen Kuczynski about 1948

Sonia (Ruth Kuczynski/Ursula Hamburger) in East Germany about 1951

Klaus Fuchs at Los Alamos, 1944 (Los Alamos National Laboratory)

Dr. J. Robert Oppenheimer and Major General Leslie Groves at Alamogordo, New Mexico, July 1945 (UPI/Bettmann Newsphotos)

President Harry S Truman and Secretary of War Henry L. Stimson, August 1945 (UPI/Bettmann Newsphotos)

Britain's Atomic Research Center at Harwell, 1948 (UPI/Bettmann Newsphotos)

FBI Director J. Edgar Hoover, February 1950 (UPI/Bettmann Newsphotos)

Michael Perrin leaving Bow Street Court, February 10, 1950 (UPI/Bettmann Newsphotos)

William J. Skardon and Henry Arnold, March 1, 1950 (UPI/Bettmann Newsphotos)

Harry Gold leaving federal court in Philadelphia, December 11, 1950 (UPI/Bettmann Newsphotos)

Clement Attlee, October 1955 (UPI/Bettmann Newsphotos)

Klaus Fuchs after his release from prison, June 23, 1959 (UPI/Bettmann Newsphotos)

Klaus Fuchs, Atom Spy

CHAPTER · 1

Secrets

Secrecy is as essential to intelligence as vestments and incense to a Mass, or darkness to a spiritualist seance, and must at all costs be maintained, quite irrespective of whether or not it serves any purpose.

— *Malcolm Muggeridge*

On January 27, 1950, a passenger got off a train in London's Paddington Station and nervously shook hands with a man waiting on the platform. The passenger, Emil Julius Klaus Fuchs, thirty-eight years old, was dark haired and balding. About five feet eight inches tall, he had a sallow complexion and wore wire-rimmed glasses. His clipped English speech was overlaid with a strong German accent. The man he had arranged to meet, William James Skardon, a counterintelligence officer assigned to Scotland Yard, was Britain's top spycatcher. Together the two men walked a few blocks to the War Office, where Fuchs dictated a long statement, which Skardon wrote down and Fuchs signed. In it, Fuchs confessed that from 1942 to 1949, while working on British and American nuclear weapons, he had deliberately and systematically given atomic bomb secrets to the Soviet Union.

The story Fuchs had to tell was as bleak as the London winter. His willingness to tell it was the result of several months of patient and sympathetic cultivation by Skardon. The process had begun on October 12, 1949, when Fuchs—head of the theoretical physics division at the British Atomic Energy Research Establishment in Harwell, Berkshire—revealed to the security officer there that he, Fuchs, might soon become a security risk. His father had been offered a professorship in theology at the University of Leipzig in East Germany and was about to move there from Frankfurt. Fuchs was worried, he said, that having a relative living in a communist country might compromise his position at Harwell. He asked the security officer, Henry Arnold, if he should resign.

Arnold, a personal friend, offered no advice but simply asked Fuchs what he would do if Soviet agents put pressure on him to reveal nuclear secrets. Fuchs said he really did not know.

Alerted by Arnold to a potential security lapse, William Skardon made an appointment to visit Harwell and talk personally with Fuchs about his situation. On December 21, in Fuchs's office, the two men met for the first time, and Skardon listened quietly to Fuchs's review of his life story. When he had finished, Skardon, in a calm voice, informed him that he was suspected of having given secret information to the Soviet Union.

Fuchs seemed surprised. He smiled and said, "I don't think so." Then he seemed bewildered. "I don't understand. I have not done any such thing." Over the course of four hours of conversation, Fuchs maintained his innocence and ignorance, indicating only that he might have to resign from his position at Harwell. On December 30 and again on January 10 he was told that it might be best if he resigned, given his father's move to Leipzig.

When Fuchs next met Skardon at Arnold's office on January 13, he appeared pale and agitated. During the morning he said little. But after the two men had lunch in the nearby town of Abingdon, Fuchs finally confessed to Skardon that he had given the Russians secret materials on the atomic bomb.

For days nothing happened. On Sunday, January 22, Fuchs rang up his friend Arnold and expressed his willingness to talk. During lunch the next day Fuchs told Arnold that he was opposed to the present policies of Stalin and the USSR. He also said he wanted to see Skardon. At 11 A.M. on Tuesday the 24th, when Skardon arrived at Fuchs's office in Prefab no. 17, Fuchs told him, "It's up to me now."

Fuchs appeared to be under considerable mental stress. "I told him to unburden his mind and clear his conscience by telling me the full story," Skardon noted. And Fuchs did, admitting that for eight years he had conducted espionage for the Soviet Union.

But the details were to emerge only gradually. On January 26, in their next meeting, Fuchs confessed that he had given nuclear information to "foreign agents" and had met six times with them before going to New York in 1943 to work on the supersecret Manhattan Project to build the world's first atomic bomb. The next day, in his statement to Skardon, Fuchs described technical data on atomic research only in very broad terms. Ironically, in Fuchs's mind Skardon did not have a sufficiently high security clearance to be trusted with such important classified information. But he agreed to make a second confession, spelling out the technical details, to Michael Perrin, deputy comptroller for atomic energy policy at the Ministry of Supply, whom Fuchs had known since 1942. Fuchs then returned alone to Harwell by train.

Late that night Henry Arnold received a report that a light was on in Fuchs's office at Harwell. Arnold promptly let himself into a room across the hall, climbed up on a cupboard, and peered over a partition into the office. Fuchs was poring over papers at his desk, smoking cigarettes in silence. Was he planning to destroy evidence? Commit suicide? Flee the country? Arnold waited, but Fuchs continued reading. He left for an hour, returned for more reading, and then drove home. After that, his office remained untouched until the day of his arrest.

On January 30 Fuchs met with Skardon once again at the War Office, where he made his technical confession to Perrin. Fuchs spent most of the day reviewing his eight-year espionage career and explaining just what he had told the Russians. Late in the afternoon he was allowed to return to Harwell, where he was kept under postal and telephone surveillance.

Signed copies of the two confessions were dispatched to the attorney general, who authorized prosecution of Fuchs under the Official Secrets Act of 1911. If the Soviet Union had been an enemy and not an ally of Britain during World War II, Fuchs might have been charged with treason, a capital crime. The charges were drawn up, and Prime Minister Clement Attlee was informed.

On February 2 Perrin telephoned Fuchs and asked, "Can you come up again this afternoon?" Fuchs arrived at Perrin's London office around 2:30 P.M. and waited for more than an hour in the outer chamber before Commander Leonard J. Burt, chief inspector for Scotland Yard, finally arrived. Perrin introduced the two men and left the room. Burt read the charges and told Fuchs he was under arrest.

Fuchs was arraigned on February 3, but little official information was given to the press. Nevertheless the case exploded in the newspapers: one of the three top scientific officers at Harwell had been arrested as an "atom spy" working for the Russians. The British press quickly compared Fuchs with Alan Nunn May, a physicist who in 1946 was sentenced to ten years' imprisonment on similar charges. The American press reported that Fuchs had worked for the Manhattan Project at Los Alamos, New Mexico, from 1943 to 1946, when the atomic bomb was being developed, and that he had represented Great Britain as recently as 1949 at the British-Canadian-American talks on declassification of nuclear information. Fuchs's arrest just before the resumption of those talks on February 9 had occurred, it was said, only because of a tip from America's own Federal Bureau of Investigation and its remarkably vigilant bulldog chief, J. Edgar Hoover. Hoover saw no reason to disavow this explanation.

At Fuchs's hearing on February 10, the prosecutor, Christmas Humphreys, read the charges and noted that only three witnesses were to be called: Skardon, Arnold, and Perrin. Fuchs's statement to Skardon was described as a "complete confession of the charges." The confession, plus the testimony of the three witnesses, would be the only evidence in the case for the prosecution.

Despite the press's interest in Fuchs's espionage activities, in Britain a curtain of official secrecy descended over the actual facts of the case pending trial later that month. Fuchs's full confession has not to this day been made available to the public. British intelligence reportedly feared that such a detailed confession, coming as it did from a trained spy, might well be simply another deception, an "overconfession" designed to provide some final bits of information to the Russians once it was declassified. Thus the case of Klaus Fuchs became a public sensation, but the details of his spying were not a matter of public record.

What actual information had Fuchs given the Russians about the atomic bomb? How much had he told them about plans for a hydrogen bomb? What were his motives? How had British and American security failed so long to discover the traitor in their midst? And how had they finally made the discovery? Why had he not fled the country? Or simply kept quiet? The answers to these and a multitude of other questions involved British and American intelligence secrets, as well as atomic espionage, and simply could not be brought up in court.

At his trial on March 1, 1950, in the grim criminal court building known as the Old Bailey, Klaus Fuchs, expressionless and seemingly nonchalant, listened quietly to the charges against him. When asked to plead, he whispered that he was indeed guilty. The presiding judge, characterizing the crime as "only thinly differentiated from high treason," convicted Fuchs as charged and sentenced him to the maximum term, fourteen years in prison.

In the United States, evidence supplied in the confession led the FBI to Harry Gold, Fuchs's American courier. Gold's confession, in turn, led to the Soviet spy ring that included David Greenglass and Julius and Ethel Rosenberg.[1] The Rosenberg case became the focus of the American public's and the historians' concern with atomic espionage, which J. Edgar Hoover called "the crime of the century." In spite of widespread doubts about the Rosenbergs' guilt, they were convicted of treason and executed. In contrast, Klaus Fuchs, after serving nine years of his fourteen-year sentence, was released from prison and allowed to leave England. He went to East Germany, where he directed a nuclear physics laboratory until his retirement. He now lives quietly outside Dresden.

In Britain the case vanished from public view within days of the verdict. Fuchs's spy contacts in England were never apprehended. British investigators, treating Fuchs's espionage as the work of a lone scientist disenchanted with his adopted country, did not pursue the case, and it was forgotten.

Today much information has recently become available, including Atomic Energy Commission files and FBI files on Fuchs's statements and on his and Gold's confessions, as well as memoirs published by Fuchs's communist associates in England. From these and other sources it is clear that many aspects of the case were kept from the public in order to conceal important political secrets, not just atomic ones.

One political secret was how Fuchs's spying was discovered in the first place. We now know that in 1949, when American government cryptographers decoded some messages sent from the Soviet embassy in New York to Moscow during World War II, they came upon a report by Fuchs on work being done at Los Alamos. To conceal from the Soviet Union that their codes had been deciphered, the American and British security services sought to have Fuchs confess to his actions. The result was the series of interviews with Skardon and Perrin. The breaking of Soviet codes was never mentioned during the prosecution of the case and remained a government secret for decades.

Another political secret was that Fuchs was known to be a communist even before he arrived in England as a refugee from Nazi Germany in 1933. From a Gestapo report and from information provided by a German agent working for the British in the city of Kiel, the British Home Office knew of Fuchs's membership in the German communist party (KPD). And Fuchs continued to express communist views while he lived in England. Even so, the British government, which was desperate to recruit scientists for the war effort, hired him in 1941 to work on the British bomb project and repeatedly cleared him for top-secret work.

Was British security merely hasty or incompetent in not ferreting out Fuchs's communist ties, or were there more sinister reasons for granting him easy access to secret weapons information? We now can see that his spying was part of a much larger Soviet effort to penetrate and control the British intelligence services, especially those sections of MI5 (domestic security, analogous to the FBI) and MI6 (foreign intelligence, somewhat similar to the CIA) that were concerned with Soviet espionage. Guy Burgess, Donald Maclean, Anthony Blunt, and H. A. R. (Kim) Philby all worked for British intelligence during the war, and all, we now know, were Soviet agents.[2] Some people in the highest realms of

British intelligence had a grave interest in making sure that the Fuchs case did not lead to disclosures about these Soviet inroads.

One of the most important facts that the British government concealed at the time of Fuchs's trial was that he was helping the British build their *own* atomic bomb, a project that was being kept secret from the public and one that the American government jealously opposed. Of course Fuchs and other British scientists at Harwell had brought back from their work at Los Alamos much knowledge and experience that was crucial to the British project. Anglo-American cooperation on nuclear research, already shaky, was further endangered by the Fuchs case. The British government was understandably eager to keep Fuchs's betrayal of secrets as quiet as possible.

The upcoming review of nuclear information exchange between the United States, Britain, and Canada was not the only political reason why the case was hushed up in England. A general election campaign was also under way, and publicity about a massive security lapse would be of little help to the Labour Party and Prime Minister Attlee.

Yet another political secret of the Fuchs case was that in fact he had *not* given the Russians any information of value concerning the hydrogen bomb. But the fear that he had done so was used to justify President Harry S Truman's decision to develop "the super." In 1950 the exaggerated news reports of Fuchs's treachery were a boon to those who argued for expanding the scope of weapons research.

The United States government had its own reasons for manipulating the public's perception of the facts in the case. In Czechoslovakia and in China, communism had achieved notable successes during the previous two years, and the Soviet Union had recently tested its first nuclear weapon. The FBI's discovery of a communist atom spy only accelerated the anticommunist sentiments being stirred up by Senator Joseph McCarthy and the Alger Hiss case. The FBI's use of wiretapping and other illegal clandestine activities to procure evidence in criminal cases seemed to be justified by these events.

In such a turbulent political atmosphere, it is not surprising that the Fuchs case seemed to offer support for the policy of maintaining national security through increased secrecy. The scientists, many said, would simply have to be brought into line if they were to be given access to national security information. The example of Klaus Fuchs stood as a warning to others that gaps in security would be identified and closed. During the Cold War the traditions of open scientific research, publication, and peer review gave way to greater classification of scientific information, restricted research, and loyalty oaths for scientists.

Yet secrecy and loyalty oaths had not kept Klaus Fuchs from perpetrating his crimes. He had worked in a world where security was supposedly maintained through secrecy, and he had publicly defended those rules, only to betray them privately. The case raises a number of disturbing questions about the sharing and concealing of scientific information from both enemies and friends. In the present nuclear age, is national security best achieved by allowing open scientific research or by imposing extensive restrictions? Put another way, what is the proper balance between security achieved through scientific advance and security assured through military secrecy? And finally, given the political as well as scientific secrets that became classified information in the Fuchs case, how do people in a democracy distinguish military and scientific secrets from political ones that simply restrict the public's right to know in the name of national security?

CHAPTER · 2

Inner Light, Party Line: The Red Foxes of Kiel

The only excitement a spy is likely to have is his last, when he is finally run to earth. An emotion similar to that experienced by the fox.

— *Alexander Foote,* Handbook for Spies, *1949*

Fuchs du hast die Gans gestohlen,
Gibt es wieder zu.

[Fox, you have stolen the goose.
Give it back.]

— *German nursery rhyme*

The story of Klaus Fuchs is in part a family tragedy that begins in Nazi Germany. He came from a long line of Protestant pastors, and his father, Emil, was a renowned Quaker leader. All of the members of his family—the "red foxes of Kiel," as a German newspaper called them for the color of their hair and the complexion of their politics—were imbued in their youth with pacifism and socialism. As adults, Emil's children became communists, mainly to resist Nazi totalitarianism.[1]

Other Soviet spies also claimed that their activities were aimed at building a new Russia or fighting Nazi Germany. In Fuchs's case, the FBI discovered in 1950 that this sense of mission was deep-seated.[2] His entire family had suffered political persecution under Hitler

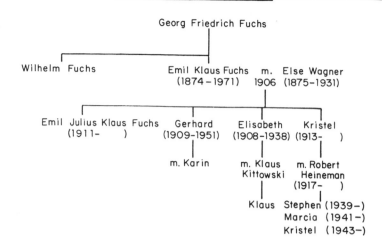

Figure 1. The Fuchs family

for their Quaker beliefs, their communist and socialist affiliations, and their organized resistance to the Nazis.

■ *Inner Light*

Klaus's father, Emil, was born in 1874 in the North German town of Beerfelden, the son of a conservative Lutheran minister, Georg Friedrich Fuchs (see Figure 1). Emil had five brothers and one sister. His mother was the daughter of a liberal army officer, and the spirit of national liberalism that had swept Germany after the 1848 revolutions and of Bismarckian unification permeated family life.

In the 1890s, when Emil Fuchs came of age, Germany under Emperor William II was beginning its drive for world power, undergoing rapid industrialization, building a powerful army and navy, and seeking overseas empire. Nietzsche's *Beyond Good and Evil* was being read in the gymnasium at Darmstadt. Emil's father wrote a brochure defending Christianity against Nietzschean amoralism, but the young man was deeply influenced by this rebel against intellectual authority.

In 1894, when Emil entered the University of Giessen to study theology, he was drawn to the ideas of one of his professors, Friedrich Naumann, the foremost exponent of German national liberalism, or liberal nationalism. Naumann, a Christian socialist who tried to reconcile the ideals of democracy and nationalism, was a leader of the National Social Association, later the German Democratic Party. His concept of "nation" was grounded in the democratic process. He believed in the inculcation of parliamentary democratic values through the educational system and in the emancipation of women and Jews from the restrictions of German society. "Naumann for me," recalled Emil many years later, "was a prophet of God."[3]

After military service in a light guard regiment, Emil Fuchs went to England in 1902 to live his Christian beliefs in the slums of Manchester. There he ministered to German immigrants working in the factories. He learned English from his Presbyterian landlady, attended Christian socialist meetings, condemned England for its capitalism and poverty, and observed the class divisions of English society. He returned from his mission in the autumn of 1904.

Emil Fuchs's two years in England deepened his sense of Christian mission and witness and moved him away from the liberalism of Naumann toward socialism. In 1904 he joined the "Christian World" circle at the University of Giessen, which was opposed to the liberal Christian theology of Friedrich Schleiermacher. The group stressed that God is ultimately love and that an ethical decision for Christ means active work and involvement in the world, not retreat from it. Emil began lecturing on these themes to trade union meetings throughout southern Germany. His home became a discussion center where ministers, students, intellectuals, and workers gathered to discuss religion and socialism, Marxism, and theosophy. In 1906 he married Else Wagner. They had four children—Elisabeth, Gerhard, Klaus, and Kristel.

In the years before World War I, Emil was deeply committed to left-wing politics as a means for living a Christian life in the world. He received an honorary doctorate from the University of Giessen in 1914 for his ministry to workers and for his interpretation of Christian theology to popular audiences. By 1914 he was a figure of some national renown for his commitment to the working classes. From 1913 to 1918 he served as an activist Lutheran minister in Rüsselsheim.

In World War I the working classes to which Emil Fuchs ministered were decimated in the trenches of the Marne and the Somme and buried in the marshes of Poland. Those who survived were traumatized by the experience. Like most socialists and liberals, including Naumann, Emil Fuchs at first greeted the Great War as a bitter necessity to defend the German nation against its enemies. But by the time of the armistice in November 1918, he had begun his transformation into a militant pacifist and socialist.

In 1918 the Fuchs family moved to Eisenach, a bastion of working-class socialist sentiment in Thuringia in central Germany. Emil renewed his work among the poor and suffering with the aid of the Quaker Relief organization. The disastrous effects of the war were compounded by a punitive peace, with heavy reparations and the assumption of German war guilt. Emil was increasingly impressed with the work of the Quakers and the packages of food and medicine that arrived from London or America earmarked for the hungry and sick of Germany. His causes multiplied: the Bund Deutsche Jugend, a youth organization; the high school movement; and, in 1921, the Socialist Party of Germany (SPD).

Emil Fuchs was one of the first German ministers to join the SPD. It was, he recalled, a difficult decision, part of a larger commitment to peace, bearing witness to inner Christian spirit against the forces of secular authority. He traveled again to Manchester that year and visited English friends. After returning to Germany, he continued his ministry among workers throughout the period of the Weimar Republic.

Emil had probably encountered the Quakers, or Friends, first in England. He was much taken by their belief that the inner light of Christ shines in the soul of every man and by their sense of mission.[4] He made a number of Quaker friends in England, among them Corder Catchpool, who was jailed in World War I as a conscientious objector. Of all religious communities, Emil felt, only the Quakers really wished to change the world according to God's will. He began attending Friends' meetings in Eisenach in 1921. The resultant sense of security and inner calling led him to join the Religious Society of Friends in 1925.[5]

Emil also became involved with a movement known as Christian socialism in the 1920s. Its founder, a Swiss socialist named Leonhard Ragaz, taught that the essence of socialism was idealism, not materialism; that Marxism was a form of religion; and that Christianity for workers must be pacifist and ethical in nature. Another influence was the young Swiss theologian Karl Barth, also an SPD member, who opposed war and capitalism and tried to reconcile the ideas of Kant and Marx. The German theologian Paul Tillich was also involved in the Christian socialist movement and became friendly with Emil Fuchs as a result.[6]

▪ Party Line

Emil's third child, Klaus, was born December 29, 1911, in the town of Rüsselsheim near Darmstadt in the province of Hesse. In his confession in 1950, Klaus Fuchs told William Skardon that his childhood had been happy and that his father was an important influence in his upbringing. His father always did what he believed to be the right thing and urged his children to follow their own consciences as well. As a child, Klaus evinced little interest in politics, except to wear the badge of the Weimar Republic at times when his schoolmates were flaunting the colors of the old imperial government destroyed by World War I. Klaus was always a top student. In 1928 he received a prize as the best high school student in Eisenach, but the award had to be presented in a private ceremony because officials disapproved of his father's socialist connections. As German nationalism and right-wing sentiment increased in the late 1920s, Klaus suffered proportionately.

Germany in 1930 was wracked by political violence and economic depression. As unemployment and inflation reached new heights, Nazis and communists fought for control of the streets of Berlin and other industrial cities. Both groups machine-gunned their victims and innocent bystanders from moving automobiles. To many German citizens, communism seemed the only force powerful enough to stop the rise of Hitler; the German communist party (KPD) received three million votes in the Reichstag elections of May 1928, then six million in November 1932, making it the third largest party in the country.

But the KPD by this time was also thoroughly Bolshevized and obedient to orders from Moscow. Those orders were to cease cooperating with the socialists and to permit Hitler to come to power, in the belief that the Nazis would preside over the downfall of capitalism. When the Nazis did come to power, in fact they decimated the KPD, which by 1933 was a "castrated giant," in the words of Arthur Koestler.[7]

Soviet military and police agents controlled a substantial network of industrial espionage in Germany in the early 1930s. Chemical and electrical industries were the most important targets. Between June 1931 and December 1932 more than one hundred cases of espionage were tried in Germany, virtually all of them involving the Soviet Union. Berlin was also the center of the growing communist propaganda empire run by Willi Munzenberg, involving dozens of front organizations publicly opposed to fascism and secretly funded by the Soviet Union. But at the same time German trade with and military aid to Russia steadily increased, and diplomatic relations between the two nations remained close.

As a student at the University of Leipzig in 1930 and 1931, Klaus Fuchs joined the socialist party, the SPD, as an organizer. He soon came into conflict with SPD leaders who supported the Weimar government's attempt to rearm the German navy. Fuchs later said that for a long time he despised the KPD for accepting the Soviet party line even when they disagreed with it. He joined the Reichsbanner, a paramilitary corps that fought street battles with Nazis on the right and with communists on the left. Theoretically open to anyone, the group was in fact staffed largely by socialists. By 1931 the Reichsbanner claimed 160,000 members across Germany.[8]

In May 1931 Emil moved his family to Kiel, where he joined the Pedagogical Academy as professor of religion; the students were generally destitute young people training for teaching careers. Because of his beliefs, Emil was increasingly popular with socialist students and unpopular with the Nazis. He began to feel genuinely concerned for the lives of his entire family. Amid these difficulties, on October 9, 1931, his deeply depressed wife of twenty-five years committed suicide. The Fuchs family was devastated.

By 1931 the young red foxes of Kiel were increasingly active politically. Elisabeth was a painter, Kristel was a student at the Odenwald School, and Klaus was a promising university student. All of them were moving from socialism toward communism in the effort to stop Hitler. Elisabeth joined the local KPD cell in Kiel in 1931 and engaged in passive resistance to the Nazis. Their father continued to speak out in lectures and the classroom for the SPD and against Hitler.

Klaus moved on to the University of Kiel. There, in 1932, he broke with the SPD when it supported General Paul von Hindenburg for Reichspresident. He argued that an alliance with bourgeois parties could not stop Hitler, that only a united working-class effort could do that. Fuchs campaigned instead for the communist candidate, Ernst Thaelmann. When Hindenburg was elected, Fuchs was expelled from the SPD. He further alienated himself from some of the socialists by chairing a student SPD-KPD group that tried to recruit Nazi sympathizers. Fuchs then joined the KPD, the only political party that still was resisting Hitler. In 1933 Hitler was elected chancellor with little communist opposition, and Fuchs was forced to go into hiding.

On February 27, 1933, the eve of a general election, a fire of mysterious origin gutted the Reichstag building in downtown Berlin. Hitler had just been sworn in as Reichschancellor. The Nazis promptly put the blame for the fire on the KPD and used it as an excuse for suspending all civil liberties, banning the KPD, and arresting thousands of party members across the country. Klaus Fuchs's name was on one of the many warrants prepared in advance. "I was lucky," Fuchs recalled years later, "because on the morning after the burning of the Reichstag I left my home very early to catch a train to Berlin for a conference of our student organization [KPD], and that is the only reason why I escaped arrest. I remember clearly when I opened the newspaper in the train I immediately realized the significance and I knew that the underground struggle had started. I took the badge of the hammer and sickle from my lapel which I had carried until that time."[9]

Hitler's election further politicized Fuchs: "I was ready to accept the philosophy that the [Communist] Party is right and that in the coming struggle you could not permit yourself any doubts after the Party made a decision." No one seemed able to resist Hitler or to "stand up for their own ideals or moral behavior."

With Hitler's accession to power, the Fuchs family became a target of Nazi persecution. Gerhard told Elisabeth that Nazi students had condemned Klaus to death. In Klaus's words, "They tried to kill me and I escaped." Gerhard fled to Berlin, Elisabeth to the home of friends in Kiel. When the police raided the Fuchs home, they found only volumes of Marx, Engels, and Lenin. Emil Fuchs had been especially careful to burn all of Klaus's papers. One night in 1933 Emil woke up screaming from a terrible dream in which he saw Elisabeth and Klaus lying on the floor covered with blood. The nightmare passed, but reality was not reassuring. Some time later the Gestapo came to the Fuchs home and asked where Klaus was. But the father did not know or would not tell.

The Nazi boot descended first on the father. In the spring of 1933 Emil was dismissed from his teaching position in Kiel and interrogated by the Gestapo in prison for five weeks. Although he was released, his passport was taken away and his trial before a people's court was delayed for two years. While Emil read the New Testament in prison, Quakers around Germany rallied to his support. Only in the autumn of 1935 did his case come to trial in Weimar. Emil was accused of having made anti-Nazi comments to a friend in Eisenach and of claiming that the KPD had not burned the Reichstag and that communism had its merits. In response, the minister read aloud his honorary degree citation from Giessen and praised German Christianity. His eight-month sentence was commuted to one, a moral victory for the large crowd of friends and sympathizers who packed the courtroom.[10]

Elisabeth and her husband, Klaus Kittowski, were arrested and imprisoned by the Gestapo in 1933. Although sentenced to eighteen months in prison, they were released at Christmas, largely through the efforts of Quaker friends. Gerhard and his pregnant wife, Karin, were arrested in 1934; they spent two years in prison, where their child was born.[11]

By 1933 Klaus Fuchs was convinced that the communist party line was correct. He was also, at the age of twenty-one, a wanted political criminal. Thus Fuchs dutifully obeyed the KPD's orders to leave Germany. "I was sent out by the party," he stated; "they said that I must finish my studies because after the revolution in

Germany people would be required with technical knowledge to take part in the building up of the Communist Germany."[12] He managed to get out of the country in July 1933, probably with the help of Willi Munzenberg's giant International Workers' Aid organization. He went first to Paris; from there he sent home a postcard, signed "Dr. Dietrich," announcing that he was safe and well. On September 21 he arrived in England, a destitute anti-Nazi refugee carrying all his worldly possessions in a canvas bag. Two weeks later his family received a letter from the director of the Friedrich Wilhelm University in Berlin informing Klaus that he had been expelled for his communist party activity.[13]

That same year, after Gerhard was expelled from law school and Elisabeth from painting school, Emil used a small inheritance to purchase two used cars and set up a car rental agency in Berlin, where he had moved with Gerhard, Karin, and Elisabeth and Klaus Kittowski. By 1934 they had acquired two more cars and were doing a brisk business smuggling Christians and Jews out of Germany. In connection with this dangerous anti-Nazi activity, Karin was arrested in May 1934, but the business continued. In 1936, however, the Gestapo confiscated all four automobiles and arrested the Kittowskis. Klaus Kittowski was sent to a concentration camp near the Elbe River; Elisabeth was released from prison and moved in with her father. Later, in a desperate effort to rescue her husband, she swam across the river to meet him in the camp and arrange his escape. The Kittowskis fled to Prague, where in 1939 Elisabeth ended her life by jumping off a bridge into the path of a moving train. Gerhard and Karin also fled to Prague, where he contracted tuberculosis and entered a sanatorium. She was put in a camp.

Kristel, who was two years younger than Klaus, had attended elementary and secondary schools in Eisenach in the 1920s, then the Odenwald School in Oberhambach. She achieved satisfactory grades, but was not the brilliant student that Klaus was. Much to her father's chagrin, she dropped out of school to apprentice herself to a bookbinder and work in a youth sanatorium at Nordhausen. In late 1933, after her father was arrested, Kristel fled to Zurich.[14] There she took education and psychology courses for two semesters at the university while working for a minister. At the end of 1934, she returned to Berlin, where she helped with the car rental agency. In 1936 Emil made an arrangement with some American Quakers to have Kristel attend Swarthmore College near Philadelphia.

In May of that year she visited Klaus in England en route to the United States. Klaus later told the FBI that he did not know Kristel was a member of the communist party until she visited him, although that seems unlikely. Through Kristel, Klaus learned the fate of the rest of his family. He wrote to the Duchess of Atholl requesting aid in obtaining Karin's release from a camp; until 1939 he continued to write to Quakers in London asking them to help Karin and Gerhard in Prague.[15]

At Swarthmore Kristel, who was not a practicing Quaker, proved an adequate student. She took courses in psychology, zoology, and biology and worked as a waitress to earn her tuition. She soon drifted into left-wing circles, and through these acquaintances she met and married Robert Heineman, a Wisconsin-born student who was a member of the Young Communist League on campus. In May 1938 she obtained a permanent residency visa.

By 1940 the Fuchs family was widely scattered. Kristel and Robert Heineman had moved to Boston, where he took graduate education classes and joined the Cambridge branch of the Communist Political Association. He made friends with Wendell Furry, a Harvard instructor whose brother-in-law, Israel Halperin, was later accused of spying in Canada. But by 1942 Kristel's husband had moved out of their house in Cambridge and rented a room in Philadelphia, where he worked for a year. He then returned to Massachusetts and worked at the General Electric plant in Lynn.[16]

Back in Germany Emil Fuchs continued to maintain his ties with both Quakers and socialists. "Our work is going on well," he wrote the American Quaker leader Rufus Jones in March 1937. "The wider fellowship is growing." Emil continued lecturing on Quaker beliefs throughout southern Germany. "We must have the courage to wait, to suffer, and to stand to our task. It is my concern to hold up the message of Quakerism till its time will come."[17]

The family Klaus Fuchs grew up in was socialist, Quaker, and then communist in its convictions. For young Klaus, moral rectitude and inner light were transformed into single-minded devotion to the authority of the party line. Communism was a means to resist the evil of Nazi totalitarianism and to build a new world. After Hitler came to power, when the KPD went underground and into exile, it was natural for Fuchs to follow party orders and seek refuge in England, where his father and other German Quakers had deep and long-standing ties.

CHAPTER · 3

Keep an Eye on Them: German Communist Refugees

Every man or woman who can hurt the Hun is okay with me.

— *William Donovan*

British security actually knew quite a bit about Klaus Fuchs in the late 1930s. From the moment he arrived in England he was befriended by fellow scientists and Quakers, and he was known to the Home Office as a destitute communist refugee from Hitler. His communism was in fact considered a political asset in the growing resistance to fascism and Nazism. Like other German refugees and communists, he was soon to become a valuable British resource in the war against Hitler.

The rise of Hitler drove tens of thousands of German refugees to England in the 1930s. Many were members of the KPD who maintained their party activities in exile. The British government was aware of this fact, but long-standing traditions of political asylum, along with the antifascist mood of the day, led them to ignore or tolerate the radicals in their midst. As early as February 1933 a Labour Party member of Parliament, Josiah Wedgwood, supported aid for the refugees from

Germany and urged that the Home Office relax the terms of the Aliens Act "to afford refuge to the Marxists from Germany." The Home Secretary, Sir John Gilmour, also noted in a memorandum to the Cabinet Committee on Aliens Restrictions that "there is, of course, a risk that the influx of refugees from Germany may include a certain number of Communists, but any who are prominent in the Communist movement are known, and would be excluded by the Immigration Officers."[1] In fact, British hospitality overcame the immigration restrictions, and very few German refugees were denied admission after 1933.

At that time communism was seen by many not as a danger but as a hope. Soviet Russia was very popular. With deep depression and unemployment throughout England, the first Five Year Plan in the Soviet Union seemed to offer a model of planned industrialization and economic recovery. Mussolini's accession to power in Italy, and Hitler's in Germany, coupled with the Japanese occupation of Manchuria, indicated to many that the danger to world peace and democratic government lay on the right, not the left. Soviet foreign policy favored peace and disarmament through the League of Nations. The Oxford Union, the university debating society, in 1933 voted overwhelmingly never to fight for king and country. For British writers like W. H. Auden, C. Day Lewis, and Stephen Spender, fascism was the real enemy, and communism a moral parable of hope in an age of anxiety.

Nonetheless, when Fuchs arrived in England, the Communist Party of Great Britain (CPGB) was extremely small and unimportant, and it remained so. Although few people actually joined the party, many attended the public meetings, cheered its speakers, joined its front organizations, and read its journals and newspapers.

■ *Bristol Exile*

When Klaus Fuchs arrived in Bristol in the winter of 1933–34 to study physics, he made no secret of his communist convictions. The Home Office learned of his party affiliation from a Gestapo report to the German consul in Bristol but later claimed that the report had not been noticed. After all, in the eyes of Nazi officials all German refugees in England were Jews and communists. But Fuchs's links with German communists in England were more extensive than MI5 or MI6 later admitted. In fact, a British security file was opened on Fuchs in 1933 when an MI6 agent in Kiel, a canal worker whose code name was Arthur, reported on Fuchs's KPD activities.[2]

Fuchs came to England through an acquaintance of his cousin, who was engaged to a German *au pair* girl living with the family of Ronald Gunn in Somerset, not far from Bristol. A Quaker relative of the Gunns told them that Emil Fuchs's son had fled to Paris, where he was registered with the Quaker Bureau. The Gunns, who knew of Emil as a highly respected Quaker, agreed to sponsor Klaus in England.[3] Not Quakers themselves, the Gunns were a well-to-do family sympathetic to the Soviet Union. Ronald Gunn, an executive of the Imperial Tobacco Company, visited the Soviet Union twice, once in 1932 with his wife on holiday, and again in 1938 on his own. Gunn persuaded Nevill Mott, a twenty-nine-year-old physicist teaching at the University of Bristol, to accept Fuchs as a graduate student in his laboratory in the autumn of 1934.[4] Mott had managed to procure research funds from a local family of some means and, with money from the Academic Assistance Council (formed to aid German refugee scholars and scientists), built up a team of young physicists from Germany at Bristol; Hans Bethe was Mott's research assistant. Years later Bethe remembered only that Fuchs had left Germany for political reasons and that he had been a brilliant, quiet, and unassuming member of Mott's laboratory. Fuchs worked for Mott and lived with the Gunns until 1937, when he went to work in Max Born's laboratory in Edinburgh.[5]

From the beginning Fuchs encountered passport problems, undoubtedly because he was a member of the KPD. In August 1934 C. Hartly-Hodder, the German consul in Bristol, refused to renew his passport without a certificate from the police in Kiel. In October Mott wrote to the Academic Assistance Council requesting aid in getting Fuchs a passport through the Home Office. His expired German passport was then returned by the German embassy in London because the Kiel Gestapo reported that Fuchs was a "Marxist." When Fuchs wrote the Home Office directly, he was told that the secretary of state was "unable to comply with your request." Mott was understandably upset, for it appeared that his graduate student would have to return to Nazi Germany. The council, however, told Mott that Fuchs was "quite safe" using his old passport and would not be forced to leave England.[6] The Home Office assured Fuchs that he could remain in England as long as Mott supported him, and in December 1934 it extended his residency for one year, as it did annually for the next four years.

Although Fuchs remained aloof from British politics, he was in fact politically active. He immersed himself in Marxist philosophy, and his left-wing views were well known in Bristol, although he spoke very little to anyone about his personal and political past. He often attended meetings of the Friends of Soviet Russia in Bristol, where student pacifism and communism were as strong as at Oxford and Cambridge. The young refugee from Nazism was warmly welcomed. Nevill Mott had no qualms about Fuchs's being a communist. "Anyone who was against the Nazis would have been. He seemed to know his stuff, so I took him on and he produced some excellent work. He was shy and reserved and I do not remember discussing politics with him." Mott himself was sympathetic to the Soviet cause and had taken a trip to the Soviet Union sponsored by the USSR Academy of Sciences in celebration of the hundredth anniversary of the chemist Mendeleyev's birth.[7]

Both Mott and Fuchs were active members of one of Munzenberg's largest front organizations, the Society for Cultural Relations with the Soviet Union. The Bristol branch, sizable and active, periodically gave dramatic readings of the transcripts of Stalin's purge trials. Mott later remembered that Fuchs always played the role of the state prosecutor, Andrei Vyshinsky, "accusing the defendants with a cold venom that I would never have suspected from so quiet and retiring a young man." Fuchs was also active in a committee that raised funds for the Republican side during the Spanish Civil War. Later, in Edinburgh, he organized a committee that distributed KPD anti-Nazi propaganda leaflets in Scotland. Fuchs considered himself a member of the KPD organization in England; he filled out its biographical data sheet, and he was aware of Jurgen Kuczynski's leading role in party affairs. Fuchs, in short, was a much more active and visible communist than the Home Office would later admit.[8]

In 1933 the KPD, driven out of Germany, established new centers of political organization throughout the world. Its international connections persisted, some through the Comintern, many through Munzenberg's front organizations. Munzenberg enrolled a wide range of antifascist sympathizers in his efforts to support communism. Like Fuchs and the KPD leaders, he had to flee Germany after the Reichstag fire. He promptly reestablished his organizations in Paris with the assistance of another German communist, Otto Katz (who wrote under the name André Simon). Within months Munzenberg and Katz had produced *The Brown Book*, detailing Nazi atrocities and persecutions. They also set up a "countertrial" in London to match the Nazi trial of the communists accused of burning the Reichstag. Not surprisingly, the countertrial found the accused innocent, winning considerable sympathy for the German communists in the struggle against Hitler.[9]

Munzenberg and Katz continued their activities throughout the 1930s. Katz organized the presentation of Soviet films and plays with revolutionary themes and visited England and America to raise money for the Comintern. In 1936, when Stalin decided to support the Republican side in the Spanish Civil War, Munzenberg's front organizations were a crucial weapon in this Popular Front campaign, subsidizing pro-Republican journalists and funneling volunteers for the international brigades of the Comintern. A German information press service monitored the fate of socialists and communists still in Germany, and a German Popular Front found widespread support among refugees.[10] Munzenberg himself, however, was chastised in Moscow for "lack of revolutionary vigilance." He was simply too influential and too independent of the Comintern and Moscow, and in October 1937 he was expelled from the KPD. But his organizations continued to prosper as Hitler occupied more and more territory in Europe. Antifascism was the order of the day, and German communists in exile were its staunchest supporters.[11]

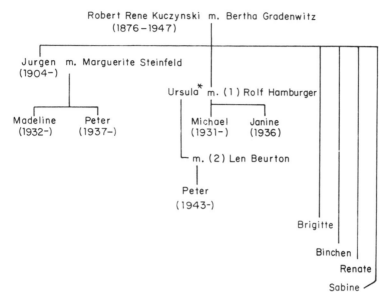

Robert Rene Kuczynski m. Bertha Gradenwitz
(1876–1947)

Jurgen m. Marguerite Steinfeld
(1904–)

Ursula* m. (1) Rolf Hamburger

Madeline   Peter   Michael   Janine
(1932–)   (1937–)   (1931–)   (1936)

m. (2) Len Beurton

Peter
(1943–)

Brigitte

Binchen

Renate

Sabine

*Ursula Kuczynski = Ruth Werner = Ursula Hamburger = Ruth Beurton

Figure 2. The Kuczynski family

- *The Kuczynskis*

One long-time supporter of Munzenberg and his International Workers' Aid was Robert René Kuczynski, a leading economic statistician who had been the director of the German Statistical Office before World War I. Munzenberg had sent him to France in 1923 to collect money for starving Germans. The Kuczynskis (see Figure 2) were a Polish Jewish family well known to British intelligence because of their left-wing involvements. MI5 opened a file on them in 1928, based on information from MI6 agents inside Germany. The file was at first simply a KAEOT—"Keep an Eye on Them"—commonly known as a K file. By the late 1930s British intelligence knew that the Kuczynski family was at the heart of the KPD's anti-Nazi activities in England.

Robert Kuczynski's son Jurgen was born in Elberfeld, Germany, in 1904. In the 1920s he studied philosophy and history at the universities of Berlin, Erlangen, and Heidelberg. In 1925 he worked for a year as a bank clerk in France, then studied economics at the Brookings Institution in Washington, D.C., where his father spent six months each year from 1925 to 1931. In 1928 Jurgen married Marguerite Steinfeld. For a time he ran the statistical section of the AFL-CIO in Washington; he also worked for the Bureau of Labor Statistics. In the process he made a number of American friends in the labor movement.[12]

The Kuczynski family also maintained close connections with the Soviet Union. In 1930 Jurgen made his first visit to the USSR, where his reputation as the author of a book on American labor statistics had preceded him. He wrote articles for the KPD newspaper *Die Rote Fahne* (The red banner) and the Soviet journal *Industrializatsiia*. He was invited to parties at the Soviet embassy in Berlin. He became close friends with Erich Kunik, head of the information section of the KPD central committee. At Kunik's prodding, Jurgen joined the party in July 1930. As Hitler moved closer to power, the Kuczynski commitment to communism deepened.

In April 1933 Robert Kuczynski fled to Czechoslovakia, then to Geneva. In 1934 he arrived in London as a refugee and found a position teaching demography at the London School of Economics. His wife stayed in Berlin to sell their house, which had already been searched by the Nazis. Jurgen's sisters, Brigitte and Ursula, also KPD members, were in China and Switzerland; his friend Erich Kunik had fled to the Soviet Union. Jurgen remained in Berlin, continuing to visit the Soviet embassy once or twice a month and editing his father's economic newsletter, *Finanzpolitische Korrespondenz*. He maintained his friendship with Soviet Ambassador Besonov and supplied political and economic reports to the Foreign Ministry.

In 1935 Jurgen Kuczynski went to Moscow at the invitation of economist Eugen Varga. There he found the KPD leadership in exile, Walter Ulbricht and Wilhelm Pieck, now calling for a Popular Front against fascism, with the ultimate goal of creating a Soviet Germany. In October the KPD in exile held its so-called Brussels conference at the village of Rublevo, near Moscow. Admitting that its earlier hostility to the SPD was a mistake, the party initiated proposals to the socialists, then centered in Prague, for joint KPD-SPD action. The SPD rejected the communists' proposals and remained suspicious of any cooperation.[13]

During his visit to Moscow Kuczynski met Ulbricht for the first time. The Stalinist leader instructed Kuczynski to leave Germany and to write him when he had found a place of refuge. By January 1936, Jurgen and his wife, Marguerite, had moved to London, where they joined his father and sister Brigitte. Jurgen, after writing to Ulbricht for further instructions, joined the CPGB. He took a job with the British government as an economic statistician specializing in Germany.[14]

During the summer of 1936 Kuczynski returned illegally to Nazi Berlin, visited the Soviet embassy, and arranged to meet Ambassador Besonov in Copenhagen. He visited Prague, Warsaw, and Danzig on KPD business before going back to England. By that time a substantial number of KPD exiles had gathered there and were reorganizing with three main goals: to send communist propaganda to Germany, to publicize Nazi atrocities in England, and to lay the groundwork within the refugee community for a future communist Germany. On Ulbricht's orders, Kuczynski then went to Paris, where the KPD central committee instructed him to become the political leader of the KPD in England. He reported directly to the KPD "foreign leadership" group in Paris.[15]

In England Kuczynski established contact with members of the left wing of the British Labour Party, including John Strachey and his wife, Celia. "In 1934," recalled Kuczynski years later, "I visited him at his house at the wish of Soviet friends who wanted to establish contacts with him." Strachey never joined the CPGB, but he was a persistent advocate of communism and the Soviet Union in his public pronouncements; Celia did join the party. Subsequently the Stracheys and the Kuczynskis became friends.[16]

Like Kuczynski, Strachey was involved in Munzenberg's organizations. He attended the antiwar congress in Amsterdam and ran a British branch of Munzenberg's World Movement against Fascism and War. In 1934 Strachey traveled to Berlin with Ellen Wilkinson, who had close ties with the KPD underground in both Germany and England. A founding member of the CPGB, Wilkinson later became minister of education in the Attlee government.[17]

In 1937 Strachey became involved in setting up a new journal, the *Tribune,* as a forum for left-wing activists who could not find a comfortable home in the Labour Party but were unwilling to join the CPGB.[18] Eventually Strachey moved away from communism and enlisted in the Royal Air Force. By the summer of 1945 Strachey was in Attlee's new government as undersecretary of state for air; his communism was considered a youthful aberration. Although he and Kuczynski did not maintain close ties after the war, they did correspond as late as the 1960s.[19] In 1950, therefore, the fact that the British secretary of state for war knew the man who had recruited Klaus Fuchs for espionage was not something the Attlee government wished to emphasize.

The number of refugees from Hitler's Germany increased substantially after the occupation of Czechoslovakia in the winter of 1938–39. In England both the KPD and the Labour Party offered assistance, especially to a group of several hundred German communists who arrived from Prague under the leadership of Heinz Schmidt. With the aid of the Czech Refugee Trust Fund, the Schmidt group provided new blood for the KPD in England and manpower for Kuczynski's various organizations. British generosity to refugees became political opportunity for the KPD.[20]

Kuczynski, the most active and best-known KPD leader in England, collected funds for Spanish Civil War veterans and for the publication of periodicals in Paris. He raised money, perhaps 100,000 marks, for Munzenberg's "Free Germany" anti-Nazi radio station, Freiheitsender, from Jewish refugees in England and America. He attended a KPD party school in Hauteville, France, and organized KPD branches in Birmingham, Manchester, Liverpool, Glasgow, and London. In December 1938 he established the Free Germany Cultural Union (Freie Deutsche Kulturbund) as a KPD front organization among the refugee community. By 1939 it claimed one thousand members, including Thomas and Heinrich Mann.[21]

Kuczynski also became a frequent speaker and writer for the Left Book Club, which took over the *Tribune* in the summer of 1938. The following summer he made a speaking tour of twenty British cities and towns for the Left Book Club. In addition to praising the Soviet Union and denouncing Hitler, he collected money for the KPD. The club published 50,000 copies of his book, *The Condition of the Workers in Great Britain, Germany, and the Soviet Union, 1932–1938*. Kuczynski was by now a well-known Marxist economist and an editor of *Labour Monthly*. He had contacts with various KPD leaders on the continent, notably Gerhard Eisler in Paris. In August 1939 he visited his sister Ursula in Switzerland and then Eisler, before returning to London just as Hitler's Blitzkrieg overwhelmed Poland.[22]

■ *Edinburgh*

Fuchs completed his doctorate at Bristol in December 1936 with a dissertation entitled "The Cohesive Forces of Copper and the Elastic Constants of Monovalent Metals." Mott recommended him for a postdoctorate position at Max Born's laboratory in Edinburgh, and in July 1937 Born wrote to Fuchs, expressing his pleasure that the young physicist would work with him for a year. He also persuaded the Academic Assistance Council to give Fuchs financial aid. Born later described Fuchs as a "brilliant young fellow" who was "extremely modest" and had "nobody to stay with during the holidays." He was "likeable, kind, harmless," a quiet man with "sad eyes" who had "suffered from the Nazis more than the ordinary refugees." Born recalled that he was "passionately pro-Russian." In 1938 Fuchs received his modest stipend of forty-two pounds per annum from the council, as well as a fellowship at the University of Edinburgh. The quality of Fuchs's work was high enough that Born had him stay an additional year (1939) at his laboratory on a Carnegie fellowship.[23]

As a scientist, Fuchs achieved only modest originality in the 1930s. His work on the quantum mechanical interpretations of cohesive forces and elastic constants in metals was largely derivative from Mott's work at Bristol. His articles written from 1939 to 1941 on quantized field equations, electromagnetic radiation, and wave functions were equally in debt to Max Born, with whom he wrote a series of papers.

During the summer of 1938, having lived in England for five years, Fuchs again approached the Home Office requesting an unlimited residence permit, and the request was granted. However, at that time the Czech government denied him a visa to visit his brother, Gerhard. In July 1939 Fuchs applied for naturalization as a British citizen, but the war broke out before this could take place, and he was then classified as an enemy alien. By that time the Home Office knew that Fuchs's passport had been revoked by the Nazis because of his Marxist leanings. But the government had no evidence that Fuchs was engaged in dangerous political activity in England, so he continued his scientific research at Edinburgh unimpeded.[24]

The Nazi-Soviet nonaggression pact of August 1939 brought about a decided cooling of Anglo-Soviet relations. The Soviet occupation of eastern Poland, the Winter War on Finland, and the British declaration of war on Germany all made the Soviet Union suspect, even in the eyes of the British left. The pact deeply divided communists worldwide, especially KPD refugees, who could not swallow Moscow's line that this was an "imperialist war." Both the KPD and the CPGB suffered a drop in membership. Fuchs persuaded himself that Stalin wanted to buy time and that the Soviet alliance with Hitler was a temporary expedient. "The Russo-German pact was difficult to understand, but in the end I did accept that Russia had done it to gain time, that during that time she was expanding her own influence in the Balkans against the influence of Germany."[25]

On June 22, 1941, when millions of Nazi forces swarmed across the Russian border, Fuchs's dilemma was resolved. "In the end," he confessed in 1950, "I accepted again that my doubts had been wrong and the Party had been right." The Soviet Union overnight became Britain's ally in the war on Germany.[26]

CHAPTER · 4

From Internment to Intelligence

Although personally I am quite content with existing explosives, I feel we must not stand in the path of improvement.

— *Winston Churchill*

Between September 1939 and June 1942 Klaus Fuchs was transformed from a German enemy alien who had to suffer the indignities of internment into a valued nuclear physicist working on the atomic bomb as a British citizen and for British intelligence. British security was well aware of his communist politics, his scientific capabilities, and his knowledge of the German physics community. After some delay, it decided that Fuchs was a security risk worth taking.

By 1939 England was home to more than 80,000 refugees from Germany, Austria, and Czechoslovakia. Although the British launched a massive campaign to help them with money, jobs, housing, and clothing, life in England for most of the refugees was not pleasant. Homesickness, unemployment, an unfamiliar language, and the humiliation of being considered enemy aliens after 1939 combined to produce feelings of isolation and frustration. The suicide rate for these refugees was high. Germans in England were increasingly under suspicion as spies for Hitler; cameras, drawings, maps, radio sets, and other belongings were confiscated. After the Nazi attack on Poland in September 1939, the minister of home security, John Anderson, set up more than a hundred one-man tribunals (usually county court judges or king's counsels) across the country to investigate all Germans and Austrians over the age of sixteen.[1]

When Fuchs was ordered to appear before an alien tribunal on November 2, 1939, in Edinburgh, it was because he was German, not because he was a communist. But until his internment the following May, Fuchs simply had to report periodically to the local police. During the winter of 1939–40 more than 70,000 refugees were examined, but only 569 were actually interned. However, the suspicion of a German "fifth column" in England mounted with every advance of the German armies on the continent.[2]

In May 1940, when the fall of France seemed imminent and an invasion of England plausible, the British panicked. Tribunals were again set up to classify all refugees in three broad categories: those in category A were interned as political risks; those in category B were subject to police restrictions; and those in category C remained at liberty. In May all those in the B category were reviewed, and most were shifted to category A and interned. By July some 43 percent of citizens polled wanted to intern all Germans living in England.[3]

■ *Internment*

On May 12, 1940, Klaus Fuchs was interrogated in Edinburgh, interned as an enemy alien, and placed in a camp on the Isle of Man. Max Born wrote to Esther Simpson at the Society for the Preservation of Science and Learning, asking her to help get Fuchs released. Born described him as "among the two or three most gifted theoretical physicists of the young generation" and a man who could do "work of national importance." Apparently Fuchs achieved a position of some authority in the camp; on June 13 Born wrote him from Edinburgh that "we are glad that you have a responsible position in the camp as a 'House Father.'" Nevill

Mott wrote from Bristol that he was dismayed at the internment of a fellow scientist. Their concern made no difference, however.[4]

The internees, both communists and Nazis, were rounded up with minimal formalities and great confusion, vaccinated, and shipped to Australia or Canada. On board ship, they stayed in crowded, airless, cockroach-ridden holds. On July 13 Fuchs landed in Canada and was imprisoned in the Canadian army's Camp L, not far from Quebec City. The internees were stripped, deloused, relieved of all possessions and money, and compelled to wear Navy pea jackets with a red patch on the back. Anti-British bitterness soon gave way to resourceful organization. A camp university was formed, and Fuchs gave physics lectures.[5]

In August his sister, Kristel Heineman, who was living in Cambridge, Massachusetts, wrote that she was glad he was at least safe in the western hemisphere and out of England. She hoped to be able to visit him. Fuchs's old friends Ronald and Jessie Gunn, who had given him refuge in 1934, were equally solicitous and wondered what their "friends in Germany" were thinking about the war. In October Fuchs was transferred to Camp N, near Sherbrooke, Quebec, where the prisoners were kept in locomotive sheds. Five faucets and six latrines served 720 men.[6]

"For a long time," Fuchs recalled later, "I was not allowed any newspapers. We did not know what was going on outside, and I did not see how the British people fought at that time. I felt no bitterness by the internment, because I could understand that it was necessary and that at that time England could not spare good people to look after the internees, but it did deprive me of the chance of learning more about the real character of the British people."[7]

Internment put Fuchs in touch with more German communists. In Canada he met another KPD activist, Hans Kahle, a forty-one-year-old Spanish Civil War veteran whose family had fled to England in the late 1930s. Kahle had helped Jurgen Kuczynski organize the KPD in England and was considered its "military authority." It may have been Kahle who later put Fuchs in touch with Kuczynski.[8]

Kuczynski was also interned as an enemy alien. On January 18, 1940, he and Marguerite were ordered to appear before a tribunal; Jurgen was promptly sent to Warner's Camp in Seaton, Devonshire, where he assumed the post of camp statistician. His KPD agitation soon got him into trouble; he lost all privileges and was set to work cleaning latrines.

But several British left leaders worked to get him released from internment. Marguerite pleaded her husband's case with Labour Party leader Harold Laski in February, and Laski wrote a letter on his behalf. John Strachey also complained to the authorities, including his friend Osbert Peake at the Home Office. In April a communist lawyer named D. N. Pritt managed to get him released from camp. Pritt called Kuczynski a "brilliant writer, labour historian, and statistician." He was appalled that Kuczynski and other communists and International Brigade veterans were interned with hundreds of Nazi prisoners of war. When Kuczynski was released, his fellow KPD internees sang the *Internationale.*

At the time Fuchs was released from internment, Jurgen Kuczynski was the official head of the KPD in England.[9] By July 1940 more than 27,000 Germans had been interned; of that number, more than 7,000 were sent abroad. Although Churchill initially agreed that enemy aliens formed a "malignancy in our midst," which must be excised, by late June he noted that "many enemy aliens had a great hatred of the Nazi regime, and it was unjust to treat our friends as foes." Churchill realized that anti-Nazi German refugees might well serve Britain's security interests rather than threaten them.[10]

By late summer Anderson's internment policies seemed excessive. Many refugees committed suicide in transit to the hastily improvised camps set up by the War Office. On July 2 the liner *Arandora Star,* laden with 1,500 internees, was torpedoed by a German U-boat off the coast of Ireland; only 71 people survived. By 1941 the panic had subsided, and nearly 20,000 refugees were released as suddenly as they had been interned. On December 17, 1940, Fuchs arrived back in England and was released, in part because of the benevolent intervention of Esther Simpson, to whom Fuchs wrote a letter of thanks. Many of the former internees became useful in the British war effort against Germany and were employed by the British intelligence and scientific establishments. One of them was Klaus Fuchs.[11]

Both Fuchs's internment and his release occurred under the direction of the British Home Office and were therefore of great concern a decade later when Fuchs's espionage was discovered. Who had released Fuchs from internment? asked a Canadian official in March 1950. George Ignatieff of the Canadian Department of External Affairs recalled that the British government had "dumped an unassorted group of enemy aliens on Canada for internment without providing any dossiers at all. Fuchs appears to have been included in this batch." In determining whether to release internees, the British had judged their "anti-Nazi persuasion" and talents that could "safely be used in the war effort." As a communist anti-Nazi and a physicist, Klaus Fuchs was doubly qualified for release. But internment remained an embarrassing wartime secret in England, characterized by "official callousness, interdepartmental intrigue, newspaper hysteria, public lies, lies told to Parliament," and general suffering.[12] Even in 1950 the British had not told the public the entire story.

- *Physics and War*

In 1941 Klaus Fuchs had great potential value for the British government as a nuclear physicist. Although he had not worked at any of the great centers of nuclear physics—the Cavendish laboratory of Ernest Rutherford at Cambridge, Max Born's laboratory in Göttingen, or Niels Bohr's Institute for Theoretical Physics in Copenhagen—he did become part of the stream of German refugee scientists who brought with them the physics necessary to build an atomic bomb.

The year 1932 had marked a turning point in nuclear physics. Bohr's model of the atom as a cloud of electrons surrounding a nucleus of protons was modified to include the uncharged neutron, which was discovered by James Chadwick at Cambridge. At Columbia University in New York, chemist Harold Urey discovered deuterium, a heavy isotope of hydrogen which, in the form of "heavy water," could slow down neutrons. (This discovery was used later to facilitate the as-yet-undiscovered chain reaction process in uranium.) Also at Cambridge, John Cockcroft showed that nuclei could be made to disintegrate artificially. In

1934 Enrico Fermi in Rome bombarded uranium with neutrons and produced a form of fission without recognizing it. In California Carl Anderson discovered the positively charged electron, or positron, and Ernest Lawrence succeeded in disintegrating nuclei with a new machine called the cyclotron, which used alternating magnetic fields to accelerate particles.[13]

In Berlin the young physicist Leo Szilard, a Hungarian, read H. G. Wells's 1914 novel, *The World Set Free,* which imagined a future of atomic bombs and nuclear reactors, but Szilard read it as merely science fiction. And at a meeting of the British Association for the Advancement of Science in September 1933 Rutherford, who was Cavendish Professor of Experimental Physics at Cambridge, proclaimed all talk of nuclear power to be "the merest moonshine."[14]

In Germany the physics community was decimated by Hitler's dictatorship, which treated physics as a Jewish and Bolshevik plot. All but the most docile and Aryan physicists were expelled from their posts. Albert Einstein resigned his position at the Prussian Academy of Sciences even as the Nazis confiscated his bank account and his house. Max Born took refuge in England; Einstein emigrated to the United States. In April 1933 Einstein wrote to Born, "My heart aches when I think of the young ones."[15]

Many German refugee scientists went to England in the thirties. Szilard worked with the Academic Assistance Council to find university positions for the newcomers. Hans Bethe accepted a temporary lectureship at Manchester, then Bristol, and Rudolf Peierls went to Birmingham.[16]

In December 1938 the world of physics was rocked by news of the discovery of fission. When two Berlin physicists, Otto Hahn and Fritz Strassmann, bombarded uranium with slow neutrons, they found that the uranium split, or fissioned, into lighter elements, such as barium, actinium, and lanthanum. A tiny mass of uranium could release enormous quantities of energy, measured in billions of electron volts. Szilard, who had moved to New York, immediately recognized that the discovery of fission implied the possibility of both nuclear power and nuclear weapons. "There was little doubt in my mind," Szilard wrote later, "that the world was headed for grief."[17]

The discovery of fission occurred in Hitler's Germany on the eve of World War II. There was concern in both England and the United States that Nazi Germany might well be engaged in research toward an atomic bomb. Indeed, in April 1939 the German physicist Paul Harteck wrote the War Ministry that uranium fission could make possible "an explosive which is many orders of magnitude more effective than the present one" and that "the country which first makes use of it has an unsurpassable advantage over the others." The German government immediately began to secure all available uranium in Germany and Czechoslovakia and banned its export. The British made efforts to secure access to uranium in the Belgian Congo.[18]

In September 1939, as Europe plunged into war, the English writer C. P. Snow observed that the discovery of nuclear fission would inevitably make possible terrible weapons of war. An atomic bomb, he wrote, "must be made, if it really is a physical possibility. If it is not made in America this year, it may be next year in Germany. There is no ethical problem; if the invention is not prevented by physical laws, it will certainly be carried out somewhere in the world. Such an invention will never be kept secret."[19]

In Britain, Russia, Germany, and America work began in committees and laboratories to find out whether a nuclear weapon was not only theoretically possible but technically feasible. Research in Britain began with the participation of two German refugee physicists, Otto Frisch and Rudolf Peierls. Frisch had emigrated in 1933 and worked with Niels Bohr in Copenhagen before settling in Birmingham in 1939. Peierls, at thirty-four, had studied with Bohr and with Max Planck, Walter Nernst, Werner Heisenberg, and Wolfgang Pauli. He had visited the Soviet Union several times to attend scientific conferences and had married a Russian physicist.

After the war broke out, Frisch and Peierls were classified as enemy aliens. They could not own cars, join a British Civil Defense team, or work on important war-related research, such as radar. But enemy aliens were allowed to work on less important projects, such as atomic research, so Frisch and Peierls began to work on the theory of an atomic bomb. "We were at war," recalled Frisch, "and the idea was reasonably obvious." Knowing that the lighter uranium-235 was fissionable and that the heavier uranium-238 was not, they conceived the idea of separating out the lighter metal by passing a gaseous form of uranium hexafluoride through tiny holes that would allow only the lighter isotope to pass through.[20]

In early 1940 Frisch and Peierls presented their ideas in a memorandum "On the Construction of a 'Super Bomb' based on a Nuclear Chain Reaction in Uranium" to Churchill's science adviser, Henry Tizard. They pointed out for the first time that the amount of fissionable uranium needed for a bomb was relatively small (a few dozen kilograms or less); that theoretically uranium-235 could be separated from uranium-238 by gaseous diffusion; that a nuclear weapon would produce considerable radiation in addition to heat and blast effects; and that the best way to create a nuclear explosion seemed to be by bringing together very rapidly two hemispheres of uranium-235.[21]

In April 1940 a top secret committee, code-named Maud, of British scientists was established under the Ministry of Aircraft Production to explore the possibilities for building a uranium bomb. For reasons of secrecy, uranium was called "x-metal" or "tube alloy" and uranium hexafluoride was known as "working gas." Upon learning that Germany had directed the Norsk Hydro plant in occupied Norway to increase its production of heavy water, a neutron moderator of great value, the Ministry of Supply began to study the possible effects of a German uranium bomb dropped on London. That summer, at the height of the blitz, Lord Lothian, the British ambassador in Washington, arranged "an immediate and general exchange of secret technical information with the United States." To promote Anglo-American cooperation, scientific liaison offices were set up in London and Washington. The British made available to the Americans certain crucial processes, including the cavity magnetron, which was essential to radar. Several months later a British mission headed by Tizard visited America and discussed the preliminary results of British and American work on an atomic bomb. Soon afterward, in May 1941, the British government gave the Metro-Vickers Company a contract to design a twenty-stage gaseous diffusion plant, and they gave Peierls funds to pursue further bomb research at Birmingham.[22]

One of the people Peierls hired to work with him on this research was Klaus Fuchs, recently released from internment and living in Edinburgh. Peierls had met Fuchs, read his scientific papers, and felt that he was a scientist with whom he could discuss theoretical technicalities. Max Born and Nevill Mott highly recommended the young German physicist. On May 10 Peierls wrote to Fuchs inviting him to join his laboratory and help with some "war work." Fuchs did not know that he was about to be drawn into the top secret project, code-named Tube Alloys, to design and build an atomic bomb for use in the war against Hitler. Later Born warned Fuchs that an atomic bomb would be a "devilish invention" and that he should have nothing to do with it. But after some delay (MI5 was reluctant to give him a security clearance), Fuchs wrote to Mott on May 25 that he was moving to Birmingham.[23]

- *Tube Alloys*

Peierls knew that Fuchs as a student had been "politically active as a member of a socialist student group [which was essentially communist] and had to flee for his life from the Nazis." But like Mott, Peierls just wanted a good scientist. He was unconcerned with Fuchs's politics, although he knew that British security might look askance at having a communist enemy alien working in his laboratory. Security instructed the insistent Peierls to "tell him [Fuchs] as little as possible." "I could not tell him what the project was until I had permission to do so," recalled Peierls, "but I described the kind of theory needed in general terms, and he agreed to join."[24]

At first Peierls had Fuchs work on some unclassified mathematical problems. In June, while he was being cleared by the Ministry of Aircraft Production, which stipulated that Fuchs should be given no more than "minimum disclosures," he signed the Official Secrets Act. He then worked on gaseous diffusion theory, mainly the mathematics of hydrodynamics. Like the other enemy alien scientists, Fuchs was technically employed by the

University of Birmingham under contract with the Ministry of Aircraft Production and was duly warned of the penalties of violating the Official Secrets Act.[25]

Even before he was cleared by security Fuchs helped Frisch and Peierls with the secret Maud committee report by solving the equation for the sphere of uranium needed for a bomb. With Peierls, he also worked extensively that summer on isotope separation. The Birmingham Germans produced their results at the same time Hitler attacked the Soviet Union. Fuchs's communism and his work on the atomic bomb melded into a single effort to defeat Nazi Germany. To the British government, Fuchs's contribution to scientific research seemed worth any security risk it might have entailed.

Fuchs's salary was 270 pounds per annum, and he was happy to have it. He moved into the Peierls home as a lodger; they found him courteous and even-tempered, a man who was usually silent unless questioned. His brief answers led Peierls's Russian-born wife, Evgeniia, to nickname him "Penny-in-the-Slot" Fuchs. Only in 1950 did the Peierlses realize that their former lodger's occasional illnesses and visits to the doctor might have had a more sinister meaning.[26]

From the outset the Tube Alloys project was dominated by Imperial Chemical Industries (ICI), a massive private enterprise directed by Wallace Akers (see Figure 3). In 1941 Akers was the director of Tube Alloys, reporting to the minister in charge, Sir John Anderson, another ICI man. Akers's assistant was Michael Perrin, an ICI chemist. Not surprisingly, the first formal research contract let by Tube Alloys in June 1941 went to ICI, which established an Energy Coordination Committee for research and development in cooperation with "work going on in the universities on the project for utilizing nuclear energy."[27]

To further complicate matters, in June 1940 two French scientists, Hans Halban and Lew Kowarski, had arrived in England to continue their nuclear research. They had brought 185 kilograms of heavy water that had been produced in a Norsk Hydro plant and smuggled out of Norway by British and French agents. Halban and Kowarski wrote up a research report for the British government and applied for British patents (as they had for French

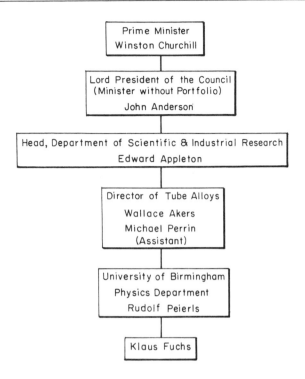

Figure 3. Tube Alloys, 1942

ones) on nuclear reactor design, isotope concentration, and the production of plutonium. In 1941 the two men worked out an arrangement whereby ICI would fund reactor research and in return would get a share of both the British and the French patents held by Halban and Kowarski.[28]

When Fuchs joined Tube Alloys, Britain was ahead of the United States in the early theoretical work on the critical mass of uranium, the gaseous diffusion process for separating U-235 from U-238, and other basic research. In June 1941 the Maud committee's report predicted optimistically that a "very powerful weapon of war" could be made by late 1943 using less than twenty-five kilograms of uranium-235 and the gun method of assembly (firing two hemispheres of uranium at each other to form a critical mass). It was generally recognized that the British were making a major contribution to nuclear weapons theory, but that production and assembly would require the more substantial and secure resources of the United States, still a neutral nation.[29]

An addendum to the Maud report by "Messrs. ICI" offered to "take executive charge of this work." In part ICI was interested in the prospects for nuclear power after the war. Perrin, in a note entitled "Nuclear Energy for Power Production (Halban Scheme)," predicted that "Halban's work can lead to the development of a new source of power of great importance in peace and war and would make possible the reorientation of world industry. It is essential that these ideas should be developed for the British Empire by a U.K. firm and ICI is prepared to do this." Nuclear research in England thus seemed about to become the commercial property of private industry and the legal property of the French government. However, after a three-day meeting in October between government and ICI officials, ICI lost control of the bomb project, which was reorganized under the Department of Scientific and Industrial Research (DSIR). All scientists working on the project now became civil servants employed by Tube Alloys. Akers and Perrin remained in charge, but the troublesome ICI link was greatly weakened.[30]

When DSIR took over, they asked British security "whether a definite clearance could be given to Fuchs." Security submitted Fuchs's case to Sir Edward Appleton, the DSIR secretary, who decided that Fuchs was so important to Tube Alloys that the security risk should be taken. Good scientists were in desperately short supply at that time, and the restrictions on Fuchs were lifted.[31]

■ A Matter of Intelligence

On June 22, 1941, when Germany invaded Russia, Winston Churchill went on the radio to proclaim that "the Russian danger is therefore our danger, and the danger of the United States." Despite his own "persistent opposition to communism," as Churchill put it, he had offered the Soviet Union "any technical or economic assistance which is in our power and which is likely to be of service to them." To this end Soviet Foreign Minister

Molotov and British Ambassador Sir Stafford Cripps agreed in July to provide mutual "assistance and support of all kinds." It is doubtful that either thought this would include informing the Soviet Union of Britain's work on an atomic bomb. But that is precisely what Klaus Fuchs decided to do.[32]

By the autumn of that year the British were providing massive military aid to Stalin, including Mark II radars, fighter planes, bombers, antiaircraft guns, destroyers, ammunition, and three million pairs of boots for the impending Russian winter. Technical assistance was coordinated by the Russian Trade Delegation in London and the British Ministry of Supply. The Cripps-Molotov agreement was formalized in May 1942 as a twenty-year treaty of mutual assistance, including military and scientific exchanges, and "close and friendly collaboration after the reestablishment of peace." By September Henry Tizard was planning an Anglo-Soviet scientific information exchange similar to the 1940 arrangement with the United States. The agreement signed that month required Great Britain and the USSR to exchange "all information including any necessary specifications, plans, etc. relating to weapons, devices, or processes which at present are, or in the future may be, employed by them for the prosecution of the war against the common enemy."[33]

In America, President Roosevelt and Secretary of War Henry Stimson did not learn of the Anglo-Soviet agreement until December. They quickly surmised that Britain might be bound by international law to provide the Soviet Union with the secrets of an atomic bomb. One result was that the United States froze all exchanges of nuclear information with Britain for the next year. A second result was that Klaus Fuchs's espionage became part of a larger British effort to provide the Soviet Union with scientific information vital to the Allied effort against Nazi Germany.[34]

On June 18, 1942, Fuchs became a naturalized British citizen, at the recommendation of Tube Alloys, so that his enemy alien status would no longer restrict his work. At the naturalization ceremony Fuchs raised his hand and declared that he would "bear true allegiance" to the British Crown "according to law." Since Fuchs was a special "national interest" case, the police and the Home Office again checked his background. His communist past was known, but the chief constable of Birmingham reported that Fuchs had no apparent communist associations there, and he was again cleared. In August 1942 Fuchs wrote to Perrin about his naturalization, and Perrin replied with congratulations. A few months later Born complained that he had not heard from Fuchs in months; he had vanished into the world of wartime secrecy.[35]

Churchill's main scientific adviser, F. A. Lindemann (Lord Cherwell), had studied science in Germany before World War I, and in the 1930s he had helped a number of German scientists, including Franz Simon, Nicholas Kurti, and Max Born, find employment at English universities and at ICI. Although in 1939 he had told Churchill that Germany was unlikely to have an atomic bomb within the next several years (a Nazi "atomic explosive" posed "no immediate danger," he felt), Cherwell became more concerned after the war began. His assistant director of scientific intelligence for MI6, R. V. Jones, whose specialty was infrared radiation, was also greatly concerned about German secret weapons including radar, the x-beams used to guide Luftwaffe bombers over English cities, and the atomic bomb. In 1940 Peierls told Cherwell that German scientists might well be working on a uranium bomb, and the Maud report reiterated that such a weapon might be developed before the end of the war.[36]

In July 1941 G. P. Thompson, chairman of the technical committee exploring an atomic bomb, wrote Cherwell that Germany was trying to acquire heavy water, and he urged Cherwell to develop a scientific intelligence program, utilizing "someone with knowledge of physics and especially of the personalities and specialties of German physicists," rather than an MI6 officer. Cherwell quite naturally turned to the German refugee community for assistance—specifically to Peierls and Fuchs at Birmingham.[37]

That autumn Peierls and Fuchs began to visit London to obtain copies of German scientific periodicals from MI6 and to deduce the location, travel, and research activity of German nuclear scientists. Together they produced a report of limited circulation in which they concluded that the importance of isotope separation in producing fissionable U-235 was "well known" in Germany and that basic research was probably centered in Berlin, Munich, and Heidelberg. When MI6 officer Eric Welsh asked Akers "what steps were being taken to find out the movements of German scientists skilled in nuclear physics," Chadwick informed Akers that Peierls and Fuchs were working on it.[38]

In February 1942 Peierls and Fuchs filed another report, concluding that a review of the scientific literature "does not give very new indications on work or interest in the T.A. [Tube Alloys] field." A month later Fuchs abstracted a paper on isotope separation by F. G. Houtermans in the *Annalen der Physik* and sent it along to Chadwick via Perrin. A further review of German literature followed. By this time Fuchs was abstracting both published German and classified American reports on early atomic bomb work.[39]

Fuchs had a phenomenal memory and so was an ideal analyst. He could understand and recall in detail the most complex and difficult documents in his field. In April 1942 Fuchs sent Perrin and Chadwick an American classified report (A-117) by Eugene Wigner and Gregory Breit, the American bomb project coordinator at the time, on the size of the sphere of uranium needed for a chain reaction. When Peierls returned to Birmingham in May after a visit to the United States, he reported that the Breit-Wigner calculations were the only advance being made on the problem of critical mass; the results were similar to those obtained by Fuchs, although Peierls said that Fuchs's results were more accurate.[40]

In spring 1943 Fuchs and Peierls continued to review the German literature. Cherwell asked Fuchs to study the implications of building a diffusion plant and a heavy water plant in Britain. A British-Norwegian commando team had successfully raided and partially demolished the Norsk Hydro plant, delaying heavy water production for Germany. R. V. Jones and Eric Welsh of MI6 and Perrin continued to have Fuchs and Peierls evaluate German progress on building a bomb. Welsh was also able to monitor the nuclear negotiations between Britain and the United States, because the coded signals passed through Welsh's office link. MI6 was upset that Britain might be forced to give up her "birthright" in atomic bomb matters to the Americans.[41] Fuchs played a key role in the British scientific intelligence effort. In September 1943, after meeting with Cherwell on August 28, he sent him a top secret report explaining ICI's plans for a heavy water plant using centrifuge and electrolysis methods, which he doubted would work.

We know now that Welsh and MI6 had a scientific-intelligence agent, Paul Rosbaud, code-named Griffin, inside Nazi Germany throughout the war. The author of the 1939 Oslo Report on the Germans' secret weapons development, Rosbaud provided continuous information on the German atomic bomb and rocket projects. Compared to Rosbaud, Fuchs was a bit player in a role he did not fully comprehend. But in 1950 Fuchs's wartime connection, however small, with MI6 was a political liability for the British government.[42]

C H A P T E R · 5

The Girl from Banbury

Ride a cock horse
To Banbury Cross,
To see a fine lady
Upon a white horse.

— *English nursery rhyme*

When Hitler's armies attacked the Soviet Union in June 1941, Great Britain and the USSR became allies rather than enemies. Sometime later that year Fuchs approached KPD leader Jurgen Kuczynski to find out how he could help the Soviet war effort. Within months Fuchs was delivering his first reports to a courier he later said he knew only as "the girl from Banbury." She was Jurgen's sister Ursula, a skilled wireless operator and a Soviet military intelligence (GRU) agent.[1]

When Kuczynski suggested that Fuchs contact the Soviet embassy, scientific and military aid to the Soviet Union was an accepted part of the great "Second Front Campaign" in Britain. As the Red Army fought desperately in the snows of Moscow, the British sent as much aid as they could spare. The Labour Party, the CPGB, the trade unions, and the *Tribune* all beat the drums for Russia. So did Stafford Cripps, the British ambassador in Moscow, and his Soviet counterpart in London, Ivan Maisky, who in April 1942 unveiled a bust of Lenin in Holford Square. That year thousands attended pro-Soviet rallies in the streets of British cities, and the BBC played the *Internationale*. During "Tanks for Russia Week" all military goods produced were reportedly sent to the Eastern Front. The Aid to Russia Fund achieved double its goal (two million pounds), and Prime Minister Churchill cabled Stalin that "you can count on us to assist you by every means in our power."[2]

During the war Kuczynski wrote numerous anti-Nazi books and pamphlets, including *The Economics of Barbarism* (1942) and *Three Hundred Million Slaves and Serfs* (1943), in which he described Germany as a vast prison camp and praised the Soviet Union. He wrote for the KPD journal *Freies Deutschland* in Mexico City, as did his wife and his father. Jurgen's analyses of the British economy were given to British officials and to the Soviet embassy, where Kuczynski frequently visited Ambassador Maisky. The Kuczynskis continued both open and secret activities on behalf of the Soviet Union and were central figures in the campaign for Anglo-Soviet cooperation.[3]

This campaign reached its peak in 1943, when Moscow established the National Committee for a Free Germany, which was controlled by KPD leaders in Russia, notably Ulbricht and Pieck. Its members included a number of German prisoners of war in the Soviet Union. Enough anti-Nazi sympathizers were found among the captured German army officers to produce a newspaper and to begin regular radio broadcasts to Germany.[4]

The British branch of the Free Germany Committee was founded in London in September 1943. Initially, the KPD hoped to cooperate with the SPD in a broad united front, but the socialists would have no part of Kuczynski's proposals. The committee, with Robert Kuczynski as president, became a communist front organization. MI5 was aware of the organization from the beginning, but British officials did not understand that its goal was to establish a communist government in Germany after the war. The Foreign Office was not willing to support publicly any German exile group. For the KPD, the Free Germany Committee remained a useful front organization until late 1944, when it ceased activity in England.[5]

- *Jurgen Kuczynski and the OSS*

In late 1944 the London branch of the American Office of Strategic Services (OSS) began to use exiled German nationals for intelligence work, a practice that was contrary to Allied policy. One of these was Jurgen Kuczynski. As early as July 1941, Stafford Cripps had explored the possibilities of sharing intelligence with the Soviet Union and of carrying out joint clandestine operations against Nazi Germany. Soviet and British intelligence organizations agreed to assist each other and not to launch subversive operations in each other's territory. An NKVD mission arrived in London, and a counterpart from the Special Operations Executive (SOE, Churchill's wartime sabotage organization) went to Moscow. Colonel George Hill of SOE helped prepare the Soviet handbook on guerrilla warfare for partisan troops in 1942. Hill also suggested to General Deane, head of the U.S. military mission in Moscow, that the OSS cooperate with Soviet intelligence wherever possible. William Donovan, who headed the OSS, went to Moscow for preliminary discussions in December 1943.[6]

When J. Edgar Hoover learned of the proposed OSS-NKVD cooperation a few months later, he was very upset. "I think it is highly dangerous and most undesirable procedure," he wrote Harry Hopkins, "to establish in the United States a unit of the Russian secret service which has admittedly for its purpose the penetration into the official secrets of various government agencies." In Great Britain, too, MI5 was highly suspicious of the OSS-NKVD arrangement and kept a close watch on the London OSS offices. Their concern was justified.[7]

The OSS frequently used German refugee communists because of their language skills, experience in partisan warfare, and anti-Nazi credentials. Both the FBI and Army Intelligence were dubious about this practice, but Donovan defended it. In regard to recruiting Spanish Civil War veterans, Donovan said: "I know they're communists; that's why I hired them." Elaborating on this philosophy later, he added: "I'd put Stalin on the OSS payroll if I thought it would help defeat Hitler."[8]

The recruitment of German communists in England was directed by Joseph Gould, a young army lieutenant assigned to the Labor Division of OSS London. Gould was referred to Jurgen Kuczynski as an economist well connected to the Free Germany Committee in both London and Paris. Gould told Kuczynski that he needed agents who spoke fluent German to be parachuted behind enemy lines. Kuczynski promptly rounded up seven exiles for him. In December 1944 Kuczynski flew to Paris with another OSS officer to rendezvous with French resistance agents. Whatever intelligence Kuczynski gleaned from this episode he passed on to Moscow via Eric Henschke, another KPD exile, and his own sister, Ursula.[9]

In addition to his OSS work, Jurgen Kuczynski worked as a bombing analyst for the U.S. Strategic Bombing Survey (USSBS) in 1944–45. His assignment, approved by Moscow as well as Washington, was to calculate the economic effects of Allied bombing on Germany, and again his reports went to the Soviet Union via Ursula as well as to Allied headquarters. Until April 1945 Kuczynski worked in London; he then moved into occupied Germany as a member of John Kenneth Galbraith's staff. Galbraith recalled that Kuczynski was not a central figure and not a very good administrator; he was a known communist. "We knew, of course, that he had very close association with the Soviets, something that in those urgent days was considered far from being a disqualification."[10]

There is no doubt that Kuczynski was as useful to the Soviet Union as to the British and Americans in 1945. "Through my sister," he wrote later, "I passed to Moscow every piece of information I received."[11]

■ *Sonia*

Kuczynski's sister's connections with Soviet espionage were far deeper than Jurgen's. After Kim Philby's defection to the Soviet Union in 1963, Ursula Kuczynski's name began to appear in connection with various spy cases of the 1950s. E. H. Cookridge, in his 1968 study of the Philby case, identified Ursula-Marie Hamburger (her married name) as a Soviet military intelligence radio operator who had served in China, Poland, and Switzerland in the 1930s before going to England, where she was Klaus Fuchs's contact. A decade later, under the name Ruth Werner, Ursula told almost all in her memoirs, *Sonia's Report*. She is currently retired and living in East Germany, safe from the FBI and MI5.[12]

In February 1985 the seventy-eight-year-old woman, in an interview on Soviet television, confirmed that she had long been a Soviet intelligence officer. For her service she had received the rank of colonel in the Red Army and two Orders of the Red Banner. "We were defending the first socialist country," she recalled. "I was an intelligence agent for twenty years and I always regarded the Soviet Union as my second homeland. I was ready to fight for it."[13]

Born in Berlin in 1907, Jurgen's sister never did like the name Ruth. Like her father and brother, she moved easily into communist party circles, becoming an agitprop leader for the Berlin KPD organization, which she joined in 1926. Because of her father's annual trips to America, she worked in a New York bookstore for a few months in 1928 before returning to Germany to marry another party member, Rudolf Hamburger.[14]

In 1930 she and her husband took a trip to Moscow, where they were persuaded to work for Soviet intelligence and move to China. In 1931 Ruth was employed at the Soviet telegraph office in Shanghai, where she soon came to the attention of Richard Sorge, Moscow's top espionage agent in the Far East. Sorge gave her the code name Sonia and recommended that she go to Moscow for further training in radio operation and espionage. Sonia left her son, Michael, with Rudolf's parents in Czechoslovakia and went to Moscow in December 1932.[15]

In Moscow she entered the world of clandestine military intelligence, complete with wireless telegraphy, microphotography, and ciphers. Officially she was a captain in the Red Army; in addition, she was a GRU intelligence agent. (GRU stands for Glavnoe Razvedyvatel'noe Upravlenie, or Chief Intelligence Administration of the Red Army, not to be confused with the secret police, the NKVD.) Headquartered in Moscow, the GRU conducted military and industrial espionage abroad through a network of military attachés at Soviet embassies. In each country the attachés provided radio sets, codes, ciphers, and money to a resident director, who was usually responsible for intelligence in a neighboring country. The attachés communicated with Moscow by radio, using agents known only by their code names. (In 1930 Ursula Kuczynski's MI6 file had been upgraded to Yellow status because she was known to be acting in the interest of a foreign power, the Soviet Union, in Shanghai, which was British territory. Her husband, as the Soviet head of station there, already qualified for a Red file, and soon Ursula did also. In 1935 the British arrested Rudolf and jailed him for espionage activities.)[16]

In 1934 Sonia traveled widely as a GRU agent. She lived first in Czechoslovakia and Trieste, then moved on to the Far East—Cairo, Bombay, Singapore, Hong Kong, and finally Shanghai. For a time she organized Chinese partisan troops fighting the occupying Japanese army along the Manchurian border. In Mukden, Manchuria, she radioed reports back to Moscow on the Japanese occupation. In May 1935 she was posted to Peking, and at the end of that year was assigned to Poland. Sonia continued her GRU radio reports there until June 1937. Then, at the height of the purges, she was recalled to Moscow for further wireless training and was awarded the Order of the Red Banner for meritorious service.[17]

By the summer of 1938 she had been promoted from lieutenant to major in the Red Army and had settled her children temporarily in the town of Felpham on the coast of England. Sonia was then told to set up in neutral Switzerland an espionage network capable of providing extensive and frequent radio reports on Nazi Germany. In due time the Gestapo would name the larger European network of which she was a part the Rote Kapelle, or Red Orchestra. In September Sonia recruited an assistant, Allan Alexander Foote, a bearded, thirty-three-year-old Yorkshireman recommended by CPGB leader Douglas Springhall, who had met him in Spain in 1936. Sonia then left for Montreux, Switzerland, where she rented a chalet, using the name Ursula Hamburger, and set up her transmitter. She was specifically instructed not to join any communist party.[18]

Foote met Sonia for the first time in Geneva in January 1939, in the midst of Hitler's takeover of Czechoslovakia. She assigned him the code name Jim and began training him in radio transmitting. Within a few weeks she asked Foote to suggest a suitable assistant. He proposed Leon Charles Beurton, age twenty-five, a naturalized British citizen of French origin. Beurton, who also used the names Len Brewer and Bill Phillips, was a handsome, wiry man with brown hair. Like Foote, he had fought with the International Brigades in Spain. Throughout 1939 Sonia ran her two British agents out of Montreux into Nazi Germany. When war broke out in September, Sonia was instructed by Moscow to remain in Switzerland and to train her operators in the techniques of shortwave transmission.[19]

▪ Allan Foote, the Lucy Ring, and the Ultra Secret

During the 1930s the Soviet Union developed espionage networks throughout Europe and the Far East. Moles recruited in England burrowed deep into the British foreign service and intelligence establishment. Anticipating war and possible occupation, the British developed their own intelligence networks in Europe. British counterespionage was particularly active during the period of the Nazi-Soviet pact, when it appeared that the Soviet Union and Nazi Germany would be common enemies of England.

All this changed in 1941, when England and the USSR joined forces against Hitler. The British intelligence networks then shared with the Soviet Union resources and information that were crucial to prosecution of the war, including the top-secret "Ultra" decrypts of German radio traffic. During the war Soviet moles in British intelligence quite consistently served both Stalin and Churchill in a common struggle. Only after 1945 did the enemies change and Soviet moles become dangerous opponents in the Cold War.

Switzerland's historic neutrality made her attractive for espionage agents of both sides. Although Swiss-Soviet diplomatic relations had been broken off in 1923, Soviet agents were numerous and multinational in the thirties. Many maintained contacts with British officials caught in Switzerland by the war. Several Soviet agents worked for the International Labour Office (ILO) in Geneva, which monitored labor conditions worldwide. (Its headquarters were moved to Montreal in 1940 when war threatened even Switzerland.) The ILO's international offices, diplomatic immunity, and readily available travel documents were especially useful to the agents.[20]

Two ILO staffers were particularly important. One was Rachel Duebendorfer, code-named Sissy, a Polish KPD member who had worked for Munzenberg's Rote Hilfe in the 1920s and had served as a stenotypist for the party central committee. She performed the same services for the ILO after 1934, serving as a Soviet (and possibly British) agent on the side. The second agent was Christian Schneider, code-named Taylor, a German translator who worked during the war for the so-called Lucy Ring. Lucy was the code name of Rudolf Roessler, a German who had lived in Lucerne since 1934, publishing books under the Vita Nova imprint. Roessler was recruited for intelligence work by Christian Schnieper, a Swiss communist.[21] Throughout the war Roessler provided a steady stream of intelligence to the Soviet Union on German military operations, but he also was linked in various ways to Swiss and British intelligence. In 1940 the Soviet resident director for Germany was the Hungarian cartographer Alexander (Sandor) Rado, who lived in Geneva and reported to the NKVD.

Whatever their sources, the Red Orchestra's information went both to Moscow and to western intelligence services, notably the Swiss and the British. Sonia's network, it turns out, was not only known to the British, but in part manipulated by them without her knowledge.[22]

On February 23, 1940, Sonia, who was then separated (but not divorced) from Rudolf Hamburger, married Len Beurton. When the Germans occupied France in the spring, Moscow ordered Sonia to make contact with Rado and to place Beurton's radio transmitter at Rado's disposal. Having married Beurton, a British citizen, Sonia was able to apply for a British passport. In the spring of 1940, however, she had a narrow escape; a woman telephoned the British embassy in Bern, denounced the Beurtons as Soviet spies, and told them where Sonia's transmitter was hidden (in a tulip bed). Fortunately for the Beurtons, the caller's broken English could not be understood, and on May 2 Sonia received her passport. She continued to draw her monthly salary of two thousand Swiss francs from the GRU. The Beurtons left Geneva on

December 18. Len, unable to obtain a transit visa through Spain because of his involvement on the Republican side in the Spanish Civil War, returned to Switzerland. Sonia and the children continued on to Lisbon, then to Liverpool.[23]

Moscow also directed Allan Foote to move from Lausanne to Geneva and train another radio operator for Rado. But Foote was no ordinary Soviet agent. The Russians suspected that he was either a double agent or a British mole inserted into the Soviet espionage network. In any case, Foote was to play a crucial role in Anglo-Soviet espionage and in the fate of Sonia and Klaus Fuchs. A woman friend described him as a "hard headed, matter of fact North Countryman with an odd streak of restless romanticism in his veins"; another said he was "physically courageous to the point of recklessness." Slightly overweight and with thin blond hair, Foote appeared not at all mysterious. He was a good listener who attracted everyone and charmed women. He had the manner of a "big friendly bear." Foote told his friends that he was in Switzerland during the war solely for his health. "No one could have been less like the popular idea of a secret agent," wrote Malcolm Muggeridge. "He was much more like an insurance agent, or possibly a professional cricketeer." "The thing that surprised me most," recalled Rado, "was his complete lack of political education."[24]

In 1936 Foote, then an airframe fitter for the Royal Air Force, had been recruited into the semi-private intelligence network of Colonel Claude Dansey, who had been involved with British intelligence since the Boer War.[25] Supposedly banished from MI6 in 1936, Dansey, under the direct orders of that agency, set up his own secret service, the Z organization, in Zurich, using his business contacts and his friendship with the head of Swiss intelligence. The idea was to have in readiness, if war came, an organization on the continent completely parallel to MI6 and capable, if necessary, of replacing it. By 1938 Dansey, with MI6 funding and approval, had agents all over Europe, including, probably, Allan Foote. During the Spanish Civil War Dansey sent Foote to Spain with the International Brigades to establish his left-wing credentials. By 1940 Foote was the chief radio operator for the Soviet network in Switzerland. Whether or not Dansey actually "ran the most important Russian spy [Roessler] of the Second World War," British counterintelligence did succeed in penetrating Soviet intelligence in Switzerland through Foote. Rado had his suspicions about Foote from the beginning, but only much later would Sonia come to realize that her agent was actually a traitor to the Soviet cause.[26]

During the first six months of 1941 Britain and the USSR were still enemies. Foote continued his radio transmissions to Moscow of information given him by Rado, but rarely received acknowledgment. The first reaction from Moscow came in March 1941 when Foote transmitted information, credited to Lucy, on German troop movements and predicted an imminent German invasion of the Soviet Union. Moscow was skeptical. Who was Lucy? Foote would not tell them.[27]

As soon as Nazi Germany attacked the Soviet Union on June 22, British intelligence began making available to Stalin the decoded German radio messages known, to a very few in Britain, as Ultra. To convince Stalin that British-generated intelligence was genuine and to make sure that Stalin could not reveal the Ultra operation to the Germans, the British needed to disguise the source of their intelligence reports to Moscow. Although the British government and its official historians deny it, other historians argue that the Lucy Ring in Switzerland was used in 1942–43 to "launder" Ultra and to convince Stalin that his intelligence sources were not British cryptographers but Soviet agents inside Germany. According to Brigadier General Walter Scott, chief of radio intelligence at Eisenhower's headquarters, "Lucy and his sources were valuable for one thing only—cover for Ultra."[28]

On the day of the Nazi attack on Russia, the British ceased to monitor Soviet radio communications, partly because the Soviet Union was now an ally and partly because resources were in desperate demand. In Switzerland Christian Schneider had given Sissy the exact date of the German attack in advance; Foote transmitted it to an unbelieving Moscow on June 17. Schneider thus established a tie to the Rado network. Roessler would give his messages to Rado, who would encipher them and send them on to Moscow through one of his three radio operators. Moscow's messages for Lucy or Dora (Rado) would return the same way.

Sissy knew Foote only as Jim, and Rado never allowed them to meet.[29]

There is no doubt that the British transmitted Ultra intercepts to Stalin to assist the Soviet war effort, though this was an official secret until the 1970s. In July 1941, Menzies at MI6 agreed to provide the Russians with Ultra traffic "on a regular basis in camouflaged form." Churchill concurred, "provided no risks are run." Intercepted German signals were sent from London to the British military mission in Moscow, their sources disguised from Stalin as a "well-placed source in Berlin" or a "reliable source." Such signals were crucial in the defense of Moscow that winter, warning the Russians of the timing, location, and disposition of attacking forces. "No one in Russia," warned Churchill, "must know about our special sources of information."[30]

How to disguise Ultra? Dansey may well have persuaded Menzies that the messages could be laundered through the Soviet espionage network in Switzerland. In the 1950s Muggeridge asked Foote point-blank if Lucy was really a cover for Ultra; Foote looked "faintly startled and then abruptly changed the subject." It is certainly plausible. In 1942 Foote had his own cipher, unknown to Rado, and could communicate with the British and the Russians on his own. All of them could have gotten intelligence information into and out of Rado's Swiss network. But did they?[31]

Kim Philby complained in 1942 that Ultra was being withheld from Stalin for fear that the true source would be compromised. In fact, this was not true, but Philby was understandably furious and wanted to aid the Russians in every possible way. As an MI6 officer, he had every motive and opportunity to provide Ultra decrypts to the Russians. British intelligence and Soviet agents all wanted to get information to Moscow as quickly and completely as possible, and Dansey and his Z organization could do it through the Lucy Ring. Radio messages could be sent from London to Moscow via Foote in Lausanne as well, without Rado's knowledge.[32]

By 1943 the Germans were beginning to close in on the Swiss network, and on November 20 Foote was arrested by the Swiss police. He was released the following year and went to Moscow, where he was thoroughly debriefed by Maria Poliakova, the GRU agent who had organized the Swiss network and had sent Sonia there. Early in 1947 Foote, who was considered a valuable agent in place, was sent to East Berlin under cover of a supposedly pro-Nazi identity. He was to travel to Mexico and serve as GRU resident director for the United States. But on August 2, 1947, Foote crossed the border into the British Zone of the divided Germanies and promptly turned himself over for extensive interrogation by MI5.[33]

Foote told the British that his Soviet masters suspected that he had been "got at" by British intelligence but that he had been cleared by Moscow for further intelligence work. He also told MI5 that two of his former colleagues, John and Sonia (Len Beurton and Ursula Kuczynski), had been living in England since 1941. Foote said that Moscow claimed both agents had been dormant during the war. After ten weeks of MI5 interviews in Germany, Foote underwent another six weeks of grilling in London before being released. He had reported Sonia to the British, but he may not have identified her by her real name. Foote later wrote that Sonia had given up spying and wished only "respectable obscurity" in Great Britain.[34]

In his 1947 *Handbook for Spies,* Foote identified Lucy as someone named Selzinger, "our source who supplied information from Berlin." The Lucy Ring became less significant, and the Ultra secret remained a secret. After the war the remaining Lucy Ring members scattered. Sissy went to the Soviet Union in 1945 and was put into a Siberian camp until Khrushchev's de-Stalinization thaw of 1956; she died in 1973. Rado spent twelve years in a Siberian camp, then returned to Budapest to teach geography in the late 1950s. Roessler and Schnieper stayed in Switzerland; they were arrested for espionage again in 1953. Foote and Roessler both died in 1958, taking many of Lucy's secrets with them.[35]

The Lucy Ring was one of the most important Soviet and British espionage operations of World War II. For several years its agents provided Stalin with top secret intelligence on German military operations on an almost hourly basis. Whether or not the source of this information was Ultra, it embroiled both Soviet and British intelligence in a Swiss spiderweb of secret information exchange. Foote may have been a British agent, or at least a double agent.

In 1950 Fuchs's arrest could have revealed publicly the existence of Soviet agents in England (Sonia and Philby), the wartime co-operation and interpenetration of the Soviet and British intelligence services, and the existence of Ultra. For Sonia had been at different times the controller of both Allan Foote and Klaus Fuchs, and she had been a wireless operator in the Soviet network through which Ultra information may have been given to Stalin.

■ *Klaus Fuchs and Sonia*

Sonia arrived in England about the time that Klaus Fuchs returned from his Canadian internment. She and her children settled in with her father, Robert, who had moved to Oxford. By the spring of 1941, therefore, one of the GRU's best agents and wireless operators was in place in England.[36]

Sonia was ideally positioned in Oxford. As "Mrs. Brewer," she was simply another Jewish refugee from Hitler. She smuggled radio parts in her baby's teddy bear and once told the local police that her transmitter was a toy. Her father continued his relationships with highly placed British officials, including Stafford Cripps, and passed Sonia information from Churchill's War Cabinet. Months went by before Sonia was able to establish contact with her Soviet control, because she had been instructed by Moscow to avoid at all costs the CPGB and the Soviet embassy in London. Her first husband, Rudolf Hamburger, had been arrested in Shanghai, and her second, Len Beurton, was stuck in Switzerland.[37]

When Sonia met her Soviet control, Sergei, in London in May 1941, he told her the GRU wanted her to build an espionage network in England. This she promptly began to do. Her first control was Simon Davidovich Kremer, secretary to the military attaché at the Soviet embassy in London. In addition to her father, she recruited her brother, Jurgen, Hans Kahle (who had been interned with Fuchs in Canada), and several others. By September 1942 Len had joined her. The Beurtons moved to a cottage in the Summertown district of Oxford, rented from Nevill Laski, brother of the Labour Party leader. According to Sonia, the Beurtons strung their aerial between their cottage and the Laskis' and began to transmit to the Soviet Union vital British wartime secrets.[38]

After D-day, Sonia says, her activity continued unabated. On November 7, 1944, she received a shortwave transmitter six times more powerful than her existing one. Because Jurgen Kuczynski was by that time working with the OSS and the Strategic Bombing Survey in London, Sonia was able to send extensive information on their activities to Moscow. Eric Henschke, another KPD leader, and Jurgen removed reports from their offices and gave them to Sonia to send on to Moscow. When Germany surrendered in May 1945, the OSS ceased using German communist agents, and Sonia turned to her other sources.[39]

In the autumn of 1941, when Fuchs asked Jurgen how he could help the Soviet Union, Kuczynski suggested that he contact the Soviet embassy in London. Fuchs did so promptly and quite openly, saying that he had important information about an Anglo-American war project that could lead to a powerful new weapon and that he wanted to share this information with Russia. He was immediately assigned a control he knew only as Alexander, a man Fuchs believed was a Russian.[40]

Alexander was Sonia's control, Kremer, who had lived in London with his wife, Evgeniia, and their two children since 1937. Nominally affiliated with the diplomatic community, Kremer was in fact employed by the Fourth Department of the Red Army, Soviet military intelligence. In 1940 Walter Krivitsky, a GRU defector who provided MI5 with vast data on Soviet espionage abroad, had named Kremer as the center of Soviet espionage operations abroad. But MI5 took no action against Kremer, who established the mechanism whereby Fuchs could provide atomic bomb secrets to Moscow.[41]

The Soviet agent had no technical knowledge of atomic bombs, but he did ask Fuchs at one point what he knew about the electromagnetic method for separating U-235 as an alternative to gaseous diffusion. Fuchs was surprised, since he himself knew nothing about it. Fuchs also reported to him that a gaseous diffusion pilot plant was being designed in Wales and that Britain and America were working together on the atomic bomb.[42]

On December 7, 1941, the day Japanese war planes attacked

Pearl Harbor, Max Born wrote to Fuchs from Edinburgh that "the news from Russia seems quite hopeful. You must be gratified that your belief in the Russians is so much justified now, even with respect to Finland." Six months later Born wrote Fuchs that he was delighted to learn of the Anglo-Soviet treaty under which Great Britain would provide significant military and technical aid to the Russian front. He had no idea that Fuchs was conducting his own technology transfer program with the aid of Kremer and Kuczynski, providing Stalin with news of the British atomic bomb project.[43]

Sonia became Fuchs's control some time in 1942, presumably because Oxford was convenient to Fuchs's work in Birmingham. They often met in nearby Banbury. Fuchs would give her his reports in writing, and Sonia would transmit them to Moscow. If the reports were mathematical, she passed them to Kremer in London, since he had the use of the diplomatic pouch and a radio. It is entirely possible that Fuchs did not know Sonia's identity; he certainly was unaware of her intelligence connections. Fuchs and Sonia met about six times at intervals of two or three months until December 1943, when Fuchs left for the United States as a member of the British mission to the top secret Manhattan Project. Before he left, Sonia gave him instructions for contacting "Raymond" (Harry Gold) in New York.[44]

Fuchs passed to the Soviets "all the information I had" about the atomic bomb. "Since that time," he later told Skardon, "I have had continuous contact with persons who were completely unknown to me, except that I knew that they would hand whatever information I gave them to the Russian authorities." "I used my Marxist philosophy," he confessed, "to establish in my mind two separate compartments." The first compartment contained friendships, personal relations, and the behavior of "the kind of man I wanted to be." The second compartment contained the dialectical necessity of correct party behavior, espionage in the name of historical determinism, which gave Fuchs a peculiar sense of being a "free man" who could be "completely independent of the surrounding forces of society." "Looking back at it now," he concluded, "the best way of expressing it seems to be to call it a controlled schizophrenia."[45]

Allan Foote named Sonia as a Soviet agent in 1947, but MI5 did nothing about it, perhaps because her real identity was unknown. Within months MI5 did trace the Beurtons to their new home at Great Rollright village, near Chipping Norton, north of Oxford. One day two MI5 officers visited her on the pretext of discussing her bigamous marriage to Beurton. When they told Sonia they knew she had been a Soviet agent, she calmly invited them in for tea. "Years ago," one of them told her, "you were a Russian agent, until the Finnish war [of 1940]. We know you were not active in England, and we don't want to arrest you, just to ask your cooperation." Sonia and Len admitted that they had known Foote, and they went along with the story handed to them: they had been Soviet agents but had long been inactive. They learned that Foote's cover had been blown and that they could no longer be effective. Foote later learned from Sonia's sister Brigitte of the Beurtons' "narrow escape." But they did not leave England until 1950.[46]

Robert Lamphere, the FBI agent who later interviewed Klaus Fuchs, believes that "Ursula Beurton" was known to MI5 "early on" as Fuchs's controller for a time and that MI5 "did not share with the FBI what they knew of her." According to MI5 officer Dick White, Sonia was never placed under surveillance, and MI5 reports on her consistently downplayed her importance. Another MI5 officer claims that Sonia did meet Fuchs in 1947 and that she turned him over to a GRU case officer at the London embassy who "was also passing information to the British, having been turned by MI6 in Ankara."[47] If this was the case, Fuchs was under MI6 control after 1947 without knowing it. Lamphere and Chapman Pincher, a British journalist, believe that the continuing ineptness of British security was the deliberate policy of Roger Hollis of MI5. Yet by 1947 Hollis was in Australia, and the curiosities surrounding Fuchs and Sonia persisted.

Sonia heard nothing from Moscow after late 1946. She and Len continued to live in England unmolested until Fuchs was arrested. Len worked at an aluminum factory in Banbury, commuting by motorcycle from Oxford. By 1948 the Beurtons had three children to raise. Len was unhappy in his job, and Sonia passed the time going to meetings of the Workers' Education

Association. They even joined the CPGB, primarily out of boredom, and in disregard of all Soviet espionage instructions. Sonia corresponded with brother Jurgen, still in West Berlin, but was unable to get a visa to see him until January 1949. When they met in Prague, she told him of the personal and political problems of being a blown agent in postwar England.[48] Sonia desperately wished to leave England. In Prague she left a letter for GRU headquarters at the Soviet embassy; using her old cipher, she asked permission to leave "Brazil" (England).

In October 1949, as the Fuchs case began to unravel, Len had a motorcycle accident and was laid up at home with a broken arm. Sonia applied for permission to visit East Germany. As soon as Klaus Fuchs became a public figure, Sonia got her visa, gathered her children, and left. That summer Len cleared out the house, burned all incriminating papers and documents, and followed his wife to East Germany and a new job with the East German News Service.[49]

We know that Sonia came under MI5 surveillance in 1947 and that she remained in England until after Klaus Fuchs confessed to espionage. She was not arrested and was allowed to leave the country in 1950. By that time the Fuchs case threatened to reveal the secret world of Kim Philby, the highly placed MI6 officer who had his own links with the Lucy Ring and the Ultra secret.

C H A P T E R · 6

Gold in Manhattan

Yes, I am the man to whom Klaus Fuchs gave the information on atomic energy.

— *Harry Gold, May 22, 1950*

F uchs's access to nuclear secrets increased significantly when he sailed for America in December 1943 as a member of the British mission to the Manhattan Project. In New York he was surprised to learn the scope of the U.S. bomb project, to which he would make major contributions. Following Sonia's instructions, within a few months he also made contact with his new courier, a man he knew only as Raymond.

- *The British Mission*

Even before Pearl Harbor, American and British scientists realized that cooperation on atomic research was crucial to success in building a bomb. Anglo-American nuclear cooperation had begun in the summer of 1940, when the British government proposed a "general interchange of secret information" with the United States. In the autumn of 1941 the two countries shared their experimental results and the Maud committee reports by the British. Vannevar Bush, director of the Office of Scientific Research and Development (OSRD), was a champion of Anglo-American liaison in all research areas. Immediately after the United States entered the war, preliminary discussions began relative to British contributions to an American atomic bomb project. Yet by December 1942 cooperation had deteriorated, as both powers pondered the postwar uses of the technologies they were developing. A central issue was the American policy makers' belief that the British would seek commercial advantages from nuclear power.[1] British research soon gave way to American engineering in the creation of an atomic bomb, and the sharing of technical information declined. The result in England was a growing sense of jealousy, frustration, belittlement, and inferiority in matters nuclear.

By the time the Manhattan Engineer District was established in 1942, under the control of the U.S. Army Corps of Engineers, the United States was thoroughly suspicious of Great Britain. Roosevelt did not appreciate Churchill's enthusiasm for a nuclear partnership, "fully sharing the results as equal partners." General Leslie Groves, the American leader of the Manhattan Project, and James Conant were particularly concerned about Wallace Akers's interest in nuclear power after the war and his powerful dual role in both ICI and Tube Alloys. "I could to some extent sympathize with American suspicions," Churchill's scientific intelligence officer, R. V. Jones, later wrote, "for in the Tube Alloys outer office the first thing that greeted the visitor was a large wall map of Britain divided up into the ICI sales divisions, its presence in fact signifying nothing more sinister than that Akers and Perrin were ICI employees seconded to the government."[2]

American officials were also worried that the British might leak nuclear secrets to the French, even though in September the French researchers Halban and Kowarski signed an agreement with the British government promising to work exclusively for the Department of Scientific and Industrial Research and to give them all patent rights outside of France.[3]

In late 1942 the British again proposed a free exchange of information on atomic bomb research, but because of American suspicions, only a "restricted interchange" was approved. The Anglo-Soviet agreement created a "very serious situation," said U.S. Secretary of War Stimson; sharing information with Great Britain could well mean that the Soviets would have access to

American secrets. Roosevelt agreed that any exchange of nuclear information with Great Britain should be limited to gaseous diffusion, heavy water production, and plutonium production. The work on bomb design at Los Alamos would be off limits. The British were being deliberately cut out of atomic research, in which they had pioneered, just when an atomic bomb was becoming a real possibility.

On December 2 a team of scientists under Enrico Fermi at the University of Chicago succeeded in creating the first controlled and self-sustaining nuclear chain reaction, using a pile of interlaced graphite and uranium blocks. The new world of nuclear energy was being discovered in America by scientists in flight from Hitler, Mussolini, and Stalin. And the British were being virtually excluded.[4]

American policy makers' concern increased when they learned that Henry Tizard was planning a mission to the Soviet Union in 1943 to exchange scientific information. In January 1943 Groves, Conant, and Akers held a stormy meeting in Washington on information exchange, and in late February Churchill wrote presidential adviser Harry Hopkins that the exchange of nuclear information should be renewed on the basis of "mutual confidence" and "complete cooperation." He suggested a formal agreement that would reconcile the needs of American national security with British and Canadian participation. Vannevar Bush told Hopkins in March that only information essential to the war effort should be exchanged.[5]

That year saw the turning of the tide in the war against Hitler. The Red Army emerged victorious from the vicious street fighting at Stalingrad, and the British launched a successful air strike against the German-controlled heavy water plant in Norway. Perrin, Welsh, and Jones were increasingly convinced, on the basis of Rosbaud's reports, that German progress toward an atomic bomb was extremely slow or nonexistent. Tizard's scientific mission to Moscow seemed less critical, and in June 1943 it was postponed indefinitely. Roosevelt, having reviewed for Groves "the highly important and secret program of research with which you are familiar," was convinced that the Manhattan Project, still in the early stages of development, must be "even more drastically guarded than other highly secret war developments."[6]

Roosevelt was thus cautious when Churchill again proposed in June that "exchange of information on Tube Alloys should be resumed." By late July, however, Roosevelt had decided that British participation in the Manhattan Project was essential to the Grand Alliance. On July 20 he instructed Bush to "renew, in an inclusive manner, the full exchange of information with the British Government regarding Tube Alloys." This crucial decision led to both the Quebec Agreement and to Klaus Fuchs's admission to the American project.[7]

The secret Agreement Relating to Atomic Energy signed by Roosevelt and Churchill at Quebec on August 19, 1943, began by stating that Britain and the United States would not use an atomic bomb against each other and would not use one against a third party without each other's consent. The agreement stated that "we will not either of us communicate any information about Tube Alloys to third parties [meaning France and Russia] except by mutual consent." Any postwar uses "of an industrial or commercial character" would be determined by the president of the United States. Finally, a Combined Policy Committee (CPC), with American, British, and Canadian representatives, would oversee the work on an atomic bomb, including the "full and effective interchange of information and ideas."[8] Canada did participate in the nuclear weapons project, but only under strict rules laid down by the Americans. The country was valued less for her scientists than for her vast uranium deposits at Great Bear Lake and the uranium refining plant at Port Hope, Ontario. But the nuclear laboratory at Montreal and the reactor at Chalk River, Ontario, provided fundamental data on neutron behavior after 1943 and contributed significantly to basic research.[9]

In September 1943 General Groves met with Peierls to discuss the design of the proposed K-25 gaseous diffusion plant at Oak Ridge. The reports of Peierls's Birmingham team had been sent regularly to J. Robert Oppenheimer and James Conant in the United States. Fuchs's contributions to the theory of gaseous diffusion were sufficiently valuable that an American team considered visiting Birmingham to consult him. But instead, the Americans decided that Fuchs, Otto Frisch, and some other scientists should come to the United States. Clearances were requested from the American embassy, and on November 18, Fuchs received a

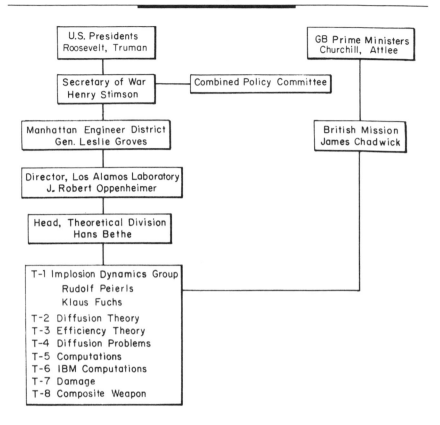

Figure 4. The Manhattan Project, 1943–1945

visa from the State Department, issued without the usual signature or photograph because of the urgency of the mission.[10]

On December 3 Fuchs disembarked at Norfolk, Virginia. Michael Perrin followed a few days later, as did the eminent physicist Niels Bohr, who had recently been flown out of occupied Denmark in a British fighter plane and was now traveling incognito as Nicholas Baker. All of the scientists were cleared by British security and accepted without further investigation by the Americans. In New York Fuchs settled into an apartment and took up his duties as a member of the British mission. (See Figure 4.) The research was administered by Columbia University and the Kellex Corporation.[11]

After a number of meetings, Fuchs was assigned to work on calculations for the Oak Ridge gaseous diffusion plant for producing fissionable uranium. He was especially concerned with the effects of fluctuations on the production rate of uranium-235, but he soon became involved in the design of the plant. His main job was to develop the theory of control, especially the mathematical hydrodynamics explaining the flow of uranium hexafluoride through the metal barriers. On December 22 Fuchs attended a meeting at the Kellex headquarters, chaired by General Groves, and heard a review of the feasibility of the K-25 plant, including the details of its pumps, valves, and control barriers.[12]

Fuchs spent Christmas in Cambridge with his sister Kristel and her family. He also established contact with his American courier, according to the plan established before he left England. By early 1944 he was in a position to pass along to the Soviet Union considerable information on the plant at Oak Ridge, which he knew only as "site x." He provided details of the sintered nickel powder membranes being constructed for the gaseous diffusion barriers, as well as copies of all reports prepared by the British mission, known as the MSN series. Fuchs's name appeared on the lists of British scientists who might visit "various establishments" of the Manhattan Project without applying to military intelligence (G-2) on each occasion, but he was not authorized to visit restricted areas or have access to classified information on these visits. He never visited Oak Ridge or Hanford.[13]

American fears of information leaks to the Soviet Union, as well as to Germany and Japan, persisted. In September 1943 Stimson wrote the president that Soviet agents were "already getting information about vital secrets and sending them to Russia." He was particularly suspicious of scientists working at Ernest Lawrence's radiation laboratory in Berkeley, California.[14]

Although Manhattan Project security was the responsibility of the War Department, the FBI remained interested in, and was informed about, all wartime security matters. J. Edgar Hoover was not satisfied with the security arrangements for the British mission. In March 1944 he asked the Manhattan Engineer District office about the mission and was again assured that all of the scientists had been cleared by British security. In late May Fuchs and Peierls went to Montreal for a conference with other British, American, and Canadian scientists involved in the Manhattan Project. By this time Fuchs had a very clear idea of the design of the Oak Ridge plant, including the size of the units, the various stages involved, and the type and size of the power unit.[15]

■ *Raymond*

Fuchs's American courier was not identified until May 22, 1950, several months after Fuchs had confessed to espionage. A frenetic search by the FBI soon focused on one man, Harry Gold, a biochemistry technician at Philadelphia General Hospital. Fuchs's identification of Gold from motion pictures shown him in London by the FBI coincided with Gold's own detailed written confession that he had been Raymond. The discovery of Fuchs's courier later led to the discovery of Julius and Ethel Rosenberg. But who was Harry Gold?

He was born December 12, 1910, to a Russian Jewish family named Golodnitzky, then living in Switzerland. In 1914 the family moved to America. In the 1930s Gold attended college at night through the Drexel Institute of the University of Pennsylvania in Philadelphia, while working full time in a laboratory for the Pennsylvania Sugar Company. In June 1940 he received his B.S. degree summa cum laude from Xavier University, a Jesuit institution in Cincinnati, Ohio. During and after World War II he worked at various laboratory jobs in the chemical and biochemical industries in New York and Philadelphia.[16]

Harry Gold's life of espionage began in 1935, when he gave information concerning sugar processing to Soviet agents who worked for the industrial espionage section, which operated out of the embassy, the New York consulate, the trading agency Amtorg, and various Comintern offices. His director was Jacob Golos, another Russian Jewish emigré to the United States. Golos, an American citizen, was a member of the American Communist Party and an employee of the front organization known as the Society for Technical Aid to Soviet Russia. After 1934 he directed a substantial industrial espionage network that included his secretary, Elizabeth Bentley, and Gold. Golos died in 1943. After

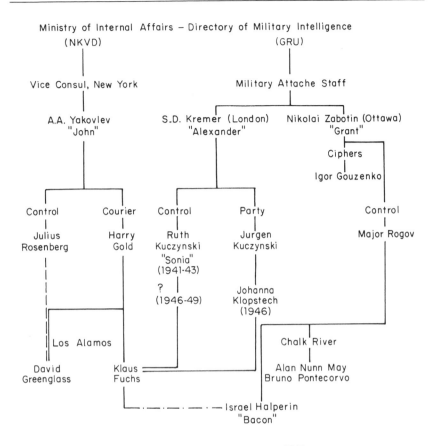

Figure 5. Soviet atomic espionage, 1945

1940 Gold was under the control of a man he knew only as Sam, who was Semon Semonov, a graduate of Massachusetts Institute of Technology who had come to the United States in 1938 to direct industrial espionage operations for the Soviet Union. In 1944 Semonov was replaced by Anatolii Yakovlev, whom Gold knew as John. Until December 1946 Yakovlev, in the guise of a vice consul, directed the most vital espionage operation of all: the Soviet quest for the secrets of the Manhattan Project (see Figure 5).

Gold said he first met Klaus Fuchs on John's (Yakovlev's) instructions in late February or early March 1944 in New York, where Fuchs was working on gaseous diffusion at Kellex. The meeting occurred on a Saturday somewhere on the East Side. "I was to carry a pair of gloves in one hand, plus a green-covered book, and Dr. Fuchs was to carry a handball in one hand," Gold told the FBI. Gold introduced himself as Raymond, Fuchs as Klaus Fuchs. After a brief walk they took a cab to a restaurant in the Fifties near Third Avenue, had dinner, and talked. After dinner they again walked the streets of New York and agreed on arrangements for further meetings, which would be brief and never twice in the same place.

Gold and Fuchs met for the second time in March at the corner of 59th Street and Lexington Avenue, then walked to the nearby Queensboro Bridge. Fuchs explained to Gold the work of the British mission on gaseous diffusion, including the "manpower setup," the process of isotope separation, and the security techniques of the Manhattan Project. Fuchs also discussed the electromagnetic separation of uranium, but brushed aside Gold's question about thermal diffusion as an unlikely process. At the time Fuchs knew nothing of Los Alamos; he said only that a uranium separation plant was being built in great secrecy somewhere in the southeastern United States, probably Georgia or Alabama. Fuchs still provided no written information on the bomb, but Gold remembered that "it was more or less mutually understood that he was to supply me with information from the work that he was doing." This written information would be passed from Gold to Yakovlev, a step that Fuchs knew nothing about.

With the mechanism of espionage established, the next meetings of the two men in New York were brief and businesslike. The third meeting, in March, took place in bitterly cold weather; both men wore heavy overcoats when they met at a corner of Madison Avenue in the Seventies. After talking with Fuchs for less than a minute, Gold walked down Fifth Avenue and delivered the documents to Yakovlev. The fourth meeting, in the Bronx in April, was more leisurely; Gold and Fuchs talked of music and chess over dinner at Rosenheim's Restaurant. Fuchs apparently did not hand over any information at that time.

By May Fuchs was able to provide handwritten copies of his own papers on the hydrodynamics of gaseous diffusion. At their fifth meeting, in Queens, Fuchs handed over a second package of documents, some forty pages of mathematical formulas, which Gold did not read. The meeting lasted only three or four minutes. Half an hour later Gold delivered the precious package to Yakovlev in the prescribed manner.

At their sixth meeting, near Borough Hall in Brooklyn in June, Fuchs told Gold that his sister might be coming to New York. He did not mention Kristel's last name (Heineman), indicating only that she lived in Cambridge, had two children, and was thinking of separating from her husband. The next meeting, in early July, was more significant. During an hour-long walk in Central Park, Fuchs told Gold that he might be transferred to a new location of the Manhattan Project "somewhere to the southwest," possibly Mexico. He also told Gold of his family problems; his brother, Gerhard, was convalescing in Switzerland after having spent time in a Nazi concentration camp, and Kristel was planning to move to New York with her children.

Fuchs never appeared for the eighth meeting, scheduled for late July near the Brooklyn Museum of Art, and he did not show up at the location in Central Park West that had been agreed on as a backup. Worried that Fuchs might have been mugged, Gold spent two hours with Yakovlev discussing the problem. In late August, when Gold visited Fuchs's apartment at 128 West 77th Street, his landlady said only that he had left town. Gold reported this to Yakovlev, who told Gold to "sit tight" and await further instructions.

In September Yakovlev obtained the Heinemans' address and instructed Gold to visit them. Gold traveled to Cambridge, but the Heinemans were on vacation and Fuchs was nowhere to be found. We now know that Fuchs had been transferred to the most secret part of the Manhattan Project, the bomb assembly and design laboratory at Los Alamos, New Mexico, and had not had time to inform Gold of his shift in duties and location.

Hans Bethe, head of the Theoretical Division at Los Alamos, had requested that Peierls replace the Hungarian physicist Edward Teller as leader of the T-1 group (Hydrodynamics of Implosion and Super). Peierls accepted on the condition that he be allowed to bring along Fuchs and Tony Skyrme, another young British scientist. In Washington James Chadwick, the British mission head, told Fuchs that he was to go to Los Alamos "provisionally until the end of December." The T-1 group, renamed Implosion Dynamics, would be Fuchs's home for the next two years.[17]

Wallace Akers at Tube Alloys had wanted Fuchs to return to England, but Peierls's wishes prevailed. "I am sorry that we took so long over letting you know what would happen to Fuchs," Peierls wrote Akers, "but you will by now have heard that he has come here. The decision was difficult because there seemed to be good cases both for his coming back and for his joining us here." On August 11 a report to Hoover on the movements of British mission personnel noted: "Dr. K. Fuchs has been transferred from New York to Y [Los Alamos]. He plans to leave New York on 11 August and should arrive for duty at Y on or about 14 August."[18]

In November 1944 Gold again visited the Heineman residence in Cambridge, identifying himself only as a friend of Klaus's visiting Boston on business. Kristel invited him in. She knew that her brother was somewhere in the southwest and that he had promised to come to see her around Christmas. Gold left her a sealed envelope and departed.[19]

CHAPTER · 7

Los Alamos: The Plutonium Connection

If Fuchs had been infinitely compartmentalized, what was inside his compartment would have done the damage.

— J. Robert Oppenheimer

The mistake that was made at Los Alamos in breaking down compartmentalization was vital to Fuchs.

— General Leslie Groves

On August 14, 1944, Klaus Fuchs settled into Room 17, Dormitory T-102, in the sprawling new barracks town of Los Alamos. Situated on a 7,000-foot mesa in the Jemez Mountains north of Santa Fe, Los Alamos was a secret town protected by barbed wire fences and guards. The location provided breathtaking views of the surrounding mountains and desert. Groves and Oppenheimer had chosen the site for its remoteness and security, its access to railroads at Lamy and Santa Fe, and its familiarity (Oppenheimer knew the area because his family's summer camp was nearby). For Fuchs the physicist, Los Alamos was a far cry from the classrooms and laboratories of Kiel and Bristol, a new world of top secret nuclear weapons research. For Fuchs the spy, the transfer to Los Alamos was a golden opportunity, of which he took full advantage.

The British mission scientists, who were allowed access to many different divisions of the Manhattan Project, often had a better overview of the research than did the Americans, who for security reasons were more compartmentalized. The British group made major contributions to the project, especially in theoretical areas. Otto Frisch joined the group that ultimately demonstrated how to achieve a critical mass of uranium-235; James Tuck developed the implosion lenses for the plutonium bomb; and Geoffrey Taylor worked with Fuchs on the hydrodynamics of implosion. Fuchs's job was to develop mathematical calculations for the yield and efficiency of an atomic bomb, for which there were two possibilities: the gun-type uranium bomb ultimately used on Hiroshima and the implosion-type plutonium bomb tested at Alamogordo and dropped on Nagasaki.[1]

Everyone knew Fuchs, but few knew anything about him. Outside his laboratory he was little noticed, as many scientists told the FBI in 1950. Compared with the likes of Bethe, Teller, Von Neumann, and Oppenheimer, Fuchs was definitely not in the front rank of scientists gathered at Los Alamos, which, after all, included twelve Nobel Prize winners. Oppenheimer saw Fuchs as a man who seemed to be carrying the world's burden on his shoulders; he supposed Fuchs was a Christian democrat, perhaps, not a "political fanatic" or a communist. Bethe, who had known Fuchs since 1934, called him "one of the most valuable men in my division." He was a quiet, industrious man whom everyone liked—brilliant but unassuming. "If he was a spy," Bethe said later, "he played his role beautifully." "He worked days and nights. He was a bachelor and had nothing better to do, and he contributed very greatly to the success of the Los Alamos project." Outside the lab Fuchs was known as a good dancer and a willing babysitter; he was popular with Los Alamos wives.[2]

Another scientist, Manson Benedict, who knew Fuchs at Kellex, found him always polite, businesslike, and shy, but also dreamy and abstract. Stanislas and Françoise Ulam remembered that Fuchs never said anything about himself and was completely unforthcoming when asked why he had left Germany. Tony Skyrme, who had also worked with Fuchs at Birmingham, described Fuchs as "very definitely anti-Nazi," but not overtly pro-Soviet or communist. The young physicist Richard Feynman, who knew Fuchs about as well as anyone at Los Alamos, once joked with him about which of the two would be the "most likely candidate as a suspect for possible espionage"; they agreed that it was Feynman.[3]

Fuchs engaged in virtually no political discussions in those years. Michael Perrin could not recall any conversations with him about the Soviet Union; Victor Weisskopf remembered that Fuchs made some positive comments about the Soviets but gave no signs of enthusiasm for communism as an ideology or a system of government. No one seemed to perceive Fuchs as a security risk. To the other scientists he was simply a quiet German bachelor.[4]

■ Security Risk

Security was a way of life at Los Alamos. All personal mail was censored, and telephones were generally unavailable. The birth certificates of all babies born there carried the same address: P.O. Box 1663, Santa Fe. The Military Intelligence Division of the War Department was responsible for all security matters, including espionage, within the Manhattan Engineer District of the Army Corps of Engineers. As the war developed, so did the levels of secret classification and counterespionage measures. In April 1943 the FBI agreed not to investigate Manhattan Project personnel unless specifically requested by the War Department.[5]

During the war the War Department investigated more than a thousand cases of unauthorized transfer of information, sabotage, or espionage relating to the Manhattan Project. Generally these concerned newspaper reporters speculating about what was going on at Los Alamos or relatives of project members caught talking at cocktail parties. Virtually any mention of atomic or uranium bombs had disappeared from American newspapers long before Fuchs arrived in New Mexico.[6]

Compared with other centers of the far-flung Manhattan Project, Los Alamos was relatively open. From the outset Oppenheimer insisted on having seminars and colloquia in which scientists from different divisions could share ideas, argue theories, and report on work in progress. The British mission members attended, although Groves kept a weekly list of which British scientists attended which seminars and what was discussed. In October 1944 the records show that Fuchs attended a colloquium led by Oppenheimer on how to create a plutonium bomb that would implode, or explode inward around a sphere, using shaped charges of high explosives known as lenses. Two weeks later Fuchs attended another colloquium run by Niels Bohr on the nuclear reactions of uranium-238.[7]

In the winter of 1944–45 morale at Los Alamos plummeted. The brilliant scientists had not yet achieved a workable bomb design for plutonium, which tended to predetonate, and no deliveries of either plutonium or uranium-235 had yet arrived from Hanford or Oak Ridge. Fuchs attended seminars on three alternatives for implosion: compression of a solid sphere; low-velocity implosion to avoid interference from jets; and shaped charge assembly using neutron initiators. A January seminar led by Bethe included calculations by Fuchs and other British mission members on jet theories of implosion. The machine shop, where Private David Greenglass worked, was casting Baratol and Composition B, the high explosives to be used in the lenses.[8]

In February 1945, when Fuchs visited his sister in Cambridge, he was also able to pass considerable written information about the atomic bomb to Raymond. When Gold and Fuchs met at the Heinemans' home, Fuchs gave his contact a report of several pages that summarized the process of assembling an atomic bomb, noting the problems with predetonation of plutonium through spontaneous fission, the advantages of the implosion method of detonation over the gun method, and the critical mass of plutonium (between five and fifteen kilograms). He also reported current ideas on how to initiate with high-explosive lenses a uniform detonation around a sphere that would compress the plutonium to critical-mass size. Fuchs told Gold that he would not be able to leave Los Alamos again for perhaps a year; they agreed to meet next in Santa Fe at the Castillo Street bridge over the Santa Fe River. Fuchs showed Gold a map of the town. Gold offered Fuchs fifteen hundred dollars for expenses, should he need it. Fuchs refused the money, and Gold later returned it to Yakovlev, along with Fuchs's new information, a "quite considerable packet," Gold remembered.[9]

In March the final designs for both the gun-type and the implosion bombs were complete. The work turned to solving the practical problems. Fuchs heard George Kistiakowsky, the Russian-born ordnance expert, explain the shaping of high-explosive charges and the casting of the sphere and lenses for the implosion bomb. He also attended seminars at which the first calculations of yield and blast effects were reported—measured in kilotons, or thousands of tons of TNT equivalent. An intense series of meetings followed in April as final experiments prior to a test were run, including a 100-ton high-explosive proof firing at the future Trinity test site in the desert near Alamogordo. By late May seminars considered the "ultimate delivery of the gadget" (dropping the bomb) and the final plans for assembling a plutonium bomb.[10]

On a Saturday in early June 1945, a month before the Alamogordo test, Klaus Fuchs drove his battered blue Buick from Los Alamos to Santa Fe and met Gold as planned at the Castillo Street bridge. Fuchs handed him another package of documents, which fully described the plutonium bomb that was to be tested at Alamogordo and the one that was to be dropped on Nagasaki, including their components and important dimensions. The bomb would have a solid plutonium core, detonated by a complex system of polonium initiators (a neutron source), a tamper, an aluminum shell, and the high-explosive lenses. Fuchs identified the two high explosives (Baratol and Composition B), neither of which he understood himself. The forthcoming Trinity test was expected to produce an explosion equivalent to 10,000 tons of TNT; Fuchs provided information on the test date and site. He told Gold that the United States intended to use the bomb against Japan. Gold remembered that Fuchs was curiously dubious about the possibilities for immediate use of the bomb; he did not think it would be completed before the Japanese surrendered. Fuchs also reported that Los Alamos was working at a frenzied pace in preparation for the test; he was putting in eighteen to twenty hours a day. When they parted, they agreed to meet again in Santa Fe on September 19.[11]

On June 4 Fuchs attended a large meeting of the Los Alamos Coordinating Council, at which Oppenheimer presided. The audience included representatives from the Departments of War and State and the White House. Fermi reported on observations at Trinity in preparation for the first test. Other seminars discussed the schedule of implosion experiments, the estimated effects of the Alamogordo test, instrumentation for measuring those effects, and the proposed dimensions of the plutonium sphere in the implosion bomb. Up to the last minute there were changes in the high-explosive detonators and problems in the pressing of plutonium hemispheres and in the manufacture of the neutron sources known as "urchins." At 5:30 A.M. on July 16 Fuchs was present at the Trinity test in the New Mexico desert, when the first atomic bomb blast turned the sky white and purple with its fury.[12]

On August 7 a huge gathering of Los Alamos scientists heard Oppenheimer report on the sucessful drop of the uranium bomb over Hiroshima. "Substantially all staff members were present," ran the security report to Groves, "and the crowd was so great that it was impossible to determine the British individuals who were there." The following weeks were full of elation and exhaustion, pride and guilt, as the scientists considered the effects of the Trinity test, the future of the Manhattan Project, and the destruction of Hiroshima. At long last their secret was out. The public learned through the press that the Manhattan Project to produce an atomic bomb had been the most closely guarded secret of the war.[13]

Much later Fuchs would recall meeting Raymond in the autumn of 1945 and spring of 1946 in Santa Fe, but he did not recall the precise dates. Gold claimed that they met only once more, on September 19. By that time the war was over. Hiroshima and Nagasaki had been obliterated by the new weapon. The two men met near a church on the outskirts of Santa Fe. Fuchs handed over a package of documents on the implosion bomb and reported his impressions of the Trinity test. The new data included the production rate of uranium-235 (about 100 kilograms a month) and plutonium (about 20 kilograms a month), his own calculations of blast waves, and the information that sintered nickel was used in the barriers for separating fissionable uranium at the Oak Ridge plant. Fuchs provided further information on the "delta phase" behavior of plutonium and the use of gallium as an alloying agent, but was not able to provide any information on plutonium metallurgy or fabrication. He also spoke about the possible development of a "mixed" bomb that used both plutonium and uranium.[14]

As they drove into the hills outside of Santa Fe, Fuchs said he had underestimated the potential of American industry in being able to construct the atomic bomb. He was greatly concerned about the terrible destruction of Japanese cities. Fuchs told Gold that a British intelligence officer had notified him that they were trying to contact Fuchs's father in Kiel, which was in the British zone of occupied Germany. The MI5 officer had hinted that it might be possible to bring the old man to England. Fuchs seemed to Gold to be very concerned about his father's welfare: Germany lay in ruins, after all, and life there was hard. He was also afraid that his father might bring up his son's communist past. "Klaus told me," reported Gold, "that as far as he knew, the British had no inkling about his past as it related to his Communist activities, and he was anxious that this continue to be so." Fuchs hoped to return to England soon.[15]

Finally Gold gave Fuchs instructions on how to reestablish his espionage contacts in England. A month after his arrival Fuchs was to go to the Mornington Crescent tube station in London at eight o'clock on a Saturday evening. In one hand his contact would be carrying five books tied with a string and in the other a copy of a book by Bennett Cerf with a yellow and green jacket. Thus instructed, Fuchs drove Gold back to Santa Fe, gave him a packet of information, and headed up the winding road to Los Alamos.[16]

We shall never know for certain what Fuchs told the Soviet Union about the atomic bomb. We do know that he had specific knowledge of the theory and design of a gaseous diffusion plant and of the implosion method for assembling a plutonium bomb. He had access to virtually all topics discussed in the seminars and colloquia between August 1944 and May 1946. According to Ralph Carlisle Smith, a Los Alamos security officer writing in September 1945, the British mission had "substantially complete knowledge of the gun assembly and implosion assembly of fissile material, the actual design of the aerial bombs employing these principles, the possible future developments, including the 'Super,'" or hydrogen bomb. But they knew only a "minimum of the engineering details." Clearly, Fuchs knew as much as anyone about the theory and design of the atomic bomb.[17]

The information Fuchs provided before December 1943 told the Russians little they did not already know from their own work and other foreign sources. He was able to tell them that a major atomic bomb project was under way in the West. His reports may well have supported Soviet physicist Igor Kurchatov's recommendations to Stalin in 1944–45 that the Soviet Union pursue its own bomb project and confirmed that an implosion plutonium bomb would work.[18]

▪ Greenglass and the Rosenbergs

Fuchs had no idea that he was not the only member of the Los Alamos community passing atomic secrets to Harry Gold. When Gold returned to New York from New Mexico in June 1945, he gave Yakovlev packets of material on the atomic bomb from two agents. Fuchs's information was by far the more valuable, but David Greenglass, a young GI working in the machine shop, provided confirming and supplementary information on the implosion bomb. Both the Fuchs and the Greenglass data, Yakovlev told Gold two weeks later, were welcomed in Moscow as "extremely excellent and very valuable."[19]

Greenglass had been drafted into the army in April 1943; a year later he was assigned to a Special Engineering Detachment unit of the Manhattan Project at Oak Ridge. During the war army personnel at the atomic towns performed a number of valuable services to support the massive scientific and engineering effort to build the atomic bomb. In August 1944 Greenglass was assigned to the E-5 implosion section at Los Alamos, under Kistiakowsky. Subsequently Greenglass worked for the X-1 and X-4 sections, which were responsible for manufacturing the high-explosive lenses for the plutonium bomb. His job was routine and menial, helping to maintain equipment and make experimental items. But he was positioned at the very heart of the developmental work on the implosion bomb, and he was able to confirm for the

Russians Fuchs's complex story regarding design and assembly of the bomb.[20]

Greenglass's letters to his wife, Ruth, during the war reveal an enthusiasm for Soviet Russia and a vague ideological commitment to communism. In June 1944 he wrote that he had been reading a lot of books on the Soviet Union and realized how "far-sighted and intelligent" Stalin and the Soviet leaders were, "geniuses, every one of them . . . I have come to a stronger and more resolute faith and belief in the principles of Socialism and Communism," he added.[21]

After being assigned to Los Alamos, Greenglass wrote Ruth that he had been "very reticent" in his letters for security reasons. He was about to work on a "classified top secret project," and his mail would be censored. They could not talk openly on the telephone and would have to use the letter C rather than the term comrade in their correspondence. He added, "Not a word to anybody about anything except maybe Julie."[22]

"Julie" was Greenglass's brother-in-law, Julius Rosenberg, who with his wife, Ethel, was part of a Soviet espionage ring operating out of New York. By November 1944 Rosenberg realized that David was a gold mine of information on the atomic bomb project, and he asked Ruth to propose that David pass along appropriate information. "My darling," David wrote Ruth on November 4, "I most certainly will be glad to be part of the community project that Julius and his friends have in mind . . . count me in."[23]

In late November Ruth visited David in Albuquerque and spelled out the details of their espionage procedure. Greenglass admitted to the FBI in June 1950 that Ruth had explained that Rosenberg wanted him to provide information on the atomic bomb to help the Allied war effort. "On that basis," he said, "I agreed to give whatever information came to me in the course of my employment at Los Alamos." At first this was simply a list of the scientists and descriptions of the buildings and layout. Ultimately it was a crude sketch of the lens molds used in making the plutonium bomb.[24]

In January 1945 Greenglass returned to New York on furlough from the army. When Rosenberg arrived for a visit, he plied David with questions about the Manhattan Project. Greenglass gave him handwritten notes and sketches on the implosion project as he knew it. Several days later, when they met again for dinner, Rosenberg told Greenglass that a courier would come to New Mexico at some point to pick up additional material; the courier would carry one half of a torn Jello box to identify himself. The other half Rosenberg gave to Greenglass.[25]

Thus when Gold arrived in New Mexico in June 1945 he was to contact Greenglass as well as Fuchs. They met in Albuquerque and established identities via the Jello box pieces. Greenglass gave Gold a package of papers, including sketches of the high-explosive lens molds, which he had written out at an apartment in Albuquerque that Ruth had rented; Gold gave him five hundred dollars and left for New York to deliver the material to Yakovlev. In Greenglass's words, "I think that I gave Gold a sketch of a high-explosive lens mold, or something of that type of thing, which was an experiment to study implosion effects on a steel tube to understand the effect it would have on uranium so it could be determined how they could arrive at a critical mass that would not explode before detonation."[26]

Greenglass's understanding of the plutonium bomb was partial and distorted. He confused plutonium with uranium, he had none of Fuchs's theoretical and scientific training, and he did not have an overview of the project. But his information confirmed what the Soviet Union had learned from Fuchs: that the United States was moving from the gun-type uranium bomb to the implosion plutonium model in its race to build a weapon for use against Japan. By September 1945, on his second furlough from Los Alamos, Greenglass was able to give Rosenberg twelve pages of description and sketches of the bomb dropped on Nagasaki. Rosenberg gave him two hundred dollars, and Greenglass returned to Los Alamos, where he remained until February 20, 1946.[27]

On June 16, 1950, after signing a confession that he had been Gold's accomplice in 1945, Greenglass was arrested. His brother-in-law was questioned by the FBI on that day, but not arrested. By the end of the year Gold had received a thirty-year sentence for espionage, setting the stage for the case against the Rosenbergs.

■ *Sharing the Secret: The Smyth Report*

Despite their generally cheerful toleration of wartime security restrictions, many Los Alamos scientists thought that the terrible weapon of war they were developing should ultimately be subject to international control. Some felt, even before the bomb was a reality, that the Soviet Union should be told about it, in order to prevent a postwar arms race. One Los Alamos scientist interviewed by the FBI in February 1950 argued that Fuchs was "perhaps the only one of the group there who acted on a theory accepted by almost all of them," and that "conversations engaged in by the scientists at Los Alamos might well have spurred Fuchs on."[28]

Leo Szilard was an early critic of secrecy in the Manhattan Project, for he felt that it only impeded the pace of scientific research. Security leaks were numerous, he believed, although not from the scientists themselves. "There is not a single case in the history of the world," claimed Szilard in February 1944, "where a scientist has betrayed the trust of the government for which he worked in wartime."[29] That sort of overconfidence certainly facilitated Fuchs's activities.

Niels Bohr was another proponent of sharing the secrets of the atomic bomb. In 1943, soon after Bohr arrived in London, he received a letter from the Soviet physicist Peter Kapitsa inviting him to set up his laboratory in the Soviet Union. Upon the advice of MI5, Bohr turned down the invitation. But in 1944 he tried to persuade both Churchill and Roosevelt to share general information on the Manhattan Project with Stalin. He was thoroughly rebuffed.[30]

The lid of official secrecy on the Manhattan Project was lifted only in August 1945 with the publication of the official history of the project, known as the Smyth Report, after its author, Henry DeWolfe Smyth of Princeton. A draft section on Los Alamos, written for the report by Richard Feynman in late 1944, pointed out that secrecy and security restrictions had been a "constant source of trouble." Scientists spent their lives investigating the secrets of nature in order to reveal them to their peers and to the public. Rationally, they could accept the need for wartime secrecy; emotionally, they were unhappy with it. But Feynman's comments did not appear in the final report.[31]

In the end Oppenheimer was the only project scientist who did not sign his approval of the Smyth report, which he found one-sided and misleading. He urged that the chapter on Los Alamos not be released unless it was significantly revised. After thorough review by the Department of War, the report, titled "Atomic Energy for Military Purposes; The Official Report on the Development of the Atomic Bomb under the Auspices of the United States Government, 1940–1945," was released to the public on August 12, 1945, a few days after Hiroshima and Nagasaki.[32]

The bombing of the Japanese cities proved that the bomb worked and that America was willing to use it; the Smyth Report told the story of its construction and production. Although the War Department assured the public that "nothing in this report discloses necessary military secrets as to the manufacture or production of the weapon," the report was breathtaking in its detail on how America had built the first atomic bomb. It claimed to tell the complete story "without violating the needs of national security." But much was omitted from the report because of "secrecy requirements," wrote Smyth, including all work on implosion and the contribution of the British and Canadian scientists. By the end of 1945 nearly 90,000 copies of the report had been sold or delivered to the public; 30,000 copies of a Russian translation appeared in the Soviet Union.[33]

In the fall of 1945 many of the Los Alamos scientists began to leave the mesa to return to civilian life. Oppenheimer was replaced as laboratory director by Norris Bradbury. But Fuchs stayed on, calculating the possible yield and damage of future bombs and working on the Los Alamos "encyclopedia," a comprehensive scientific report on the bomb project. He attended seminars on the future of nuclear power and on the possibility of new types of nuclear weapons, including a thermonuclear, or hydrogen, bomb. He viewed films of the "combat drops" at Hiroshima and Nagasaki, and he signed the British memorandum calling for international control of atomic energy and an end to secrecy.[34]

The autumn and early winter of 1945–46 were taken up with

talk of the future of Los Alamos under a projected civilian Atomic Energy Agency, the subject of great debate in Congress. Design improvements were made in the Nagasaki bomb, and the damage in Japan was interpreted, in part based on calculations performed with the aid of new IBM computers. On November 20 Fuchs left Los Alamos on a well-deserved vacation. He went first to Montreal, where he conferred with John Cockcroft, who wanted him to take charge of theoretical physics at the proposed Atomic Energy Research Establishment in England. Fuchs then went to Mexico for two weeks with Rudolph and Evgeniia Peierls. When he returned to Los Alamos in December, many of his British colleagues had gone home.[35]

Originally Fuchs planned to return to England in February 1946. This deadline was extended to June because he was needed to help plan the Bikini Islands tests of the atomic bomb against warships, scheduled for that spring. Chadwick agreed to let Fuchs stay on, even though he noted that the British wanted their scientists back in England. "In Dr. Fuchs's case," wrote Norris Bradbury, "we are anxious to retain his services at least until the completion of the Naval Tests." These services included advice on weapons theory, new models of the current atomic bomb, and other matters on which the Theoretical Division was "seriously short of personnel."[36]

In March Fuchs heard Edward Teller discuss "the possibilities of thermonuclear reactions in water and air" and participated in discussions on the declassification of secret research conducted under the Manhattan Project. Together with William Penney, Fuchs ran the calculations of the blast effects at Hiroshima and Nagasaki and analyzed the radiation effects of the Alamogordo test. Fuchs continued to do good work, and Bradbury continued to press for keeping him as long as possible.[37]

Fuchs finally left Los Alamos on June 14, going first to Washington, where he conferred with Chadwick. He then visited Kristel in Cambridge and Hans Bethe at Cornell. Bethe and Fuchs were deeply saddened by the radiation accident at Los Alamos that had recently killed one of their co-workers, Louis Slotin. Eager to return to England, Fuchs decided to travel by air rather than by sea. On June 28, the British Supply Office in Washington informed General Groves that Fuchs had flown by bomber from Montreal.[38]

The FBI was also informed of Fuchs's departure. On July 2 Lieutenant Colonel Charles H. Banks of the Department of War, in a memo to Hoover on the movements of British personnel, noted that Fuchs was flying to London. In July the FBI requested a list of "individuals who had access to information not contained in the Smyth Report" from C. W. Rolander of the Manhattan Project. The list naturally included Klaus Fuchs.[39]

- *The Gouzenko Case*

On September 5, 1945, while Fuchs was still at Los Alamos, Igor Gouzenko of the Soviet embassy in Ottawa, Canada, walked out of his office, taking with him substantial files that demonstrated the existence of widespread Soviet espionage in Canada during the war. As principal cipher clerk, handling all embassy cables for Ambassador Georgy N. Zarubin and the military attaché, Colonel Nikolai Zabotin, Gouzenko had access to the most sensitive secret information. He had come to Ottawa in 1943; in August 1945, upon learning that he was about to be recalled to Moscow, he and his wife, Svetlana, had decided to defect. After considerable tension and confusion, they were granted asylum by the Canadian government.[40]

Gouzenko would normally have been interrogated by the MI5 officer in Ottawa, Cyril Mills. But Mills was retiring, so the case was referred to the MI6 counterespionage officer in Washington, Peter Dwyer, who flew to Ottawa to interview Gouzenko. Dwyer reported his findings to Kim Philby, the head of Section 9 of MI6, in London. Philby, who was secretly working for the Russians, was then under threat of exposure by another defecting Soviet intelligence officer in Istanbul; to concentrate on this threat, Philby referred the Gouzenko case to Roger Hollis, director of MI5's F Division. Hollis flew to Ottawa to consult with the wartime head of British security in the United States, William Stephenson. Under interrogation Gouzenko later testified to the existence of a Soviet mole in MI5, code-named Elli (in recent years Chapman Pincher has suggested that Elli was actually Hollis). The Gouzenko affair publicized the fact that Soviet agents had penetrated the Manhattan Project, but the existence of Soviet agents within British security was not yet known.[41]

After some months of investigation of Gouzenko's files, the Canadian government in February 1946 arrested thirteen citizens on charges of espionage. In England, Scotland Yard detained a British physicist, Alan Nunn May, who had worked in Montreal for the Manhattan Project. He denied any knowledge of Soviet espionage activities. Nunn May was a shy, serious, and reserved experimental physicist, the same age as Klaus Fuchs. Like many other Englishmen in the 1930s, he was a communist sympathizer and a supporter of Soviet Russia, but not a party member. In April 1942 Nunn May joined Tube Alloys in Cambridge and became an insider at the British bomb project. In January 1945 he went to Canada as part of John Cockcroft's team. There he was recruited for espionage by Ambassador Zabotin. Nunn May visited Chalk River and the Chicago Metallurgical Laboratory, and he was able to provide considerable information on the Manhattan Project to the Soviet embassy in Ottawa. He reported on the Alamogordo bomb test in July 1945, and Zabotin conveyed the news to Moscow on August 9, three days after Hiroshima had made the bomb public knowledge. Nunn May also provided samples of uranium-233 and 235. Gouzenko's files revealed that on August 2 Moscow had asked Zabotin to "take measures to organize acquisition of documentary materials on the atomic bomb! The technical processes, drawings, calculations."[42]

When Nunn May returned to England in September he was already under surveillance because of information the British and Canadian intelligence officers had gained from Gouzenko. On September 30 Canadian Prime Minister Mackenzie King met with President Truman and Assistant Secretary of State Dean Acheson for a two-hour briefing on the Gouzenko case and on atomic espionage within the Manhattan Project. They identified Anatolii Yakovlev as the chief Soviet agent in the United States. Truman was alarmed but did not act impulsively. He warned against any "premature action" and urged that there be a "complete understanding" with Prime Minister Attlee before Nunn May was arrested.[43]

On the afternoon of March 4, 1946, Nunn May was arrested, taken to the Bow Street magistrate's court, and charged with violating the Official Secrets Act. He made and signed a confession. At his trial he pleaded "not guilty," but he was convicted and served several years in prison. Upon hearing of this at Los Alamos, Fuchs said only that he did not think Nunn May could have told the Russians very much about the atomic bomb, which was true. The arrest of Nunn May and the publication of the Royal Commission's report on the Gouzenko case that March caused a public sensation. For a month there were headlines about Soviet espionage operations in Canada and trials of the principal suspects. Eighteen persons were brought to trial, and eight were sent to prison.[44]

One of the people arrested because of Gouzenko's revelations was Israel Halperin, a mathematics professor at Queens University in Kingston, Ontario. In 1942 Halperin had joined the Canadian army and had risen to the rank of major while engaged in a number of secret ordnance research projects. In 1945 he was one of a group of Canadians recruited by the Soviet embassy for espionage. He had been given the code name Bacon. At one point he was asked to provide samples of uranium-235 from Chalk River, but unlike Nunn May, Halperin was either unwilling or unable to do so. He was placed on trial, but the espionage charges against him were dismissed.[45]

When he was arrested, in February of 1946, Halperin's address book was seized by the police. Among the 436 names in the book were those of Klaus Fuchs, with his Edinburgh address, and Kristel Heineman, in Watertown, Massachusetts. Canada's External Affairs Minister Lester Pearson said in 1950 that the list of names had been sent to both British and American security officials. On the basis of this information the FBI in 1946 began investigating Kristel Heineman and her husband, presumably because they were living in the United States. According to the FBI, which reported this information to the CIA after Fuchs's arrest, Kristel said that Halperin had "befriended" her brother while he was interned in Canada and had sent him scientific journals and cigarettes.

What was the origin of this relationship, and what was its significance? Although Fuchs was at Los Alamos in the spring of

1946, he was not investigated in connection with the Gouzenko case. When the Canadian connection was revealed after Fuchs's arrest in 1950, it raised further suspicions about the lapses of British security in failing to identify Fuchs before 1949. And it suggested that the case might involve more than atomic espionage.[46]

CHAPTER · 8

Harwell: Building the British Bomb

If we had decided not to have it, we would have put ourselves entirely in the hands of the Americans.

— *Prime Minister Clement Attlee*

A central political secret of the Fuchs case was that Great Britain was building her own atomic bomb, a key status symbol in the postwar years of socialism at home and declining empire abroad, and that Fuchs was a leading scientist in the British bomb project. As early as January 1944 project leader John Anderson had told Tube Alloys scientists and officials that high priority would be given to a "T.A. plant" in Great Britain after the war. In February 1945 Churchill notified Roosevelt that the British intended to build their own nuclear weapon; the Combined Policy Committee (CPC), which had been established under the 1943 Quebec Agreement to coordinate nuclear cooperation, was informed of this intent in April. A few months later the new prime minister, Clement Attlee, created a supersecret committee called Gen 75, to plan the project. In October Parliament learned that an "atomic energy research establishment" would be set up at Harwell and other locations. By January 1946 a full-scale nuclear weapons program was under way, but

Parliament was not informed of that. Aside from the scientists, only Attlee, Foreign Minister Ernest Bevin, and perhaps a half dozen other Cabinet members knew that Britain was building a bomb. Wrote Bevin afterward: "We simply could not acquiesce in an American monopoly on this development."[1]

Attlee's nuclear program was a massive one; a budget of one hundred million pounds was allotted without Parliament's knowledge. The project was placed under the Ministry of Supply and based in London. Akers and Perrin remained in charge, Lord Charles Portal became controller of production, and Cockcroft was named director of Harwell. As in the United States, functions were geographically divided. An air-cooled research reactor began operating at Harwell under the auspices of the United Kingdom Advisory Committee on Atomic Energy, chaired by Anderson. Plutonium production reactors were constructed at Windscale, and a gaseous diffusion plant to make U-235 was built at Capenhurst in Cheshire. Aldermaston would be the weapons design center. But Harwell, located on an RAF base in the Berkshire Downs, a few miles south of Oxford, was the intellectual and administrative nerve center (see Figure 6). Harwell became a boom town of military barracks, but it was virtually unknown to the British public. Curious visitors saw only research and power reactors. The real goal, though, was a plutonium bomb; the target date was 1952.[2]

On May 12, 1948, in response to a question in Parliament, the minister of defense, A. V. Alexander, admitted that "all types of weapons, including atomic weapons, are being developed." This was the only official British announcement of the project prior to the Fuchs case. British secrecy far exceeded that in America. "The policy of secrecy," concluded Margaret Gowing, the official historian of atomic energy in Britain, "went beyond rational explanation." All discussion in the press was regulated by the system of D-notices, which forbade publication of references to official secrets. D-notice 25 of April 29, 1948, explicitly ruled out any public discussion of, or reference to, atomic weapons work in the United Kingdom, including research, personnel, locations, and raw materials. All atomic energy research establishments were barred to the public under the Official Secrets Act.[3]

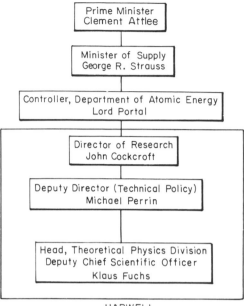

Figure 6. British atomic energy research establishment, 1950

How much President Truman knew about the British bomb project is unclear. Publicly Attlee urged Truman to utilize nuclear energy for peace, to rid the world of nuclear weapons, and to continue sharing nuclear information. But in September 1945 Truman established a policy of security through secrecy, excluding all other nations from access to American classified scientific information, engineering skills, and industrial resources. At their meeting in Washington in November 1945, Truman briefed Attlee on the Quebec Agreement, agreed to work toward international control of atomic weapons, and promised "full and effective cooperation" in nuclear matters through the CPC. But this was largely the rhetoric of good feelings. The American desire to monopolize the "winning weapon," as Bernard Baruch called it, preceded the existence of the weapon. The Anglo-American special relationship was coming to an end. The Americans had no intention of giving up their atomic monopoly, and the British had every intention of building their own atomic bomb.[4]

The CPC was almost as little known as the Quebec Agreement that had created it. It provided a forum for American, British, and Canadian planning of the acquisition and allocation of nuclear resources, sharing of information, and joint progress toward nuclear weapons. All nuclear policy matters came before the CPC. When the committee met in February 1946, the American representatives refused to renegotiate the Quebec Agreement to allow the British greater access to nuclear information. The U.S. Atomic Energy Act of 1946, known as the McMahon Act, was supposed to tighten American control of nuclear weapons material and information. Attlee warned that if Congress passed it, Britain would indeed build her own bomb. A few months later, when the United States refused to provide nuclear reactor data requested by the British government, Attlee was "gravely disturbed." By spring it was apparent that Great Britain had not broken the American monopoly on nuclear weapons and that Congress did not wish to share classified nuclear information with any other nation. The Combined Development Trust, also established under the Quebec Agreement, continued to assure joint discussion and control of world uranium and thorium supplies and American support for heavy water research at the Canadian Chalk River plant. But passage of the McMahon Act on August 1, 1946, was, from the British point of view, a declaration of nuclear rivalry.[5]

In May 1947 the U.S. Congress Joint Committee on Atomic Energy (JCAE) first learned of the secret British bomb project. For many it was their first knowledge of the Quebec Agreement and of the fact that America had shared its nuclear secrets with Britain for nearly four years. Some congressmen were shocked and outraged, especially at the notion that the United States could not bomb Moscow without British permission. Senator Hoyt Vandenberg called the restrictions "astounding" and "unthinkable." "The somewhat incredible truth," Secretary of State Dean Acheson wrote in his memoirs, "was that very few knew about it (due, in part, to so many changes in high office), and those who did thought of it as a temporary wartime agreement to be superseded by broader arrangements currently and constantly discussed."[6]

On January 7, 1948, a so-called *modus vivendi* was drawn up by British and American officials to replace the Quebec Agreement. Under the new arrangement Great Britain gave up her right to veto American use of the bomb and gave the United States access to two-thirds of all uranium production from the Belgian Congo and South Africa for 1948 and 1949. In return, the United States agreed to furnish additional information on reactors, plutonium metallurgy, and nuclear explosion detection. The British felt that they "acquired very little and conceded a great deal," as one historian put it.[7]

■ From Los Alamos to Harwell

When Fuchs left the United States to begin work at Harwell, most members of the British mission had returned to England, with the accumulated knowledge of the Manhattan Project in their heads. The British scientists were especially irritated that Manhattan Project security, under Groves's orders, refused to let them remove even their own research papers from Los Alamos. Many did so on their own. Fuchs told the wife of one British scientist that it was really "very easy" to remove documents from Los Alamos; she assumed that he meant documents for his work in England. As the British mission returned home, U.S. War Department officials warned of a "definite security risk" if Britain began building her own "atomic energy plants."[8]

For Fuchs, the scientific community at Harwell became a surrogate family. He soon immersed himself in planning the program and recruiting personnel. His salary was fifteen hundred pounds a year, and he took up residence first in the bachelors' quarters of the staff club, then in a boardinghouse in nearby Abingdon. He became the head of the theoretical physics division and a member of virtually every committee available. He was friendly with the entire staff, including the chief security officer, Henry Arnold, who became his next-door neighbor after Fuchs moved to Harwell. Although Fuchs's later conceit that "I am Harwell" was excessive, he was a major figure in the project, where scientists sometimes believed they were gods in control of the greatest power on earth, nuclear energy. In August 1946 Fuchs gave his first scientific report, on the properties of fast reactors, and predicted that all power stations would be using nuclear fuel by the 1980s.[9]

In the summer of 1946 Arnold reported to MI5 that one of the staff members was a German who had been naturalized during the war. This triggered a new security check on Fuchs, lasting some five months. Again MI5 reportedly turned up only the 1934 Gestapo report and nothing else adverse. Before he left for Australia, Roger Hollis, advised by Perrin, for the sixth time went through the MI5 file on Fuchs. Again he cleared him for secret work.[10]

In November 1947, MI5 vetted Fuchs yet again so that he could be given a permanent civil service appointment at Harwell, as requested by the Ministry of Supply. Arnold pressed for a more attentive investigation of Fuchs as a security risk; he felt that Fuchs was simply too zealous in his own concern for security, too much of a loner, too correct in his relations with the friendly and personable Arnold, whom Fuchs later said was the only man he ever trusted. MI5 again investigated, and Fuchs was cleared.[11]

Attlee's announcement in March 1948 that known communist and fascist party members would be dismissed from any civil service post that was vital to national security had absolutely no effect on Fuchs. When a Los Alamos friend, Martin Deutsch, attended a cocktail party at the Peierlses' home in December 1948, he was surprised to learn that Fuchs had belonged to the KPD before World War II and that his activity and associations were the subject of a security investigation.[12]

In May 1948 a startled American visitor from the Atomic Energy Commission discovered that the research reactors at Harwell were designed to produce plutonium, not power. AEC chairman Lewis Strauss was astonished and called for further limits on any exchange of nuclear information, such as the recent British request for consultation on plutonium metallurgy. Senator Bourke Hickenlooper joined Strauss in urging minimal sharing of information with Great Britain. The British scientists found it very difficult to get the Americans to declassify the reports they needed, even of work done in America by the British mission. One scientist, James Tuck, complained to Lord Cherwell that this was a "very serious matter" and that "we are likely to find ourselves in the position of working for the next two to five years to find out things already known." Peierls also noted that parts of Tony Skyrme's dissertation were still classified by the Americans; "very fortunately, the dissertation has, in fact, not been shown to anybody except Fuchs."[13]

The British scientists' enthusiasm for declassification of wartime nuclear documents convinced Strauss that "the primary purpose of our friends is no longer benign use but, on the contrary, the production of plutonium for bombs." It was a "sacrifice of security" to share further nuclear information with the British. Strauss's friend William Golden agreed, noting that "disclosures, with little or nothing in return," were "beyond my comprehension." Sharing data from the 1948 Sandstone bomb test series was, "at best, grossly improvident."[14]

Fuchs was active in advising on declassification of papers on gaseous diffusion, thermonuclear reactions, and other matters. In September 1948 he attended the second declassification conference at Harwell. Fuchs was flattered when Oppenheimer, on a visit to Harwell, invited him to come to the Princeton Institute for Advanced Study as a research fellow, but he declined the invitation. By this time Fuchs had achieved a fine scientific reputation because of his work at Harwell. Peierls wrote Cockcroft that Fuchs was probably the "strongest candidate" for a university chair in mathematical physics, should one become vacant in England, for he was "one of the few men well suited to build up a strong school of theoretical physics." A few months later he proposed Fuchs for membership in the Royal Society, a proposal that was seconded by Cockcroft.[15]

By early 1949 Anglo-American nuclear relations had reached an impasse. Oppenheimer convened a high-level meeting at Princeton to discuss the problem with a number of AEC and State Department officials. There was concern that both the British and the Soviets might have a bomb in the near future. The Americans feared that the British bomb program would assist the Russians, both because British security was lax and because in the event of war the Soviet Union might invade and occupy Great Britain. The United States sought to stall the revision of the *modus vivendi*, which would facilitate the British project, and Britain continued to push for a more complete exchange of information. But by March 1949 President Truman had decided that the United States should be the only country making nuclear weapons, with some bombs stockpiled in Great Britain and joint planning for possible war with the Soviet Union.[16]

In 1949 the Cold War was at its height. The Berlin blockade was coming to an end, but Soviet-American relations remained tense. In April the North Atlantic Treaty Organization (NATO) was established to defend European security against Soviet aggression. The willingness to use atomic weapons to defend Europe later became a cornerstone of NATO policy. For the moment it was essential that Great Britain and the United States cooperate in building up a larger stockpile of nuclear weapons. The British proposed a joint weapons project, whereby Britain would give up the idea of an independent deterrent, send scientists to Oak Ridge to study, provide plutonium produced at Windscale to the United States, and station American nuclear weapons on British soil. At a top secret meeting in Washington on July 15, Truman and Acheson pushed hard for a full nuclear partnership with Britain; Lilienthal, Eisenhower, and Johnson were supportive, and Strauss was strongly opposed. Despite some isolationist Republican resistance to sharing nuclear secrets, a joint nuclear weapons program did seem possible.[17] When, therefore, in September the Soviet Union tested its first atomic bomb, code-named by the Americans Joe 1, Britain was apparently prepared to concede her atomic bomb program if she could obtain weapons through a joint project. Measuring and analyzing the fallout from Joe 1 was done by the two countries together. On September 20 discussions began in the CPC on full sharing of nuclear information, but ten days later the negotiators adjourned without agreement, in part because the Americans wanted to keep all plutonium production in the United States.[18]

The agreement on sharing fissionable raw materials was due to expire on December 31. When talks resumed in late November, the revised British position was that Britain would continue to develop her own bomb, cooperate in weapons testing, provide plutonium for building warheads in the United States, and permit some twenty American atomic bombs to be stockpiled in Great Britain. But the Americans wanted control over plutonium production and over any joint weapons program. "Even without Fuchs," concluded the official Atomic Energy Commission historians, "the chances of close cooperation were problematical."[19]

There were other problems as well. The joint Patent Advisory Panel was embroiled in legal complexities, and the third declassification meeting, at Chalk River in December 1949, which Fuchs did not attend, continued to argue over how much information should be declassified. Certainly the Russians had acquired whatever they needed to build a plutonium bomb. When British ambassador Oliver Franks on December 29, 1949, submitted to the State Department a draft proposal for "complete collaboration" in nuclear matters, there was still talk of a "full partnership" between the two countries; but a month later, after the Fuchs case erupted, such talk was no longer possible.[20]

■ *Contact and Conflict*

Whether MI5 lacked hard evidence, was careless, was penetrated by traitors, or was fiendishly clever in manipulating a Soviet espionage ring, it allowed Klaus Fuchs to continue to deliver the goods after 1946. Upon his return to England in June of that year, he tried to locate his old KPD contact, Jurgen Kuczynski, as Gold had instructed him to do. (Kremer had returned to the Soviet Union, and Sonia's whereabouts were unknown.) In early 1947, after Fuchs had learned that Kuczynski was no longer in England, he took a step that was against all the rules of espionage. He approached another member of the KPD in England, Johanna Klopstech, a thirty-seven-year-old woman who had been a stenotypist for the KPD refugee organization in Czechoslovakia in the 1930s and for the Czech Refugee Trust Fund in London after she emigrated in November 1938. She also helped run the Freie Deutsche Kulturbund in London. She was sufficiently well known as a communist to be "considered dangerous by MI5" and was included in a list of twenty-one subversives supplied to the American embassy in London as early as December 26, 1940. According to Fuchs, Klopstech put him in touch with the agent who served as his last contact in England.[21]

When Fuchs and the new agent first met at the Nagshead Pub—

the contact carrying a book with a red cover, Fuchs bearing a copy of the *Tribune*—Fuchs was reprimanded for having approached Klopstech. Until early 1949 Fuchs had six meetings with this as yet unidentified individual, often at the Spotted Horse Pub or the Kew Gardens tube station. They even worked out a bizarre emergency signal: Fuchs would throw a copy of the magazine *Men Only* over a wall if he suspected he was being followed. At one point he accepted one hundred pounds to establish that he was a bona fide agent.[22]

As a top-ranking scientist at Harwell, Fuchs was able to give the Russians key information on the plutonium bomb. He described equation-of-state mathematics, the probability of predetonation, and the blast calculations of the Hiroshima and Nagasaki bombs. He also gave the formula for radiation intensity as a function of distance, based on his work prior to the Bikini Island tests of 1946. The Soviet Union, engaged in building its first atomic bomb, asked Fuchs for the full derivation of the formula whereby the yield, or explosive power, of the bomb was calculated; later Fuchs said he provided the net yield but not the derivation. He reported the figures for plutonium output at the Windscale plant and outlined the debate that had led the British to decide on air-cooled rather than water-cooled piles.[23]

Fuchs's espionage abated somewhat in 1948. He did not pass along much information on plutonium production at Harwell, perhaps because the Russians had sufficient data and asked few questions about it. Nor were they interested in uranium reprocessing and recovery, canning techniques, uranium pile rods, the preparations, purity, and dimensions of graphite, and basic nuclear physics data on a chain reaction. His agent's questions about pile production at Harwell and Chalk River convinced Fuchs that the Russians were getting information from another source or sources.[24]

At this point, Fuchs later told Skardon, "I began again to have my doubts about Russian policy." His controlled schizophrenia for a time prevented him from facing the facts about Stalinist totalitarianism. But eventually he got to the point where "I knew I disapproved of a great many actions of the Russian government and of the Communist Party." He still believed in a communist "new world," but he was no longer sure that he was "doing right" in passing information to the Soviet Union. He missed one appointment with his courier in 1949 because he was ill, probably with tuberculosis or pneumonia, then he decided not to keep another appointment.[25] He became brooding and unsociable; his physician urged him to take a rest.

■ Father and Son

In October 1949 Klaus's father, Emil, moved to the newly formed German Democratic Republic (DDR). Klaus's emotional ties to his German family now came into conflict with his ties to the Harwell family. He decided to approach Henry Arnold to suggest what Arnold had long suspected, that Klaus Fuchs could be a security risk. Like his Quaker father, Klaus wanted to do the right thing.

Until 1943 Emil had managed to eke out a living in Nazi Germany, living with various friends and continuing to resist Hitler. He fled to Switzerland in 1943 and did not return until after the war. By that time he was convinced that his children no longer cared for him, especially Klaus and Kristel, from whom he had been separated for a decade or more. In December 1945 he wrote to them, upset that he had not heard from them recently. He had received food packages from the Quakers, but why wasn't Kristel writing anything about her children? Why was Klaus in America and what was he doing there? Until well after Klaus left Los Alamos, Emil apparently knew nothing of his son's wartime activities.[26]

In early 1946 Klaus wrote to his father via their mutual Quaker friend in England, Corder Catchpool, assuring him that he was well and that he would try to arrange for Emil to visit England soon. By this time Emil was busy with numerous activities, including reorganizing the Odenwald School and creating a "united workers' party" for the rebuilding of Germany. His son told him of the frightening power of the atomic bomb, which he had seen tested at Alamogordo. "I only hope that we can concentrate on the peacetime use of this tremendous force in the future," Klaus added. He also wrote to British officials, asking for help in getting his father to England.[27]

In August, shortly after his return to England, Klaus and his father were reunited in Germany at Bad Pyrmont, where the Friends' annual meeting was under way. According to Emil's memoirs, Klaus arrived wearing a British army uniform, saying that he was on his way to see the German nuclear physicist Otto Hahn at Göttingen. Hahn, the discoverer of nuclear fission, had been arrested in April 1945 by a team of British and American scientists whose mission was to find out whether the Germans were building an atomic bomb. Hahn was interned in England with other German scientists, then returned to Germany early in 1946. Michael Perrin had been a key member of the scientific team, and Fuchs may have been sent to interview Hahn in connection with the British bomb project, inasmuch as Fuchs had helped monitor the German bomb project for British intelligence during the war.[28]

Bureaucratic red tape delayed Emil's trip to England. In May 1947 Klaus saw his father at the Bad Pyrmont Friends' meeting, which greatly cheered the old man. A few weeks later, in June, Klaus again visited his father, saying only that he was in Germany "on a scientific errand that was fixed for certain days." In August 1947 Emil finally received his visa. He spent the autumn with Klaus in Abingdon, not far from Harwell, and he lectured to Quaker gatherings. And he learned about Klaus's involvement in the Manhattan Project.[29]

Since 1940 Emil had wanted to go to the United States to lecture and meet other Quakers, and especially to visit Kristel. In 1948 he made the long-awaited trip, stopping en route to see Klaus for three days in Abingdon. The official purpose of Emil's visit was to lecture under the auspices of the American Friends' Service Committee. But he managed a visit in October to Kristel in Cambridge, where he also toured the slums of Boston and paid calls on local Quakers. During his American tour, which lasted until July 1949, Emil visited a number of cities and gave lectures. He told of the suffering of German Christians under the Nazis, of the Quaker spirit still alive there, of the future of workers in a new Germany. During the spring he gave courses at Pendle Hill. He was well received and widely publicized.[30]

By this time Emil was seriously considering a move to the Soviet zone of Germany. He had been invited there in 1948, when a campaign was launched to appeal to German Christians to help build and legitimize a new German communist state. Presumably Emil discussed the possibility of the move during the month he spent with Klaus in the summer of 1949. Democracy, he felt, was bankrupt in the West. True freedom lay in the East and the new communist society being constructed there. "My friends call me to the East," he told Klaus. By October 15 Klaus knew that his father had moved to Leipzig, carrying all his worldly possessions in his knapsack. Little did Emil know that his action had triggered the time bomb ticking in his son's divided soul, bringing to an explosive end the double life of Klaus Fuchs.[31]

■ *Klaus Fuchs in 1933, twenty-two years old*

Jurgen Kuczynski about 1948

Sonia (Ruth Kuczynski/
Ursula Hamburger) in East
Germany about 1951

■ *Klaus Fuchs at Los Alamos, 1944*

■ *Dr. J. Robert Oppenheimer and Major General Leslie Groves at Alamogordo, New Mexico, after the first atomic bomb test, July 1945*

■ *President Harry S Truman and Secretary of War Henry L. Stimson, August 1945*

■ *Britain's Atomic Research Center at Harwell, 1948*

■ *Michael Perrin (left), leaving Bow Street Court after testifying at Fuchs's pretrial hearing, February 10, 1950. Man at right is unidentified.*

■ *William J. Skardon and Henry Arnold after Fuchs's trial, March 1, 1950*

■ *FBI Director J. Edgar Hoover, February 1950*

■ *Harry Gold leaving federal court in Philadelphia after sentencing, December 11, 1950*

■ *Clement Attlee, Labour Party leader, October 1955*

■ *Klaus Fuchs after his release from prison, June 23, 1959*

CHAPTER · 9

The Super
and the Soviet Code

We still don't know if the Super can be built, but now we don't know it on much better grounds.

— *Edward Teller*

Nuclear weapons development in the United States remained under military control until January 1, 1947, when the Manhattan Engineer District ceased to exist and the civilian Atomic Energy Commission took over. The Atomic Energy Act of 1946 established two potentially contradictory goals: active support of atomic research and development and restriction of data to those cleared to receive it. Violators were to be punished under the Espionage Act of 1917. Thus the U.S. government was committed to both the "free discussion of basic scientific information" necessary to the advance of science and to restricted data "born classified" that could not become the subject of public discussion or peer review.[1]

The fundamental question was whether national security can best be achieved by keeping scientific information secret or by allowing science and technology to develop openly, perhaps more rapidly than military secrecy allows. In general, the government and the military opted for secrecy, and the scientific community for openness. In October 1948 Karl T. Compton, president of the Massachusetts Institute of Technology, argued that "secrecy and progress are mutually inimical" in science, which requires "free inquiry and free interchange of ideas." Compton and other scientists feared Truman's new loyalty oaths and the "chilling and crippling effect of secrecy upon scientific work." "Secrecy is the enemy of both science and democracy," they argued.[2]

In the spring of 1949 the Joint Committee on Atomic Energy held hearings on AEC security procedures (see Figure 7). The committee chairman, Senator Brien McMahon, argued for greater public access to atomic information, including the size of the current nuclear weapons stockpile, which was much smaller than generally assumed. How could Congress legislate intelligently without such information? he asked. "Secrecy is not security," wrote Hanson Baldwin of the *New York Times*, "nor is the bomb

Figure 7. U.S. Atomic Energy Commission, 1950

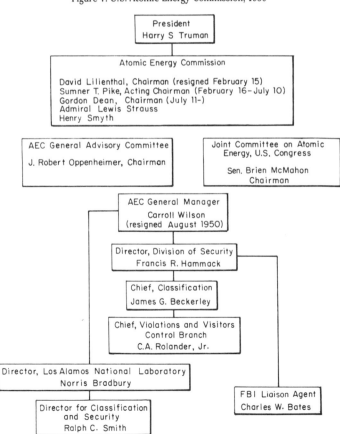

an impregnable rampart. Security is things, and people, and bombs, and weapons, and research and bases, intangibles as well as tangibles. Security above all is spirit and morale and progressive, advanced, and imaginative thinking, and secrecy is the enemy of these." Baldwin wrote that it was fallacious to imagine that the bomb ensured security or that security required secrecy. Excessive secrecy could weaken security.[3]

In August 1949 the first Soviet atomic test accelerated the debate. Harold C. Urey and Harrison Brown of the University of Chicago warned against the "excessive emphasis" on secrecy. Even if all Manhattan Project records had been given to the Soviet Union, they said, the Russians could not have produced a bomb any sooner, for it required an enormous engineering and industrial effort. Physicist Robert Bacher argued that "security is actually diminished when information only remotely related to weapons and fissionable material production is included with highly secret data and treated in the same way." S. K. Allison, director of the wartime Metallurgical Laboratory at Chicago, added that secrecy retarded science and was "not to be confused with security except in some military minds."[4]

Republican politicians were not convinced. Senator Hickenlooper continued to charge David Lilienthal with "incredible mismanagement" at the Atomic Energy Commission. Lewis Strauss argued for more secrecy, not less, "now that others may possess atomic weapons." In October 1949 the JCAE cleared Lilienthal of all charges, including lax security, with McMahon voting in favor of Lilienthal and Hickenlooper against. The final report concluded that "no evidence hints that Russia had acquired information from the commission."[5]

■ *Joe 1 and the Super*

Joe 1 shocked the United States as a sign of Soviet strength and American weakness. As early as October 1945, the Joint Chiefs of Staff had predicted that the Soviets would have an atomic bomb within five years, even if the United States "does not give the secret of atomic energy to the Soviets." In 1949 they predicted that a Soviet test was imminent and that the USSR would have a stockpile of about a hundred bombs by 1953; after the Fuchs case they revised their estimates upward. The size of the American stockpile, reportedly low, was a closely guarded secret.[6]

The Soviet test played a major role in convincing President Truman and other officials that the United States must proceed to develop an even more awesome weapon: the hydrogen bomb. After Joe 1, many observers felt that the Russians might be in a position to move rapidly toward that weapon. In fact, neither the Soviet Union nor the United States was close to making a hydrogen bomb, but each side thought the other might be.

The idea of a "super" bomb based on the fusion of light elements, rather than the fission of heavy ones, was at least as old as the Manhattan Project. At Los Alamos Teller and a small team of physicists working in Bethe's Theoretical Division conceived of a weapon thousands of times more powerful than the atomic bomb. But they first had to be able to create an atomic bomb in order to raise temperatures high enough for a thermonuclear explosion.

Since the late 1930s Bethe had studied the process of nuclear fusion that occurs in the sun; he discovered that at temperatures near forty million degrees centigrade (the sun's interior was estimated to approach a temperature of thirty million degrees), hydrogen could be converted into helium. The most likely fusion elements were the hydrogen isotopes deuterium and tritium, as well as lithium. Physicists theorized that at very high temperatures these isotopes could be fused to create heavier elements, with a consequent release of energy many times greater than could be achieved through fission.[7]

In a seminar on the theory of an atomic bomb in July 1942 Teller raised the possibility that a fission bomb could be utilized to trigger a fusion bomb. At a time when many believed that even a fission bomb could ignite the atmosphere, this idea seemed both awesome and preposterous. From the summer of 1942 on, Teller pursued his monster weapon with the support of Bethe and Oppenheimer, although Oppenheimer said that the idea of a thermonuclear weapon using deuterium had a "pretty fantastic sound."[8]

In the spring of 1943 Teller suggested that a deuterium bomb exploded at temperatures approaching 400 million degrees Fahrenheit could produce at least five times the yield of a uranium bomb. By that autumn Teller was prodding Bethe and Oppenheimer for greater support, even though a fission weapon was still a theory and the Los Alamos lab was still under construction. Teller warned that the Germans' interest in basic research on deuterium might mean that they were working toward a super bomb.[9]

During the winter of 1943–44, studies at Ohio State University indicated that the ignition of deuterium would be unusually difficult. Both Groves and Oppenheimer felt that resources should not be diverted from the main mission of producing an atomic bomb, but that some work on the super should continue; Teller and his small staff were taken off implosion work in June 1944 to pursue this research. Teller began imagining an implosion-type bomb that would contain deuterium and tritium as a fuel, thus using a fast neutron chain reaction to ignite a thermonuclear one.[10]

By spring 1945 Teller was quite convinced that a super bomb could yield at least ten megatons of explosive power, compared to the twenty-kiloton yield of the first atomic bombs. Even before the atomic bomb was successfully tested, Oppenheimer wrote Secretary of War Stimson that new weapons "quantitatively and qualitatively far more effective than now available" would be possible after the war and that there were "quite favorable technical prospects of the realization of the super bomb."[11]

The hydrogen bomb research at Los Alamos consisted largely of theory, talk, and patent applications for untested processes. In December 1945 Teller filed a patent application based on an idea conceived in 1943: that the reaction of deuterium and tritium would produce additional neutrons to react with the plutonium or uranium in a fission bomb, thus adding greatly to the bomb's efficiency. In 1946 a German scientist, Hans Thirring, speculated that a fission bomb could indeed be used to trigger a thermonuclear reaction.[12]

In April 1946, shortly before Klaus Fuchs returned to England, a conference was held at Los Alamos to discuss the history and future prospects of a super bomb. The conference concluded that "it is likely that a super bomb can be constructed and will work," and that the yield would be limited only by the amount of deuterium fuel used. In theory the bomb could be as powerful as its builders wished. But work on the super would divert a "considerable fraction of the resources" away from atomic bombs, which were still in very short supply.[13]

The Los Alamos conference was preliminary and optimistic. Fuchs undoubtedly reported the theoretical physics data to the Russians, as he did to Chadwick in May 1946. Fuchs also took part in a conference at Harwell in January 1947 on "plans for work on thermonuclear reactions," mainly deuteron-deuteron ones. But a super bomb was still far from reality, as Teller said in a report written in September 1947. Although the mathematical work on a hydrogen bomb was "virtually completed" by December 1949, computers adequate to the task did not become available until 1952.[14]

▪ The Hydrogen Bomb Debate

President Truman's first major decision regarding nuclear weapons had been to use the atomic bomb against Japan in 1945; he had not known about the bomb until one month after Roosevelt's death on April 12 of that year. The decision was heavy with bureaucratic momentum; in light of a two-billion-dollar expenditure and the belief that the atomic bomb would shorten the war and save American lives, Truman could only confirm a commitment already made. Now, in the autumn of 1949, Truman faced a decision that was his alone: whether or not to develop the most destructive nuclear weapon imaginable. Officially, the United States reacted to the Soviet test explosion with calm. The State Department informed American embassies that the new development was not viewed with alarm, that there was no reason to believe that it was the result of anything "stolen or copied from us," and that total security could never be achieved by nuclear weapons alone.[15]

The pro-super lobby began to form in October 1949. Edward Teller and Ernest Lawrence led the Los Alamos contingent in favor of the new project, with strong support among the military. The Joint Chiefs of Staff argued for increased nuclear weapons production, as did the National Security Council (NSC). Admiral

Lewis Strauss wrote the Atomic Energy Commission on October 5 that "we should now make an intensive effort to get ahead with the Super," a "quantum jump" and a "commitment in talent and money comparable, if necessary, to that which produced the first atomic weapon. That is the way to stay ahead." On October 17 Truman decided to accelerate the production of atomic warheads. The Soviet-American arms race had begun, and momentum was building toward a thermonuclear weapons program.[16]

The owlish Strauss, age fifty-four, was to play a crucial behind-the-scenes role in both the Fuchs case and the hydrogen bomb decision. Strauss was a highly patriotic American Jew for whom Nazi Germany and Soviet Russia were the embodiments of evil. He did not think much of the British, who had frustrated his efforts at Jewish resettlement in the 1930s, and he favored a complete American monopoly of the atomic bomb. In 1945 he had become the Navy representative on the Interim Committee on Atomic Energy, and from 1946 to 1950 he served as the sole Republican on the Atomic Energy Commission. He was alone among the five commissioners in his single-minded support of the super, to which chairman David Lilienthal was especially opposed.[17]

Many of the scientists who had built the first atomic bomb were opposed to the super. In a letter to Harvard President James Conant, Oppenheimer noted that he was "not sure the miserable thing would work" or could be "gotten to a target except by ox cart." He objected that the hydrogen bomb would also interfere with the production of atomic bombs, would have very few suitable targets (large Soviet cities), and would imply that America intended to make the first strike. Yet he felt that it would be "folly to oppose the exploration of this weapon," concluding that "we have always known it had to be done."[18]

Oppenheimer finally opposed the hydrogen bomb on both practical and moral grounds. In late October 1949 he persuaded other scientists on the AEC General Advisory Committee to recommend against it. The committee's October 30 report expressed the overwhelming conviction that "the super program itself should not be undertaken." The hydrogen bomb would extend much further the atomic bomb's capacity for "exterminating civilian populations."

The global effects of fallout would be massive and indiscriminate. A thermonuclear weapon might well become a "weapon of genocide." But the committee hedged its bets on whether a hydrogen bomb should be explored in a limited fashion or developed at a later date. "It would be wrong at the present moment," the report concluded, "to commit ourselves to an all-out effort toward its development." One scientist, Luis Alvarez, thought the program was dead in the water. It was not.[19]

Within a week of the GAC report, the voices of three major critics of the hydrogen bomb were stilled: Secretary of the Navy James Forrestal committed suicide, George F. Kennan retired from the Policy Planning Staff of the State Department, and Lilienthal announced that he would resign from the AEC as soon as a decision on the super was reached. Lilienthal was "flatly against this project," he wrote in his diary, because such a terrible weapon would merely create a "false sense of security" among Americans while increasing the danger of a nuclear war.[20]

Others disagreed. Secretary of the Air Force Stuart Symington argued for an "adequate air defense" against the Soviet Union and predicted that "the question of the survival of the United States may be involved." A subcommittee of the congressional Joint Committee on Atomic Energy visited Los Alamos and announced its "enthusiasm for an immediate program." The atomic energy commissioners were deeply divided. Lilienthal, Sumner Pike, and Henry Smyth shared the GAC's opposition to the project; Strauss and Gordon Dean favored an immediate crash program. And it was Strauss the president would listen to in the months ahead.[21]

Truman further committed himself to the super on November 19 when he appointed a special National Security Council subcommittee to respond to the GAC report. The recalcitrant Lilienthal was ultimately outvoted by the more enthusiastic secretary of state, Dean Acheson, and the secretary of defense, Louis Johnson. Truman warned the three men that any publicity would be "seriously prejudicial to the national security." In other words, the public would remain ignorant of the crucial debate over the hydrogen bomb. Security would be defined in secret.[22]

The very few congressmen who were aware of the debate were

in favor of the super. Senator McMahon, chairman of the JCAE, warned Truman that "if we let Russia get the Super first, catastrophe becomes all but certain—whereas if we get it first, there exists a chance of saving ourselves." But McMahon also felt that public debate should be encouraged in order to stimulate Soviet-American arms control measures. General Omar N. Bradley of the Joint Chiefs told Johnson that it would be "intolerable" for the Soviet Union to have the super and noted that "a unilateral decision on the part of the United States not to develop a thermonuclear weapon will not prevent the development of such a weapon elsewhere."[23]

In a letter dated November 25, Strauss urged Truman to direct the AEC to "proceed with the development of the thermonuclear weapon, at highest priority." Paul Nitze of the Policy Planning Staff at the State Department also urged an "accelerated program to test the possibility of a thermonuclear reaction." Thus when the NSC subcommittee met for the first time on December 22, Lilienthal's voice of opposition was hardly audible amid the chorus of pro-super opinion reaching the president's ears.[24]

The year 1950 opened with national security the central concern. In response both to Joe 1 and to the emergence of communist China, the National Security Council prepared a full-scale report on the global balance of power between East and West and its bearing on American national security. Yet Truman proposed a defense budget of $13.5 billion for fiscal year 1951, a reduction of nearly $1 billion from the previous year. The trend at that time was still toward "economy at the expense of national security programs," and the super would cost money, even though it might ultimately produce a "bigger bang for the buck."[25]

On January 13 the Joint Chiefs of Staff recommended that the United States proceed to determine the technical feasibility of the hydrogen bomb, including its delivery vehicle. Truman told Sidney Souers, his national security assistant, that the memo "made a lot of sense" and "that was what we should do."[26]

The final decision was more complex. On January 31 the NSC subcommittee drafted its recommendations: that the president direct the AEC to determine the technical feasibility of the hydrogen bomb; that the secretaries of state and defense be instructed to reexamine American objectives in the light of the Soviet atomic explosion and the "possible thermonuclear bomb capability of the Soviet Union"; and that the president "defer decision" about actually producing the new weapon. The last point, which ran counter to the JCAE's recommendation of mass production as soon as possible, was stricken from the final recommendation to the president.[27]

That afternoon Acheson, Lilienthal, and Johnson met for seven minutes with Truman and Souers at the White House. A few hours later the White House announced that the president had directed the AEC to "continue its work on all forms of atomic weapons, including the so-called hydrogen or super-bomb." The decision was now public knowledge. "I carried the good news into the GAC," wrote Lilienthal. "It was like a funeral party— especially when I said we were all gagged. Should they resign? I said definitely not, on the contrary. This would be very bad."[28]

"We were really shocked when President Truman decided in favor of a crash program," recalled Bethe, who now led a movement among prominent atomic scientists urging the U.S. government to issue a no-first-use declaration regarding the new weapon. Einstein proclaimed the idea of security through nuclear weapons to be a "dangerous illusion." But Teller argued for the weapon as a necessary defense against Russian tyranny, and the Nobel-prize-winning chemist Harold Urey proclaimed that "the hydrogen bomb should be developed and built." Like the policy makers, American scientists were divided over the hydrogen bomb. But they articulated their views in public, not in secret.[29]

A series of articles in *Scientific American* that spring pointed out the dangers of secrecy in making such a momentous decision. Louis Ridenour called Truman's decision "authoritarian"; the public had no idea what questions were even being asked. In an informed democracy, true security lay not in the "bankruptcy of our secrecy policy," but in international control of atomic weapons. Bethe called the hydrogen bomb a weapon of "total annihilation" useful only in destroying such population centers as New York, Moscow, and London. He also called for less secrecy and for a Soviet-American relationship of "mutual trust." The physicist Robert Bacher called the hydrogen bomb a "grossly over-rated" weapon that would not contribute much to American security; he felt that it should be debated in public, and he derided "the fallacy that there is security in secrecy." Ralph Lapp noted that hydrogen bombs would be better suited to American targets than Russian ones, with population dispersal the only defense.[30]

In general, the scientists opposed Truman's decision and the military supported it, as did the public. Polls showed that 73 percent of those sampled favored building the hydrogen bomb; 18 percent opposed it. A smaller majority favored continued negotiations with the Soviet Union for international control of nuclear weapons. When Bethe visited Los Alamos in April 1950, he discovered a "universal hostility" to the GAC report recommending against the hydrogen bomb; the entire laboratory "seemed enthusiastic about the project and was working at high speed."[31]

In retrospect, the decision to go ahead with the hydrogen bomb has appeared to some historians virtually inevitable. The GAC report, classified until the 1970s, indicated resistance to it by top scientists, but not by those in the laboratories. The AEC was divided. For our purposes it is important to remember that the Fuchs case was unknown to either the president or the American public until several days after the January 31 announcement. But that decision was not yet a commitment of resources; the Fuchs case would hasten and support that commitment.

In 1954, when the Atomic Energy Commissioners met to consider what effect the Fuchs case had had on the 1950 hydrogen bomb decision, they noted that the AEC had been informed of the FBI's suspicions in early November 1949. Carroll Wilson, the AEC general manager, had reported to the commissioners that a British scientist had spied on the Manhattan Project and described it as "one of the most important" espionage cases pending. But the significance of the case was "evidently not apparent." In fact, on November 1, 1949, a secret memorandum by the AEC's Security and Intelligence Division had reviewed, at the FBI's request, Fuchs's work on the atomic bomb. The memorandum concluded that Fuchs and Peierls made up "two thirds of the team which handled the hydrodynamics in the Theoretical Division which made the implosion developments possible. They both contributed heavily to all phases of the weapon development including implosion and super."[32]

The evidence thus strongly suggests that Lewis Strauss, at least, was aware of the developing Fuchs case well before he began urging the president to proceed with the super. Fuchs's espionage was not reported to the General Advisory Committee until January 30, on the eve of his arrest. The FBI had not officially communicated to other agencies or the White House at this time, but reports of Fuchs's imminent arrest circulated at the NSC subcommittee meeting on January 31 which recommended to the president that he proceed with the super. That same day Strauss tendered his expected resignation as AEC commissioner, effective April 15. The next day Strauss wrote Truman that "the recent word from the FBI as to the espionage case involving a prominent British scientist only fortifies the wisdom of your decision. The individual in question had worked on the super-bomb at Los Alamos."[33]

Truman apparently did not learn of Fuchs's confession and arrest until February 1. Hoover telephoned Souers and suggested that he "might want to pass this information on to the president." Souers was shocked. That afternoon he called Hoover back from the White House, concerned that in the light of the new information on Fuchs the Russians might have "gotten going on the hydrogen bomb even before the other [atomic bomb]." Hoover also told Senator McMahon that it was "significant" that Fuchs was at Los Alamos while "some work was being done on the hydrogen bomb." Hoover added that he thought the Fuchs case would "strengthen the president's hand" in choosing a new AEC chairman to replace Lilienthal and in "tightening up all along the line" in security matters.[34]

■ *Discovering Klaus Fuchs: The Soviet Code Break*

How had Fuchs been discovered? According to his confession, his father's move to the Soviet zone of Germany had driven him to tell all to the British authorities. But why had he not fled the country? Or simply kept quiet? And how had the British and Americans discovered that Fuchs was an atom spy?

According to American press reports, the hunt for Fuchs had begun because of an FBI tip, probably a wiretap, or "technical surveillance," as it was euphemistically called. Hoover saw no reason to disavow that explanation; the bureau had been under fire in recent months for wiretapping, and the Fuchs case precipitated an avalanche of mail in favor of government wiretapping. The FBI's public announcement said only that "the case involving Dr. Fuchs was developed by the British on information originally furnished them by the FBI." To understand this terse explanation, we must return to World War II and the world of cryptography.[35]

Until 1945 American and British code-cracking efforts were directed against the Germans and the Japanese. The British, with Polish help, had succeeded early on in recreating the German Enigma machine that was used to encipher all military wireless traffic. Thousands of cryptographers and translators worked around the clock at a secret center in Bletchley Park on the code intercepts known as Ultra.

But in 1945 the Soviet Union, a wartime ally, became the enemy. It was not long before attempts to crack Soviet codes and ciphers began in earnest. American and British code breakers independently sifted through mounds of intercepted Soviet traffic, including wartime messages to Moscow from the Soviet consulate in New York. This slow, painstaking work was code-named Bride in America and U-traffic in Great Britain. In 1948 the U.S. effort was coordinated under a new, highly secret cryptographic organization known as the Armed Forces Security Agency, headed by Admiral Stone. The code-breaking project was run by a top cryptanalyst named Meredith Gardner.[36]

Soviet messages normally utilized a method known as the one-time pad. These were notepads with groups of five-digit numbers used by an agent in conjunction with other numbers referring to a code book held by the receiver in Moscow. The enciphered message was impossible to crack without having both the code book and the pad. In 1944 FBI agents, with the aid of documents stolen from the Soviet Purchasing Commission in New York, had acquired a duplicate set of one-time pads together with a batch of messages. After the war, by comparing these with intercepted messages from the Soviet consulate to Moscow from the same period, American cryptanalysts were able to begin reconstructing the Soviet cipher system, which Robert Lamphere of the FBI and Meredith Gardner succeeded in cracking in the summer of 1949.

In the process the cryptanalysts discovered a remarkable document: a report on the Manhattan Project written by Klaus Fuchs from Los Alamos during the war, sent from New York to Moscow. The intercepted report did not necessarily mean that Fuchs was the Soviet agent. But other FBI intercepts of Soviet messages indicated that the agent was a scientist whose sister had attended an American university; it was known that Fuchs's sister, Kristel Heineman, had attended Swarthmore College in the 1930s and was now living in Cambridge.[37]

This was not the first time that the FBI had seen Fuchs's name. During the war Hoover had shown steady interest in the British mission to the Manhattan Project; a list of all the British scientists was reported to the FBI in December 1943, and in late March 1944 Hoover received an updated list with the usual assurances that all of the scientists had been cleared by British security. The movements of all British personnel were reported to Hoover, including Fuchs's transfer from New York to Los Alamos, and, after the war, his return to England.[38]

At the time there was no reason for the FBI to take special notice of Fuchs. But on June 15, 1945, John Cimperman, the FBI agent in London, forwarded to Washington copies of two captured German documents that had been prepared for the invasion of Russia in 1941. They included a two-volume list of thousands of names of people suspected of communist activity by the counterespionage branch of the Gestapo. The Philadelphia FBI office translated the list, and in Volume 1 appeared: "210. FUCHS, Klaus, student of philosophy, December 29, 1911. Russelsheim, RSHA IVA2, Gestapo Field Office, Kiel." The list was sent to Hoover as part of a report on "Soviet Intelligence Activity" on July 31. Fuchs's name, of course, was only one of thousands. But in 1946 Israel Halperin's address book, discovered in connection with Gouzenko's defection, listed Klaus Fuchs and Kristel Heineman. The FBI did not investigate Fuchs, but agents were sent to question his sister.[39]

In January 1949 Rear Admiral John Gingrich, security chief of the Atomic Energy Commission, asked for a report on the activities of British and Canadian scientists assigned to the Manhattan Project in 1945 and 1946. The report noted that the British had made major contributions, especially at Los Alamos, and included a list of all the scientists, with their arrival and departure dates. The Los Alamos report was substantiated by Hans Bethe and by Carson Mark, director of the Los Alamos laboratory and former member of the British mission.[40]

The AEC did not pursue the matter of the British mission until late summer, when the FBI's suspicions of Fuchs, coupled with the Soviet bomb test, set off a new alarm. By September 13 the AEC, at the FBI's request, had searched its files for information on Fuchs and had assembled a list of his reports written for the Manhattan Project. The FBI was particularly interested in a 1944 document on effluent fluctuation, probably the same report that had turned up in the Soviet cipher traffic. The FBI did not tell AEC security why it was interested in Fuchs, but it made it plain that "no other inquiries outside the Division of Security [are] to be made at this time." FBI agent C. W. Bates also requested that AEC Security "obtain discreetly any record of Dr. Fuchs' activities at Los Alamos."[41]

On September 22, one day before President Truman announced the successful Soviet bomb test, the FBI opened a case on Fuchs. It was listed under "Espionage—Russia" and was code-named Foocase. Hoover notified President Truman several months later that FBI agents Robert Lamphere and Ernest Van Loon had begun investigating Fuchs "on the basis of information indicating that he had been active as a Soviet espionage agent while in the United States." The FBI instructed its offices in New York, El Paso, Knoxville, and Washington to begin an all-out investigation of Fuchs, but not to make any public disclosures or interviews. The initial information obtained was sketchy. Reports came in that Fuchs had been a "medical physicist" in England and that he had gone either to Los Alamos or to Oak Ridge (which he never visited) in 1944. Until the public announcement of Fuchs's arrest in February, the FBI was largely limited to a paper chase through available records. Nevertheless, by late 1949 a fairly detailed picture of Fuchs's travels had begun to emerge.[42]

In the meantime the FBI notified its British intelligence contacts in Washington, Kim Philby of MI6 and Geoffrey Patterson of MI5, of the case. In early September Robert Lamphere wrote a

top secret memorandum to MI5 about the Fuchs report, the Gestapo file, and the Halperin notebook and delivered it to the
British embassy in Washington. The memorandum was duly reported to Stewart Menzies, the head of MI6 in London, and on
September 6 Michael Perrin told Menzies' deputy director, Dick
White, that "it looks very much as if Fuchs of Harwell is working
for the Russians." "After careful consideration" Prime Minister
Attlee authorized Scotland Yard to interrogate Fuchs. The trick
was to persuade Fuchs to confess to information that had already
been obtained by deciphering. Otherwise the British could not
arrest him without Moscow's deducing that someone had broken
their codes.[43]

CHAPTER · 10

Confession and Trial

The Fuchs trial did nothing to acquaint the public with the true nature of his offense. Indeed, it did something to disguise it.
— *Rebecca West,* The New Meaning of Treason

On December 29, 1949, Klaus Fuchs quietly celebrated his thirty-eighth birthday with friends at Harwell. Seemingly relaxed, he showed no outward sign of the turmoil that had overtaken his life in recent months. Fuchs's friends might not have felt so comfortable on the occasion had they known that eight days earlier, on December 21, Fuchs had met with William James Skardon, an MI5 intelligence officer assigned to Scotland Yard. During their conversation Skardon had informed Fuchs that he was suspected of having given secret information on nuclear weapons to the Soviet Union.[1]

As an MI5 officer (see Figure 8), Skardon had no power of arrest, and he had no evidence with which to confront Fuchs. The challenge was to coax a confession of his crimes from Fuchs himself. But a confession was not to be the outcome of that first meeting. Fuchs denied having passed along secrets to the Russians. The only way he could be a security risk, he maintained, was as a result of his father's recent move to East Germany. Emil Fuchs had accepted a professorship at the University of Leipzig, and the Soviets might see this as an opportunity to blackmail Klaus. Skardon later testified that Fuchs said during their conversation that he considered his oath of allegiance to Great Britain to be a "serious matter." But he felt he still had the "freedom to act in accordance with his conscience" should circumstances arise in Britain "comparable with those which existed in Germany in 1932 and 1933." In that case Fuchs would feel free to act on "a loyalty which he owed to humanity generally."[2]

On December 30 Skardon arrived at Harwell once more, this time to inform Fuchs that the Ministry of Supply, which directed

Figure 8. MI5 (British Security Service), 1950

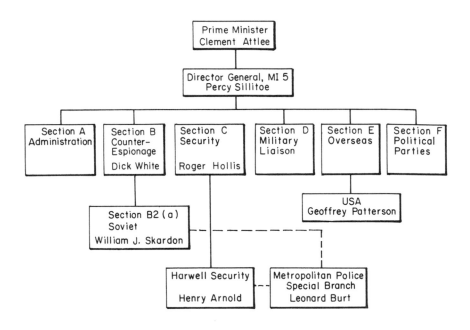

atomic matters, was "likely to dismiss" him because of his father's recent move. Fuchs seemed upset, but again denied that he had engaged in espionage. On January 10 Sir John Cockcroft, the Harwell director, told Fuchs that, under the circumstances, it would be best if he resigned; Cockcroft offered to retain him as a consultant.[3]

Three days later, on January 13, when Fuchs met with Skardon again, he finally admitted that he had given the Soviets secret materials on the atomic bomb. Then, to Fuchs's confusion and distress, for eleven days nothing happened. By the time talks with Skardon resumed on January 24, Fuchs was under considerable mental stress, and when he was given an opportunity to make a formal written statement about his espionage activities, he accepted. On January 27 Fuchs and Skardon met on the platform at Paddington Station and walked to the War Office. There Fuchs dictated a long statement, which Skardon wrote down and had Fuchs sign. (The FBI's version of this confession is given in Appendix A.)

■ *Confession*

Fuchs noted in his statement that he had never known any of his contacts by name. At first he had told them simply that work on an atomic bomb was proceeding. But when they wanted more details, he agreed to supply them. Initially Fuchs transmitted copies of only his own research papers. Subsequently, at Los Alamos, he did what he considered "the worst I have done, namely to give information about the principles of the design of the plutonium bomb." And he had continued to provide information until March 1949. His father's decision to move to East Germany made him face some facts about himself. "I was not sure whether I would not go back." At that time, recalled Fuchs, his father's and his own political views were closer than ever; his father too believed that the East German government was a least "trying to build a new world." Fuchs became more and more convinced that he would have to leave Harwell, especially when he was "confronted with the fact that there was evidence that I had given away information in New York" on the Manhattan Project. "I was given the chance of admitting it and staying at Harwell," said Fuchs, "or of clearing out. I was not sure enough of myself to stay at Harwell and, therefore, I denied the allegations and decided that I would have to leave Harwell."

Fuchs concluded his confession by saying that he hoped to "repair the damage" somewhat by telling the authorities what information he had given the Russians from 1942 to 1949. Perhaps this would help uncover other spies who were "still doing what I have done."

After Fuchs signed his confession, Skardon made a note that Fuchs had read it, made alterations, and initialed each page. The two men agreed that Fuchs would make a second, more technical, statement to Michael Perrin. Perrin, who had worked for Tube Alloys and ICI, had the proper security clearance for the highly classified information Fuchs would divulge.

In many ways Fuchs did not realize the magnitude of his crimes. His vagueness and confusion about what he had done probably kept him from flight or more drastic action, such as suicide.[4] The public Klaus Fuchs was the scientist, the naturalized British citizen. Outwardly personable but inwardly shy, withdrawn, and egocentric, Fuchs had been virtually imprisoned in the atomic towns of Los Alamos and Harwell for five years. He had many admirers but no real friends. Cut off from his own family by exile, Fuchs had adopted Harwell, where he was a scientific leader surrounded by younger researchers. He came to believe that he was essential to Harwell, but he was not. The private Fuchs was a political true believer in communism whose Quaker upbringing reinforced his sense of rectitude and moral idealism. Dominated by the religious and ethical righteousness of his father, devastated by the suicides of his mother and sister, Fuchs had retreated into the world of communism and espionage, where he felt morally virtuous, politically active, and personally fulfilled. The public Fuchs obeyed the rules of British secrecy; the private Fuchs followed the party line. By the time he met Skardon, these two selves were in deep conflict. When he confessed his double life, he described himself as having been in a state of "controlled schizophrenia."

On January 30 Fuchs met Skardon once again at the War Office, where he made his technical confession to Perrin (the FBI's version of this confession is given in Appendix B).[5] Fuchs told Perrin in more detail what information he had passed to the Russians during his eight-year espionage career, as Perrin took notes. (Only later did Perrin learn that MI5 had tape-recorded the entire session, although in a form so garbled as to be unintelligible.)[6] Fuchs said he originally gave information to Soviet agents in early 1942, a few months after he began working for Tube Alloys. At first he handed over only the results of his own research on the mathematics of gaseous diffusion. He was also trying to determine the critical mass and efficiency of an atomic bomb and to estimate the explosive yield. At that time Fuchs knew nothing of plutonium, which had recently been discovered in America, or how to produce it.

When Perrin asked Fuchs what he knew about the Soviet atomic bomb test the previous August, Fuchs agreed that it was probably a plutonium bomb. (Measurements of airborne fission products collected by an American WB-29 airplane seemed to confirm this.) But Fuchs said he had been extremely surprised that the Soviets had exploded a bomb so soon, for that meant they had made great headway in engineering design and in industrial facilities for producing plutonium.

"I formed the impression," concluded Perrin in his summary comment, "that throughout the interview Fuchs was genuinely trying to remember and report all the information that he had given to the Russian agents with whom he had been in contact, and that he was not withholding anything. He seemed, on the contrary, to be trying his best to help me to evaluate the present position of atomic energy works in Russia in the light of the information that he had, and had not, passed to them."

MI5 did not wish to create complications by having Fuchs arrested at Harwell, where he might have co-conspirators. Because it did not have authority to arrest anyone, MI5 traditionally called upon Scotland Yard for this formality. It was decided to have Fuchs go to London again and to arrest him there. Perrin telephoned Fuchs and asked him to come for another session on February 2, this time at Perrin's office at the Shell-Mex House in

London. When Fuchs arrived, Commander Leonard J. Burt of MI5, who was also chief inspector for Scotland Yard, read Fuchs the charges and told him he was under arrest. Shaken and ashen, Fuchs had only one question for Perrin: "Do you realize what this will mean at Harwell?"[7]

■ *Arraignment and Hearing*

Few were present in the Bow Street magistrate's court on February 3 when Fuchs was arraigned and sat listening to charges that at least four times between 1943 and 1947 he had "communicated to a person unknown information relating to atomic research which was calculated to be, or might be directly or indirectly, useful to an enemy," and that he had done something similar "on a day . . . in February 1945 . . . in the United States of America." Fuchs's appearance in court was brief, and the only witness was Commander Burt.

"Do you want to ask any questions?" asked Sir Laurence Dunne, chief metropolitan magistrate. "No," replied Fuchs quietly. "Do you want the court to do anything about legal representation for you?" "I don't know of anybody," Fuchs replied weakly. At this point the prosecutor, Christmas Humphreys, noted that a hearing would be held the following Friday, February 10, until which time Fuchs would be remanded to prison. "I shall not listen to any representations unless they are of a very extraordinary nature that will justify a further remand," he said.[8] Fuchs quietly left the courtroom. Later he was transferred to Brixton Prison in southeast London, and the curtain of secrecy dropped once again. The Ministry of Supply informed the British public only that Fuchs had been arrested and charged. It made no comment on either the man himself or the specific charges; indeed, comment might have prejudiced a fair trial.[9]

The Americans wanted a representative present at Fuchs's hearing. The U.S. Department of State planned to send the legal attaché from the London embassy, John A. Cimperman. But Cimperman was actually the FBI representative at the U.S. embassy, and he argued that his appearance in a British court would blow his cover. Hoover instructed him to "obtain complete details of proceedings" without actually appearing in court. Cimperman had Matt C. McDade of the American Embassy staff attend the hearing and take notes, which Cimperman the next day wired to Washington.[10]

Humphreys began the case for the prosecution by reading the two charges brought under Section 1 (1) C of the Official Secrets Act. He noted that only three witnesses were to be called: William Skardon, Henry Arnold, and Michael Perrin. Fuchs's statement to Skardon was labeled a "complete confession of the charges." The confession, plus the testimony of the three witnesses, would be the only evidence in the case for the prosecution. Humphreys briefly traced Fuchs's career as a German refugee communist, who had been interned in 1940. Because he was "one of the finest theoretical physicists living" and therefore of immense value for Tube Alloys, "after a very careful scrutiny of his background and apparent mental makeup, he was then taken from internment and his great brain was harnessed to atomic research."[11]

In July 1942, Humphreys told the courtroom, Fuchs had become a naturalized British citizen and had sworn to "be faithful and bear true allegiance to His Majesty King George VI, his heirs and successors, according to law." He had subsequently "signed the usual security undertaking" and "always impressed his superiors as being security minded." Yet such behavior "meant nothing to a man whose mind was irrevocably wedded to Communist principles." To emphasize the point, Humphreys read snippets from the confession to Skardon, demonstrating that Fuchs had passed information to the Russians from 1942 to 1949. It was "undesirable" and "unnecessary" to reveal what that information was, but it was "of the highest value to a potential enemy." Fuchs had committed "planned and deliberate treachery to the country of his adoption" because his real motive was "unswerving devotion to the cause of Russian Communism."

Humphreys went on to philosophize about Fuchs's self-confessed "controlled schizophrenia," a Jekyll behaving like a normal citizen and scientist, and a Hyde behaving like a "political fanatic on the payroll of a foreign power." His confession was a process of "mental crisis." Humphreys then read further excerpts from Fuchs's confession, skipping the first six pages on his political

activity in Germany and England and beginning with his espionage in 1941. He called upon William Skardon, who reviewed
the process of interviewing Fuchs and briefly described Fuchs's
meetings with Soviet agents in England and America. At this point
Humphreys stated that the confession should be regarded as secret, and it was handed to Commander Burt for safekeeping. Burt
produced a statement by the attorney general consenting to prosecution, along with Fuchs's certificate of naturalization.

Arnold and Perrin made brief statements confirming Fuchs's
confessions. Perrin gave only a brief outline of the chronology of
espionage and none of the scientific details. Humphreys asked
Perrin if the information Fuchs gave the Russians would be "of
value to a potential enemy." Perrin said it would. Humphreys
concluded by asking for a trial during the next session of the
Central Criminal Court, which was to begin February 28. Fuchs's
court-appointed defense counsel, J. Thompson Halsall, declared
that the defendant had nothing to say and no evidence to present.
Fuchs stood in the dock as Humphreys again read the two charges.

At one level the press ridiculed Fuchs as an "atomic wizard"
who could not fix his own car; at another he was a traitor who
had sold Russia "atomic secrets," a villain who had betrayed the
country that gave him refuge. His espionage was said to be of
major significance. The atomic bomb secrets were "priceless," and
the published quotes from his confession to Skardon hinted at
systematic and prolonged threats to national security. In court
Fuchs spent the two hours of the hearing gripping his knees
occasionally with his left hand, a curious figure in wrinkled brown
suit and dark red tie, almost lost in the crowd of sixty reporters
and note-passing prosecutors. On the front pages of the world
press he became larger than life: a communist spy of shattered
faith, split personality, and enormous influence on world affairs.[12]

The New York Times editorialized that Fuchs's confession and
hearing had a surrealist quality. He was no "controlled schizophrenic," but the "dupe of a soulless philosophy." He had betrayed himself, his colleagues, his adopted country, and the world.
His motive was not money, but the force of an idea, communism.
"The Fuchs case teaches us that specific security measures must
be tightened," the newspaper continued, although an "alarmist
witch hunt" would only play into Russian hands.[13]

■ *The Trial*

The FBI wanted to have an American observer at Fuchs's trial on March 1. Hoover offered Percy Sillitoe, director general of MI5, all possible assistance and proposed that an FBI man, Lish Whitson, attend the trial officially. The British refused; they clearly intended to try Fuchs without American assistance or interference, and in a manner designed to divulge as little as possible. The British authorities even claimed that they had broken the Fuchs case without FBI assistance. Hoover fumed. Some FBI agents suspected that Lord Portal and Michael Perrin had known of Fuchs's culpability as early as February 1949; Hoover's men wanted to tell the MI5 officers to "put up or shut up" and stop spreading rumors. Whitson was finally allowed to attend the trial when the U.S. Department of State appointed him an attaché and designated him an official observer.[14]

The trial lasted only an hour and a half, from 10:30 A.M. until noon, in courtroom number one of the grim criminal court building in London known as the Old Bailey. The proceedings were open to the public, and the audience included the Duchess of Kent, sister-in-law of King George VI; some eighty newspaper reporters, including one from TASS; two American embassy representatives, including Whitson; the mayor of London in his plumed cock hat, medallions, and black robe; and a German woman, Fuchs's cousin, who was often in tears. The silence was broken only by an occasional cough or the rustling of papers.[15]

Fuchs sat in the dock of the Senior Assize Court of the British Empire. The presiding judge, Lord Chief Justice Goddard, robed in scarlet and ermine and wearing the traditional white wig, sat in a massive oak chair. The crown's chief prosecutor, Attorney General Hartley Shawcross, was widely known for his role at the Nuremberg war crimes trials. Derek Curtis Bennett, the chief counsel for the defense, was equally famous for his ability to obtain acquittals for a wide variety of accused criminals.[16]

The four-count indictment was read:

1. On a day in 1943 in the city of Birmingham [Banbury in the original version] for a purpose prejudicial to the safety or interests of the State, he communicated to a person unknown information relating to atomic research which was calculated

to be, or might have been, or was intended to be, directly or indirectly useful to an enemy.

2. On a day unknown between 31st December, 1943, and 1st August, 1944, he being a British subject in the City of New York in the United States of America, committed a similar offense.

3. On a day unknown in February 1945, he being a British subject, at Boston, Massachusetts, in the United States of America, committed a similar offense.

4. On a day in 1947 in Berkshire, he committed a similar offense.[17]

Because the dates and the names of those to whom Fuchs had given information were unknown at the time, he could not be charged with conspiracy. The indictment made no mention of the fact that Fuchs had admitted committing espionage from 1942 through 1949, not just on four occasions between 1943 and 1947. Like so much else about the Fuchs case, the indictment was as significant for what it omitted as for what it included.

In presenting the case for the crown, Shawcross argued that the prisoner was a communist, which was both the explanation and the tragedy of the case. Klaus Fuchs was a scientist serving a false cause, communism. He had given information to the Soviet Union, which, though a British ally at the time, was later an enemy. Shawcross stressed that Fuchs had confessed to Skardon while he was at liberty, a "free man"; he had not been coerced.[18]

The defense argued that Fuchs was an anti-Nazi refugee fighting Hitler, that the USSR had been an ally of Great Britain during the war when Fuchs began his espionage, and that he had rendered "valuable practical assistance" to the state in giving his confession. Curtis Bennett pointed out that Fuchs was on record at the Home Office as having been a member of the German Communist Party and that he had never joined the CPGB. He had made no secret of his communism during an era when it was hardly unusual to be one or to sympathize with the Soviet Union. If anything, being a communist during the war made him a more reliable anti-Nazi in the eyes of the British. After all, Fuchs had come to England to build a communist Germany, not to build atomic bombs.

Asked to plead guilty or not guilty, Fuchs stated softly that he was indeed guilty, that he did not want to hurt his friends at Harwell, and that he had received considerate treatment in prison and a fair trial. He hoped that his confession would help atone for his wrongdoing, and he alluded mysteriously to additional crimes he had committed which were not mentioned in court.

In passing sentence, Goddard heaped scorn on the defendant. He stated that Fuchs had betrayed British protection with "the grossest treachery," following the "pernicious creed" of communism. His atomic espionage had done "irreparable harm" to both England and America. He had imperiled the right of asylum and liberty for other refugees from tyranny. His crime was "only thinly differentiated from high treason." When Fuchs's lawyer asked him what penalty he expected, Fuchs said the death penalty. On the other hand, he still seemed to believe that his value to Harwell and his confession would save him from a harsh sentence. Within minutes he was sentenced to the maximum fourteen years and led off to prison.

Fuchs said he had gotten a fair trial. But it was an unusual trial in that there was no jury (a fairly common procedure in cases involving official secrets), no evidence was presented other than his confessions, and no witnesses were heard except Skardon. The prosecutor read in court only part of Fuchs's confession to Skardon, omitting the section on his communist party membership in Germany before 1933, which showed that he had come to England on party orders for political reasons, and his statement that the worst he had done was "to give information about the principles of the design of the plutonium bomb" to the Russians. No part of the technical confession to Perrin was read in court. These omissions were crucial, for it was widely believed that Fuchs had acted alone and that he had given away the secrets of the hydrogen bomb.

Fuchs did not know that the British government had not allowed him a jury trial because he had betrayed political secrets that they could not risk having brought up in court. A jury trial with cross-examination and witnesses might have revealed that Fuchs was working on Britain's secret atomic bomb project at Harwell; that Fuchs's controllers were German communist refugees who had contacts with members of Attlee's cabinet; that Soviet agents had penetrated British intelligence and the foreign service; and that the still-secret Ultra intelligence had been shared with Stalin during the war, possibly through the same Soviet agents who controlled Fuchs. The advantage to the government of calling him a lone violator of security and giving him a quick trial was that he would be unable to reveal further secrets.

■ *Treason and Liberty*

Many people thought that Fuchs should have been charged with treason and sentenced to death. Why was he not so charged? In British law, treason is defined by a 1351 statute of Edward III: "If a man do levy war against our Lord the King in his realm or be adherent to the King's enemies in his realm, giving them aid and comfort in the realm or elsewhere," then he has committed treason. In 1945 the Old Bailey had been the scene of the treason trial of William Joyce, known to British radio listeners as Lord Haw Haw, a Nazi broadcaster during World War II. Joyce, who clearly "did traitorously adhere to the King's enemies," was tried by a jury and executed.[19]

Because treason is a capital crime, juries sometimes have acquitted a defendant rather than impose such a severe penalty. In addition, treason traditionally has meant an act in time of war to aid the enemy. But the Soviet Union had been an ally during the war. Indeed, the Anglo-Soviet Treaty of 1942 provided for explicit and significant sharing of secret military information and technology with the Russians. If Fuchs had given the secrets of Los Alamos to Germany, Italy, or Japan, he could have been executed for treason. Instead, he was brought to trial under the Official Secrets Act (originally passed in 1889 and amended in 1911, 1920, and 1939). This law, the British government's response to the need for security in an age of political crimes, was commonly employed in cases of espionage: the 1938 case of Percy Glading, a Soviet agent working at the Woolwich Arsenal; the 1939 case of John Herbert King, a Foreign Office cipher clerk who passed documents to the Soviets; the 1941 case of Douglas Springhall, a

British communist engaged in industrial espionage; and the 1946 case of Alan Nunn May.[20]

The defense in the Nunn May trial had taken the line that the Soviet Union was an ally of Great Britain when the crimes were committed and that Nunn May had simply been overzealous in carrying out Churchill's policy of sharing scientific and technical information with Stalin. The chief justice found this unsatisfactory and sentenced Nunn May to ten years at hard labor. (When Nunn May was released in 1952, after six years, he still felt he had "acted rightly" and expressed no remorse. Many British scientists, including Rudolf Peierls, had agreed with him earlier.)[21]

For political crimes in the twentieth century British law shifted toward nonjudicial regulation by police and censorship organs under the executive administration of the Official Secrets Act. Leniency gave way to preventive administration through emergency legislation, control of the press, and stiffer penalties. State security became as important as individual liberty. The police played an ever-increasing role in initiating prosecution and gathering evidence, which formerly had been done by the judicial system. Yet great care was taken to establish reasonable grounds for guilt before the suspect became the accused, formally charged with a crime and arrested. Confessions were admissible evidence, as long as they were obtained voluntarily in writing with the appropriate cautions about being potentially incriminating. Police interrogation thus became crucial to the prosecution's case, ideally resulting in a signed statement by the suspect that would establish guilt beyond a reasonable doubt.[22]

Thus even Fuchs, who had threatened the liberties of all Englishmen by his betrayal of official secrets, found his own liberty protected under the law until found guilty. "We must all bear in mind," wrote Percy Sillitoe of MI5, "if we cry out against the people who have abused their liberty in this country, that had we deprived them of that liberty without legal evidence against them we should have been taking steps which would, inevitably, have threatened the liberty of every one of us in Britain."[23]

In understanding Fuchs's failure to appreciate British liberty, we must remember that he had inherited the peculiarly German attitude toward freedom articulated by Leonard Krieger and other scholars. According to Krieger, the German notion of *Recht* (right) was traditionally a formal attribute of the state; rights were designed not so much to protect the individual from the state but to preserve the state itself. Conformity to legitimate political authority, in short, was not the antithesis of liberty, but its very source. Fuchs had no sense of individual liberty in opposition to the state and no sense of politics beyond the transcendent truths of the communist party.[24]

The novelist Arthur Koestler, who joined the KPD in Berlin at about the same time as Fuchs, recalled the experience as an epiphany: "The new light seems to pour from all directions across the skull." All questions suddenly had correct answers determined by the party with its infallible knowledge of history. The result was an individual's "readiness to sacrifice" all values and goals to those of the party. Unlike Koestler, however, Fuchs did not lose his faith. In his confession Fuchs did not state that he had broken the law, nor did he renounce communism. Rather, he told Skardon that in 1933 "I was ready to accept the philosophy that the Party is right and that in the coming struggle you could not permit yourself any doubts after the Party had made a decision." For Fuchs the communist party of Germany, with its knowledge of history and its dream of a classless society, was the source of true liberty, not its enemy.[25]

■ The Prisoner

Fuchs did not seem to fully comprehend the nature of his crime. He seemed surprised that Arnold was the only person who visited him in prison after 1950. Fuchs felt guiltier about deceiving Arnold than about betraying the British government. Arnold continued to look after Fuchs's affairs while he was in prison.[26] At one point Fuchs told Peierls, with a mixture of arrogance and naiveté, that he regretted his espionage. "You must remember what I went through under the Nazis," he told his former mentor; "besides, it was always my intention, when I had helped the Russians to take over everything, to get up and tell them what is wrong with their own system."[27]

For nine years Fuchs sewed mailbags with other prisoners, read physics journals, and organized classes for his cellmates. There were rumors, vigorously denied by the Home Office, that a diary and scientific papers had been found hidden in the hollow leg of his bed. In the winter of 1957–58, Emil Fuchs visited him in prison and began negotiations for a new life and career for his son in East Germany. Because Fuchs was a model prisoner, always on good behavior and in charge of prison education programs, his sentence was reduced to nine years. Fuchs feared that upon his release he would be extradited to the United States and executed. The FBI suspected that the British would continue to employ Fuchs as a nuclear physicist. The British press reported that the government wanted to send him to West Germany to obtain citizenship and then on to Canada to do scientific research.[28]

Instead, Klaus Fuchs went to live with his father in East Germany. Arnold helped make the arrangements to spirit him out of England, where Fuchs may well have wished to stay; he told Arnold that losing his British citizenship was the deepest wound he had suffered. On June 24, 1959, traveling as "Mr. Strauss," Klaus Fuchs was driven to Heathrow Airport and placed aboard a Polish Convair airplane, which flew him to East Berlin. There a Russian Ziv limousine with drawn curtains whisked him away to join his father. "In a way I'm sorry to be leaving Britain," observed Fuchs. "I bear no resentment whatsoever against Britain." The forty-eight-year-old scientist, dressed in a cheap brown suit, appeared pale, yet genial in mood. Asked what he had done all those years in prison, he replied: "I read a lot."[29]

CHAPTER · 11

A Serious Mistake

England is a family with the wrong members in control.

— George Orwell

Attlee's government was predictably defensive about an embarrassing security lapse that could, if made public, reveal even more embarrassing political secrets. The Labour Party in 1950 faced a growing barrage of criticism from the Tories, who charged that Britain's postwar experiment in socialism was financially bankrupt, pro-Soviet, administratively incompetent, and politically authoritarian. The Attlee government did manage to eke out a narrow margin of victory, but nobody expected the new government to last very long.[1]

- *Anglo-American Cooperation*

An important concern was that the British-Canadian-American talks on exchange of nuclear information were to begin in Washington on February 9. The Fuchs case clearly placed the exchange in jeopardy. In Washington, British ambassador F. Hoyer Millar warned that "Congressional resistance to 'sharing secrets' with us will be increased." The independent British atomic bomb program, begun five years earlier, was still a state secret; the case also threatened to reveal the British drive for nuclear independence and Fuchs's role in it.[2]

As Fuchs awaited trial, the fourth Anglo-American declassification conference, meeting at Harwell, liberalized the restrictions regarding low-power reactors used in research and design. But the AEC commissioners, led by Strauss, angrily demanded "full information on the disclosures made by Dr. Fuchs" and a "full and current report on the technical information believed to have been disclosed to the Russian government," including information on the hydrogen bomb. The AEC representative to the Harwell conference returned to say that "detailed information concerning the data transmitted to the Russians by Dr. Fuchs had not been released or furnished to the United States, in order that the Crown's case against Dr. Fuchs might not be prejudiced by discussion in advance of the trial." By the end of February the talks on nuclear cooperation "returned to square one, where there was a deep freezer from which they did not emerge in my time," as Dean Acheson said. Although the talks were suspended indefinitely, the *modus vivendi* continued in effect.[3]

By March AEC commissioners Dean and Strauss felt that the time was right to press the British to supply more uranium for thermonuclear weapons development, to revise the *modus vivendi*, and to amend the Atomic Energy Act. But when Strauss learned that John Strachey, minister of war in the Attlee government, had a long history of flirtation with the communist party and had complete access to all nuclear information, he suggested suspending Anglo-American technical cooperation. The other commissioners did not agree and voted Strauss's suggestion down.[4]

By April the policy of information sharing was being reviewed both by the CPC and by the senior responsible reviewers of the AEC; all were trying to learn what Fuchs had told the Russians. When Acheson visited London in May, he reported that Attlee felt the British government was now in a "difficult position" because of the "Fuchs affair." But he hoped that nuclear cooperation would be revived. At the tripartite talks on security standards held in Washington in June, the British admitted that the Fuchs case had been a "serious mistake." It had obviously torpedoed any chances for a joint nuclear weapons program along the lines of the Manhattan Project. The net result of the complex negotiations was that Great Britain produced slightly less plutonium than she might have, and the United States continued to receive essential uranium and thorium supplies under the trust agreement.[5]

When Winston Churchill returned to power in October 1951, he attempted, unsuccessfully, to revive the Quebec Agreement. Neither the AEC nor the Defense Department was willing to cooperate, and they were not surprised in October 1952 when the British tested their first nuclear weapon in the Montebello Islands off Australia. The British independent deterrent became a reality three years after Joe 1, in part because of Fuchs's work at Harwell. In 1954 Churchill persuaded the British cabinet that work should begin on the hydrogen bomb.

The devastating effect of the Fuchs case on Anglo-American nuclear cooperation clearly served the Soviet Union well. After Joe 1, Fuchs could have told the Russians very little that they did not already know about a plutonium bomb. He was expendable. For the British, too, Fuchs was less valuable than he had been in 1946. His major contributions at Harwell had been theoretical, and now the Los Alamos work had been assimilated. Ahead lay the practical work of designing, engineering, and testing a bomb.

■ *The British Reaction*

In the postwar years many British scientists felt that the Official Secrets Act was unnecessarily restrictive and that it inhibited research. They also objected to the Atomic Energy Bill of 1946. "As soon as the Bill becomes law, roughly everything we do in nuclear physics will become illegal [classified]," complained Peierls. The act's "sweeping restrictions" on information disclosure were "ridiculously out of proportion" and should be "rectified," regardless of whether that meant "running even a small risk."[6]

The Fuchs case shocked the British scientific establishment. Sir John Cockcroft, Fuchs's superior at Harwell, was astounded to learn of Fuchs's suspected espionage in September 1949. He called the case "a great shock to us all." Otto Frisch, a colleague at Los Alamos, was "dumbfounded" when he learned of it in January 1950 from Perrin and Eric Welsh. Frisch believed that Fuchs had acted out of "sincere motives" based on his conscientious belief in Christianity and communism. Max Born said he now understood what Fuchs meant when he said he could not leave Harwell for a university position because he had a "greater service to perform." British scientist Philip Dee noted an "unfortunate blindness" among those who knew of Fuchs's "extreme communist views" for years but did nothing. Any idea that Fuchs was innocent vanished after an American colleague, Edward Corson, wired Fuchs in jail that he did not believe the accusations of espionage. He received a return telegram from Fuchs that read: "Thank you. The evidence will change your mind. Fuchs."[7]

Peierls, shaken by Fuchs's arrogance and naiveté, could not imagine that his colleague was a spy. At first he thought Fuchs was lying or suffering from a nervous breakdown, but two visits to Fuchs in prison convinced him that "the story he told was substantially correct." Fuchs's various absences from home and office because of illness made sense in retrospect.[8]

Peierls wrote to Bethe and Nevill Mott that the Fuchs case was a "complete shock to me" and that "I had not known there was anything wrong until the day of his arrest." The case was a "dreadful blow" to Harwell, where Fuchs had built up a team of good young physicists who admired his leadership. For Peierls, Fuchs remained an "unselfish man with a passionate devotion to his work."[9]

In public, Peierls stated that the Fuchs case showed that "present methods of security checks are not adequate to prevent leakage." But he warned against additional "secrecy in science" and an "iron curtain" of new security regulations. To that, nuclear scientist George Thomson replied: "What is the connection between secrecy and the Fuchs case? Nobody ever suggested that work on the atomic bomb was anything but secret."[10]

Lord Cherwell was especially upset about Fuchs, from whom he had received valuable scientific intelligence during the war. The Americans had "unfairly blamed" Britain for Fuchs's perfidy, he felt. Yet British security was certainly to blame for keeping him on. "The mere fact that our people thought he seemed all right when we took him on is no excuse for their failing to watch him and prevent his activities several years later."[11]

Two days after the trial George Strauss, Minister of Supply, briefed Attlee on questions that might be asked in the House of Commons. Windscale would produce plutonium by late 1951, he reported, and Aldermaston was working hard on "military aspects of atomic energy." As to Fuchs: "The employment of this particular man was arranged at a time when his valuable contributions to the wartime project were urgently needed, and that until the autumn of last year [1949], there was no reason to suspect that he was anything but a loyal member of the organization."[12] On March 6 Attlee told the House of Commons that "a proper watch was kept at intervals" on Klaus Fuchs. Only in the autumn of 1949 did the British learn from the Americans that there had been a wartime leak at Los Alamos. Once MI5 had identified Fuchs as the source of the leak, security acted "promptly and effectively" in arresting him. The Fuchs case was a "deplorable and unfortunate incident," but British security had done its job; "all the proper inquiries were made and there was nothing to be brought against him."[13]

"The storm over the Fuchs case is dissipating over here slowly," wrote James Tuck, a Los Alamos veteran of the British mission, to Cherwell. "A witch hunt is in full cry." Tuck wondered if it was a case of the Russians "sacrificing a backsliding agent for the benefit of worsening Anglo-U.S. relations," allowing Fuchs to be caught so nuclear cooperation would suffer. For Esther Simpson of the Society for the Preservation of Science and Learning, it was a matter "not of the defection of a German refugee, but of a dedicated communist, whose nationality is irrelevant." By April 1950 the excitement had "settled down surprisingly rapidly," wrote Peierls. On April 22 he withdrew his nomination of Fuchs for the Royal Society "in view of what has happened."[14]

In general, British scientists saw no need for greater secrecy or security. Citing Bohr's critique of nuclear secrecy, Peierls called for continued "openness in the field of international relations, particularly in scientific matters." The Fuchs case, argued Peierls, "gave proof again, if proof was needed, that in democratic countries it is impossible to keep large projects secret for long." The Fuchs case should not lead to the illusion of greater security through greater secrecy. The British government's predictable response was to tighten security so that no other such incident could occur, although scientists argued that a civil service "purge" of suspected communists would be of no avail and would create a "dangerous precedent." Security measures should be limited to those institutions concerned with important military secrets.[15]

In fact, most Britons knew so little about the Fuchs case that there was little to debate. D-notices forbidding press coverage of secret matters were still common, and nuclear weapons were not a topic for public discussion. As the *New York Times* observed, British justice required a fair trial, and comment by the press was restricted while the trial was pending.[16]

▪ Roger Hollis and the Penetration of MI5

Why was British security so tolerant of Klaus Fuchs for so long? Why did it not pursue his accomplices as vigorously as the FBI did in 1950? Why is his case still closed to public scrutiny in England? Such questions have yielded only answers supplied by the British government or the silence of official secrecy. For in 1950 it was not yet evident that some of the very individuals responsible for discovering men like Fuchs were themselves more loyal to the Soviet Union than to England.

Until the 1960s one could assume that MI5 was merely lax, tolerant, or disorganized in its approach to German communists who were necessary Allied resources. In 1950 MI5 argued that the only evidence against Fuchs was the 1934 Gestapo report on his Marxist leanings and that this was hardly enough to prevent Tube Alloys from using his expertise for war work. Since Philby's defection to Moscow in 1963, however, evidence has mounted that British security was penetrated at a high level by Soviet agents and that the failure to uncover Fuchs was deliberate. The most provocative argument has been that Sir Roger Hollis, head of Section F of MI5 from 1940 to 1945 and later director general of MI5, was a Soviet mole.[17]

It was Hollis who declared the Fuchs case resolved in Washington in June 1950. In meetings with American military, atomic, and intelligence officials, Hollis argued that the Gestapo report on Fuchs was "tainted" evidence; that Fuchs's release from internment in 1940 was a "mistake" resulting from the "confusion" of the time; that Fuchs was admitted to Tube Alloys in 1941 because there was "no positive adverse information on his activities in the United Kingdom"; that the unusual step of granting an enemy alien British citizenship in 1942 was taken because there was "no adverse information"; that in 1946 Fuchs was "very specially considered" by MI5 in a security check and that "nothing derogatory" was found. Hollis admitted that "a serious mistake had undoubtedly been made" in letting Fuchs work on the atomic bomb.[18]

In 1950 Hollis seemed convincing, contrite, and persuasive. But Robert Lamphere, the FBI agent who interviewed Fuchs in London, now sees Hollis's argument as self-serving and unconvincing. "If MI5 knew in 1934 of allegations that Fuchs was a communist, why did they not at least in 1941 really check it out with a thorough investigation? And why did they tell General Groves that they had carried out a full investigation?" Suspicions persist in the British press that the man responsible for monitoring the KPD in England was a Soviet agent. Lamphere now believes that Hollis "provided the earliest information to the KGB that the FBI was reading their 1944–45 cables" after 1949.[19]

The son of an Anglican bishop, Hollis was educated at Clifton College at the University of Bristol and then Worcester College at Oxford. He dropped out in 1926 at the age of twenty-one and went to China, where he worked for the British American Tobacco Company. After several years he contracted tuberculosis; he went to Switzerland for a cure, then returned to England in 1936. He then joined MI5, at a time when clublike conviviality and the old boy network dominated British intelligence. By 1940 Hollis had risen to the position of acting head of Section F, responsible for overseeing all Soviet and communist party operations, including the CPGB, the Comintern, and other pro-Soviet activities, in the United Kingdom and the commonwealth. In 1940 Hollis assisted the Home Office in categorizing German enemy aliens according to their political sympathies, for possible internment. Throughout the war he was responsible for monitoring the activities of the KPD in England.[20]

When Fuchs was hired to work for Tube Alloys in 1941, there were already suspicions that he might be a security risk. In May

Hollis reviewed Fuchs's file with Perrin and was reluctant to clear him, but Peierls was insistent. As a result, Fuchs was cleared without restrictions, although Home Office suspicions were aroused.[21]

The slippage continued. When Fuchs became a British citizen in 1942 because Tube Alloys needed his services, Nevill Mott vouched for him and signed his certificate. Fuchs and four other German refugee scientists had to be cleared by the Home Office because they were enemy aliens. A July 1943 police report from Birmingham revealed no adverse information on Fuchs. In early 1944, as Fuchs prepared to go to Los Alamos, Perrin asked MI5 for the latest and most detailed views on him so that "we do not slip up in any way." The report was again favorable, based on Fuchs's good behavior, political inactivity, and scientific value. Thus he was vetted several times by security, with due warning but without action, and there was no "positive vetting" of his background.[22]

Fuchs continued to avoid attention in 1946, even though his name was one of five on the list sent to MI5 from Halperin's notebook and even though the FBI opened a file on his sister. It was Hollis who was sent to Ottawa to handle the Gouzenko case. (Gouzenko later testified that there was a Soviet agent inside MI5 who had "something Russian in his background"; Chapman Pincher suggests that this was Hollis, who had traveled to Russia in 1934 and whose family members believed they might be descended from Peter the Great.) If Hollis were the agent, he would be unlikely to turn Fuchs in.[23]

On the eve of Fuchs's return to England in 1946, Prime Minister Attlee appointed a new director general of MI5, Percy Sillitoe, a likable chief constable who disliked and distrusted Hollis. Attlee had given Sillitoe the task of ferreting out communist subversion in England, and Sillitoe promptly asked Hollis for a report. The result was a mere listing of foreign communist parties with a brief description of each. Sillitoe was disappointed. Hollis was made director of Section C (Security) and sent to Australia to monitor Soviet cipher traffic and assist security officials there. But from 1955 to 1965 he was director general of MI5. In the wake of the spy cases involving Philby and call girl Christine Keeler in 1964,

Hollis himself was investigated as a possible Soviet mole. The case against him was not proven, but journalists and historians continued to speculate. Chapman Pincher, in particular, claimed that Hollis was responsible for the successive clearances of Klaus Fuchs and for the lax surveillance of the KPD in England; he attributed the many failures of British security to deliberate Soviet penetration rather than to incompetence, inefficiency, or calculated risk.[24]

Some people have argued that after 1946 the British allowed Fuchs to pass information to the Soviets in order to assess Russian progress on the atomic bomb. Certainly MI5 and MI6 knew a great deal about Fuchs, as they did about Jurgen Kuczynski, even in the early 1930s. (MI6's file on Fuchs had begun in 1932 with a report on his communist party membership by an MI6 agent in Germany, a lock operator on the Kiel Canal. When Fuchs entered England, the file shifted from MI6 to MI5.)[25]

For whatever reasons, British security failed to move against Fuchs until after the Soviet bomb test, and then only when prodded by the Americans. They continued to clear him, though with some reluctance. More than this, they chose to characterize Fuchs as a lone wolf, failing to tell the FBI, even after the Fuchs investigation began, about his communist background. In the wake of the Maclean-Burgess-Philby-Blunt-Hollis revelations and speculations, it is no longer possible to consider him a loner. Fuchs was part of a network, which included Jurgen Kuczynski and Sonia, that British security allowed to operate in England during and after World War II.

- ### The Canadian Connection

On February 3, 1950, FBI agent Lish Whitson wrote a memorandum recommending that the bureau inquire into Fuchs's activities in Canada, to which J. Edgar Hoover added a handwritten note: "Yes, and by wire." The Canadian government was also interested in press reports that Fuchs had been released from a Canadian internment camp in 1940. "Let us know if you are being pushed for details about his release," Ottawa cabled the Canadian ambassador in Washington. "It is the hope here that you will not be."[26]

But speculation about Fuchs's internment was widespread. A man who had been interned at the same time told a New York newspaper that he was not surprised that Fuchs had been arrested as a Soviet spy. "He was known to all of us as a strong Communist. But I was completely amazed to learn that he ever attained such an important position with the British government." The Canadian ambassador in Washington was told that Fuchs might well have been among those German aliens rounded up by the British government in 1940 and sent to Canada; he was instructed to say only that Fuchs had been interned in Canada and that he had been returned to the United Kingdom in December 1940 at the request of the British government; the Canadian government did not clear, vet, or release him. British security was solely responsible for interning and releasing Fuchs. In 1950 the subject of internment generally, and in particular Fuchs's internment and release, was an unwelcome reminder of a sad chapter in wartime British policy.[27]

Even more embarrassing, potentially, was Fuchs's connection with the Gouzenko affair of 1946. Shortly after Fuchs's arrest the Canadian consul general in New York wired Ottawa, asking what he should tell the American press about that connection. The Canadian Department of External Affairs replied that the Royal Commission on Espionage had "found no evidence whatsoever that would involve the name of Dr. Karl [sic] Fuchs, nor has he ever been associated with the Canadian atomic energy project." These assertions were false.[28]

On February 12 columnist Drew Pearson telephoned the FBI and said he had learned that in 1946 Fuchs's name had appeared on a list given to both MI5 and the FBI. Not surprisingly, the FBI had no comment. When the House of Commons in March asked Attlee whether or not the British government had "received any warning regarding Dr. Fuchs from His Majesty's Government in Canada when the Canadian Royal Commission was sitting in 1946," Attlee's answer was a decisive "No." And Lord Chancellor Viscount Jowett echoed his denial. Both were wrong. Whether or not Attlee and Jowett knew it, Fuchs's name had emerged in connection with the Gouzenko affair, because he was listed in Israel Halperin's address book. On February 28, when Canadian police interviewed Halperin, he maintained that his connection with Fuchs was scientific, that he had sent Fuchs some technical journals during his internment.[29]

Press speculation on the Halperin address book began shortly after Fuchs's trial. The most sensational rumor was that next to Fuchs's name in Halperin's notebook appeared the handwritten annotation in Russian, *nash,* meaning "ours." Hoover queried Glen Bethel, FBI liaison officer in Ottawa, and Lish Whitson in London about the rumor: what was the source of it? A frantic search at the FBI revealed that the word *nash* did appear in some of Gouzenko's documents next to the names of agents working for Soviet military intelligence. But Fuchs's name did not appear in any of these documents, only in Halperin's address book.[30]

Bethel and Whitson could add nothing more on the *nash* story, which had first appeared in *The Ensign,* a leading Canadian Catholic weekly journal of opinion. The story implied that Canada had suspected Fuchs of espionage in 1946 and had so informed the United States. Bethel assured Hoover that this was "entirely incorrect" and surmised that Gouzenko might have started the rumor to implicate the Soviet Union.[31]

On April 5, 1950, Jowett retracted his denial in the House of Lords, admitting that MI5 had in fact received a list of names from the Canadian government in 1946. This was confirmed in great detail by Lester Pearson, who stated that Canada had turned over all the Royal Commission evidence to both the United States and Great Britain, including Halperin's address book, which "contained a great many names, among which was Dr. Fuchs." Fuchs's name was one of only five of people living in Britain. Why had MI5 not noticed? Or had it? On May 11, 1950, Clement Attlee was asked in the House of Commons if "the spy operations of the four names, other than Dr. Fuchs, sent by the Canadian authorities, have ceased," and why Fuchs had not been apprehended in 1946. Attlee begged the question, saying he had nothing to add to Jowett's April 5 reply to the House of Lords.[32]

Hollis and Perrin did review Fuchs's file again in 1946 in connection with his work at Harwell. But even if this file included Halperin's reference to Fuchs, there was no real evidence against him. The reluctance of British security to pursue Fuchs in 1946 became significant only with hindsight. In 1950 no one would have believed a suggestion that British counterespionage was being run by Soviet military intelligence. Only Philby's defection in 1963 confirmed that this was one of the great political secrets that the Fuchs case threatened to reveal.

- ### Kim Philby

During the war MI6, which was responsible for liaison with Claude Dansey's secret Z organization, the Lucy Ring, and the cryptographers at Bletchley Park, employed communists, fellow travelers, and Soviet agents. One of the people responsible for liaison of MI6 with Bletchley Park and with the Red Orchestra network was Kim Philby, who throughout the war played the double role of Soviet intelligence officer and British counterintelligence expert. Until 1945 the two parts of this role were quite consistent. After 1945 this rising star of MI6 became a dangerous traitor within the British security establishment.

It is well known now that Philby was one of the "Cambridge Comintern," young men who were recruited at Cambridge University in the 1930s to serve as Soviet agents within British intelligence and the Foreign Office. In London in 1933 Philby established contact with S. D. Kremer, who later also served as Fuchs's control. Philby, an unemployed journalist, at first made no secret of his communist sympathies. He was probably recruited for espionage by his wife, Litzi Friedman, or by Anthony Blunt around 1935.[33]

When the war broke out, Philby obtained a position with MI6 on the recommendation of his friend and fellow Soviet agent, Guy Burgess. In September 1941 he joined Section V of MI6; its main job was counterespionage against enemy agents, presumably Nazis in England. Philby was a superefficient counterintelligence officer whose left wing sympathies were well known and unremarkable.[34]

In late 1941 Philby learned about the Red Orchestra and the Lucy Ring. Soviet friends at the London embassy, perhaps Kremer, suggested that he contact Alexander Rado in Switzerland; Philby suggested to his MI6 superiors that Rado could supply information to the British military attaché in Bern, H. A. Cartwright, who was an MI6 station officer. Philby, who also knew Christian Schneider, the ILO man working with Rado, played a key role in maintaining the links between MI6 and the Swiss network of Soviet agents. He certainly knew about both Ultra decryption at Bletchley Park and about the Swiss network. With access to Ultra intercepts, his Section V soon became an "unwitting extension of the KGB" in England. Security clearances were provided quickly, with the notation "N.R.A."—Nothing Recorded Against.[35]

In the spring of 1944, Philby moved to MI6 headquarters, where he was in charge of a new counterintelligence section to be directed against Soviet Russia. In this capacity Philby in November 1944 arranged the safe conduct for Rado and Foote from Switzerland to Paris, then to Moscow. By 1945 Soviet intelligence had achieved an astounding victory: a Soviet agent was running British counterespionage against the Soviet Union.[36]

In 1949 Philby became directly involved in the Fuchs case. He claimed in his memoirs that he "had no ideas about Los Alamos," but he certainly knew about Donald Maclean's Soviet espionage at the British embassy in Washington and in the Atomic Energy Commission. In September 1949 Philby, together with Peter Dwyer, MI6's man in Washington, were heavily involved in analyzing information and data on the Soviet bomb test. The physicist W. B. Mann conveyed the Americans' analysis of fallout to Attlee via Philby's MI6 communications channel. On October 10, 1949, Philby was appointed first secretary at the British embassy in Washington, replacing Dwyer, who had helped the FBI identify Fuchs, as the MI6 officer. Philby's main task was to serve as liaison between the fledgling CIA and the presumably more experienced MI6. Frequently briefed by CIA director Walter Bedell Smith, Philby continued to have access to the highest classification of Anglo-American intelligence secrets.[37]

Philby knew that any revelations by Fuchs about the Kuczynskis and Kremer could quickly lead to him. After the Fuchs case broke, Philby adamantly told Hoover that the FBI could not interview Fuchs in England, undoubtedly helping to delay that interview until May. Philby was concerned that the Fuchs case might reveal the major political secret of Anglo-Soviet intelligence cooperation during World War II and the persistence of Soviet agents afterward. He could not save Fuchs without risking the far greater secret of Soviet penetration of British intelligence. "I enjoyed an enormous advantage over people like Fuchs," wrote Philby later, "who had little or no knowledge of intelligence work."[38]

In 1951 Philby was recalled from Washington under suspicion. He was interviewed by William Skardon, but no evidence was found against him. On May 25, tipped off by Philby, Maclean and Burgess defected. Although Philby did resign from MI6, he was in effect cleared again in 1955 by Prime Minister Harold Macmillan and readmitted. But in 1963 he fled to Moscow.

Whether Sonia and Philby ever met is not known, but both were part of the Soviet penetration of British intelligence. We now know that the GRU and the NKVD placed literally hundreds of agents in England during and after the war. "Had MI5 kept itself sufficiently aware of their activities too," wrote the British communist Douglas Hyde, "it is probable that the Fuchs case would never have occurred."[39]

We are now better able to answer the question of MI5's apparent inability to discover Klaus Fuchs before 1949. Obviously, Hollis and Perrin knew a good deal about him from the time they first reviewed his Home Office file in 1941. He was a needed communist scientist. They took a calculated risk in clearing him and they knew it. We do not need to assume that Hollis was a Soviet mole or that he was inept. Both Fuchs and Sonia were unwittingly on the fringe of MI6 foreign intelligence operations during World War II, Fuchs working for Perrin and Cherwell on assessing the German atomic bomb project, Sonia as a wireless operator for the Lucy Ring. By 1947 MI5 had interviewed Sonia, but under British law there was no case against her that it could actively pursue; her espionage had been against Nazi Germany in inadvertent cooperation with MI6, which may have known about Fuchs through a turned Soviet agent. We have seen that MI5 discussed turning Fuchs in 1949 and sending disinformation to the Russians, but rejected the idea.[40]

The Fuchs case threatened to become an MI6 case as well as

an MI5 one. Jurgen Kuczynski and Sonia were a problem both for British internal security, which had apparently failed to act against them, and for counterintelligence, whose anticommunist activities were increasingly under Philby's control. This may have included running the unwitting Fuchs after 1947.

CHAPTER · 12

Science, Secrecy, and Security

If it weren't for our work in Canada and the United States, the Soviet Union would still not have the atom bomb.

— *Lieutenant General Peter Fedotov (1952)*

The Fuchs case created a great furor in America. The Soviet atomic bomb, the fall of China to the communists, and the widening hunt for internal subversion all provided a context in which atomic secrets seemed essential to American security. Fuchs's espionage was revealed at precisely the time that American officials were secretly debating the merits of the awesome technology of the hydrogen bomb.

■ *The Super*

It has long been assumed that because Truman's public announcement of the hydrogen bomb preceded news of Fuchs's confession, the case played no real role in Truman's decision. But this was not the case. Truman's announcement on January 31, 1950, which marked a clear political choice for a strategic arms race with the Soviet Union, was primarily influenced by the first Soviet atomic bomb test. But Truman was making a limited commitment to conduct a feasibility study. On March 10 he made public his decision to commit resources to develop the new weapon. Between those two dates the Fuchs case had a major impact, convincing many concerned observers that the Soviet Union might well be ahead of the United States in thermonuclear weapons research.[1]

On February 2 reverberations from the Fuchs case began to be felt in Washington. "The roof fell in today," wrote David Lilienthal in his diary when he learned of Fuchs's confession. This was truly a "world catastrophe," he added, and a "sad day for the human race."[2]

Hoover and the FBI applauded the British announcement of Fuchs's confessions. Hoover wired Cimperman in London, asking him to convey to Sir Percy Sillitoe "congratulations on a job well done." The Central Intelligence Agency, the Office of Naval Intelligence, the armed services, Congress, and the president were duly informed of the FBI's coup in tipping off the British. Attorney General Peyton Ford wished to prosecute Fuchs in the United States, but neither he nor the White House seemed to know whether Fuchs was a British or an American citizen. If Fuchs was not a British citizen, Ford wanted to "bring the s.o.b. back to the United States and prosecute him."[3]

At the White House Stephen Early, the president's press secretary, was miffed that the CIA had known about the Fuchs case for two days before Truman was informed. Not so, said the FBI; the CIA had been informed at the same time as the Navy and the Air Force. At that time American intelligence gathering was divided among the FBI, the fledgling CIA, and the armed services; Hoover must have taken great pleasure in leading the charge. "I am God damned glad to see Edgar is in it," crowed Early. "I have been fighting a battle for a long time that he is the only one competent to handle this kind of matter and this will strengthen my argument."[4]

Hoover summarized the Fuchs case for President Truman on February 6 in a long memorandum to Sidney Souers, reviewing the particulars of Fuchs's life. The intelligence aspects of the Fuchs case were especially important because of the Soviet bomb test. There was even talk of "exploiting Fuchs in order to determine what type of information he was able to furnish to the Russians, which would indicate the interest they have in the bomb and also the scientific aspects of the information passed on by Fuchs."[5]

On February 4, 1950, the *New York Times* headline was "BRITISH JAIL ATOM SCIENTIST AS A SPY AFTER TIP BY FBI HE KNEW OF HYDROGEN BOMB." The story, more cautious, noted that Fuchs had acquired "certain basic information dealing with hydrogen bomb development and thus was in a position to pass it on to the Russians." Again Hoover was quoted. Similar stories appeared in the *Washington Times-Herald* ("BRITON ADMITS GIVING REDS H-BOMB DATA") and the *Boston Post* ("SPY GAVE REDS H-BOMB DATA"). "Why don't we just deliver the hydrogen bomb secrets by uniformed messenger?" asked columnist Victor Riesel. Never one to miss an opportunity to strengthen the FBI, Hoover asked Congress for money to hire three hundred new special agents. For a few days there was talk in the newspapers of extraditing Fuchs, under a 1931 treaty with Great Britain, to stand trial in the United States. But the treaty exempted persons "still under trial" in either country, so the idea was not pursued.[6]

The fear that Fuchs had given the Russians the lead in developing an awesome new thermonuclear weapon spread quickly. Democratic Senator Millard Tydings, chairman of the Senate Armed Services Committee, proclaimed that Fuchs's information would "cut a great deal of time off" the Soviet hydrogen bomb program, perhaps a year or more. The fear was fed by dramatic rumors that the Soviet Union already had three hydrogen bombs and had tested one; that batteries of antiaircraft guns were being installed around Oak Ridge, Hanford, and Los Alamos to protect our atomic towns; that Fuchs had co-conspirators in America; and that he had given Russia a "secret hormone ray" capable of "feminizing" opposing soldiers. Even such a sober and well-informed observer as *New York Times* science editor William Laurence speculated that Klaus Fuchs had single-handedly advanced Soviet nuclear weapons development by three to ten years. By March the Fuchs case and the hydrogen bomb decision had become firmly linked in the public mind. The Soviet Union, wrote the *Brooklyn Eagle*, "may have gained a head start over the United States on hydrogen bomb research through information furnished by Klaus Fuchs."[7]

The AEC agreed. The commissioners were "agitated," according to Lilienthal. Fuchs was clearly the real thing, "no periphery guy, or a courier, or a dumb spy, but a scientist who knew most of the weapons stuff." Lilienthal hoped that the Fuchs case would not "disturb the Los Alamos outfit" or hold up the new super program, which he had opposed earlier. The AEC's problem was to determine as quickly as possible what technical information on the hydrogen bomb Fuchs might have obtained at Los Alamos. Meeting in executive session, the commissioners decided that it would be "undesirable to mention in the Commission press release Dr. Fuchs' association with early work on the 'Super' bomb."[8]

The AEC told the FBI that the Fuchs case was a "matter of great concern" and asked to be kept fully informed. Its Division of Security began collecting all wartime memoranda on the British mission at Los Alamos and any technical memoranda written by, or accessible to, Fuchs. At a meeting on February 14 Strauss called for all information that Fuchs might have passed to the Russians. The commissioners also requested a staff report on all information on the hydrogen bomb that might have been available to Fuchs before he left Los Alamos in 1946. AEC acting chairman Sumner Pike also asked the State Department for any technical information Fuchs had transmitted.[9]

Strauss was both elated and concerned. He told Hoover that the Fuchs case would "very much reinforce the hands of the president on the strength of the [hydrogen bomb] decision he made a few days ago." But at the same time he suspected that Fuchs knew as much about the hydrogen bomb as any American scientist and that therefore the Russians might well be ahead in the hydrogen bomb race. During the evening of February 16, Strauss removed from AEC files four documents on the hydrogen bomb to which Fuchs had had access and showed them to Gordon Dean and Carroll Wilson. He apparently made them available as well to Truman and Louis Johnson, for on February 21 the National Security Council telephoned the AEC and requested the "documents discovered by Admiral Strauss." Pike agreed that it might be useful to reconvene the NSC subcommittee on the hydrogen bomb to discuss the implications of the Fuchs case.[10]

The FBI thought the AEC was interfering in its case. Not so, Pike wrote Hoover on February 28. The AEC wanted to have the technical data compromised by Fuchs because it "may have an important bearing" on decisions related to the hydrogen bomb. But Hoover was adamant, and the AEC had to limit itself to rummaging through its own records for material on Fuchs, including the report on the 1946 Los Alamos conference on the super. According to the report, the numerous meetings Fuchs had attended at the conference covered design of a thermonuclear weapon, ENIAC computer calculations, necessary experiments, neutron cross-sections, tritium-deuterium reactions, and other matters. Norris Bradbury, the Los Alamos laboratory director, wrote Wilson that Fuchs had probably known the full story of the hydrogen bomb as of the time he had left Los Alamos. He concluded that "the relative position of this country with respect to Russia in an atomic armament race may be considered to be worse as a result of our knowledge of the Fuchs situation."[11]

In March copies of Fuchs's confession to Skardon and a summary of the confession to Perrin began to circulate among a few top officials in Washington, first at the FBI and then within the AEC. Hoover sent the Perrin memorandum on to the White House, including Perrin's statement that Fuchs had described "current ideas in Los Alamos when he left on the design and method of operation of a super bomb, mentioning, in particular, the combination fission bomb, the tritium initiating reaction, and the final deuterium one."[12]

Strauss also sought to use the Fuchs confessions to bring outspoken or recalcitrant scientists into line. He was particularly concerned about Hans Bethe, the leading scientific critic of the hydrogen bomb. Bethe and other top scientists had issued a statement calling the super "no longer a weapon of war but a means of extermination of whole populations." Bethe admitted that Fuchs was a first-class scientist whose information had probably given the Soviet Union a year's advantage in building an atomic bomb, so that there were "no longer secrets" concerning the hydrogen bomb. Strauss suggested bringing Bethe to Washington to show him the paragraphs on the hydrogen bomb from the Perrin memorandum. For Strauss the conclusion was evident: "In 1947 Fuchs had given the Russians the information on the hydrogen bomb." Strauss also felt that the news of Fuchs's confession would have a "salutary effect" on scientists engaged in classified research and would serve as a warning to the potentially disloyal or indiscreet.[13]

Robert Oppenheimer disagreed. On February 27 he told the State-Defense Policy Review Group that secrecy in government was becoming excessive, and he reiterated that the hydrogen bomb should not be built. In addition, he speculated that the Soviet Union could not have proceeded very far in developing thermonuclear weapons and that what Fuchs had learned at Los Alamos would not have helped them significantly. But Oppenheimer and Bethe were definitely in the minority as voices of reason and restraint. Most high civilian and military leaders continued to believe that Fuchs had given away the secret of the hydrogen bomb.[14]

In mid-March the AEC sent the Perrin memorandum to Los Alamos for review by a committee. W. F. Libby urged that an "expurgated version should be circulated within the project" in order to tighten up security; "reading these documents," he noted sadly, "has been one of the most shocking experiences of my life." Both the committee and the AEC director of classification, J. G. Beckerley, recommended declassification of the Perrin memorandum "with appropriate deletions." But that did not happen.[15]

Many members of the Joint Committee on Atomic Energy also wanted to make the Perrin memorandum public. Brien McMahon wrote to Sumner Pike that the Soviet Union probably possessed whatever technical information was in the document anyway. In a democracy, he cautioned, the public was entitled to this information. Publication would improve security far more than continued secrecy and classification. But the AEC refused, saying it needed to study the documents in more detail, seek the advice of other agencies, and receive permission from the British, whose documents they were. Despite McMahon's pleadings, the AEC continued to withhold the Fuchs confessions from Congress. Publication, the AEC argued, would be "unwise." Not even a summary statement should be issued. To this day the American government has refused to release the confessions, because they are still classified by the British government.[16]

Some officials at the Pentagon also thought that the Soviet

Union might already have a thermonuclear weapon in production. Brigadier General Herbert B. Loper wrote a memorandum to that effect on February 16, and Robert LeBaron, chairman of the Pentagon's Military Liaison Committee to the AEC, reported to Louis Johnson that Loper's memorandum "shows what the Soviet capabilities for atomic weapons might be if we make certain assumptions that now seem possible in the light of the Fuchs espionage case." An earlier CIA estimate of Soviet nuclear weapons capability, added LeBaron, was much too low and optimistic.[17]

On February 24 Secretary of Defense Johnson wrote President Truman that "certain developments, which you and I have discussed," namely the Fuchs case, "make it apparent that the Soviets may already have made important progress in this field of atomic weapons" [thermonuclear]. On this basis the Joint Chiefs of Staff "most urgently" recommended that Truman direct appropriate agencies to proceed with the "immediate implementation of all-out development of hydrogen bombs."[18]

The NSC subcommittee on the super, meeting on March 9, recommended that the hydrogen bomb be developed as "a matter of the highest urgency." Specifically, this meant that the president would direct the AEC to begin construction of reactors to produce tritium and to plan a program of bomb tests. On March 10 Truman endorsed the recommendation. What role did Fuchs's confessions play in the final decision? We know that at the meeting on March 9, Secretary of State Acheson mentioned that Strauss had telephoned him in February about the hydrogen bomb documents Fuchs had had access to, which Strauss had removed from the AEC building. Strauss accused Hoover of withholding the Perrin memorandum from the AEC for some time and demanded the "full confession" of Fuchs. Sumner Pike discussed the memorandum with the JCAE on March 10, the day of Truman's second announcement on the hydrogen bomb. It was also circulated to the AEC commissioners for their information, but kept within a restricted circle of AEC specialists.[19]

During the spring research continued on the super. The mathematicians Stanislas Ulam and John von Neumann, meeting at Princeton in April, concluded that "the model considered is a fizzle." Teller and Fermi were unable to do any better. There was no workable model of a hydrogen bomb. On May 18 Ulam wrote von Neumann that "the thing gives me the impression of being miles away from going." Whatever secrets Fuchs had given away, there was no workable hydrogen bomb in either America or the Soviet Union in 1950.[20]

In May, as the FBI was preparing to interview Fuchs in London, Pike wrote the AEC commissioners that the Fuchs case was a "lamentable milestone in atomic energy weapons matters." The Los Alamos committee had completed its review of possible damage, and the AEC suggested to the FBI topics for their interrogation of Fuchs, in hopes of learning precisely what he had told the Russians.[21]

On June 16 Hoover wrote the White House that when questioned by the FBI, Fuchs stated that he had furnished no information on the hydrogen bomb to his Soviet contact in America because he "did not have a clear understanding of the research being done in this regard" and was generally "confused" about the super. Fuchs refused to tell the FBI what information he had provided the Russians after his return to England because at that time Britain and America were not cooperating on atomic energy research. In July an Oak Ridge laboratory report on gaseous diffusion reviewed Fuchs's confession and concluded that he probably did not tell the Russians the exact or even the approximate concentrations of uranium-235 produced at Oak Ridge "as it exists today." Fuchs's information was "of an early vintage" and theoretical. Many of the secrets of making a hydrogen bomb were embedded in complex industrial and engineering processes that had not yet been developed.[22]

The real secret of the hydrogen bomb, the use of radiation coupling to ignite fusion fuel from the primary fission weapon, was discovered only in 1951 by Teller and Ulam. The first successful test of a hydrogen bomb, which was not a deliverable weapon but a huge refrigerated warehouse, occurred on a Pacific island on May 8, 1951. The entire island vanished. Neither the United States nor the USSR had deliverable thermonuclear weapons until the mid-1950s. Whatever Klaus Fuchs had told the Russians about the hydrogen bomb was evidently theoretical,

partial, and preliminary. But the technical data were less important than the political fallout. The Fuchs case had played a major
role in accelerating the Soviet-American race for the hydrogen
bomb.[23]

■ *Donald Maclean and Declassification*

In its first press release on the Fuchs case, in February 1950, the
AEC admitted that Fuchs had visited Washington in November
1947 as a member of the British delegation to discuss a new
Declassification Guide. The guide had been developed in 1945
and 1946 to determine what nuclear information might be shared
among the three partners: Great Britain, Canada, and the United
States. In 1950 officials realized that Fuchs had been one of the
scientists actively involved in determining the limits of nuclear
secrecy. A number of scientists attended the first declassification
meeting, including Fuchs, Cockcroft, and Peierls from Great Britain. Donald Maclean of the CPC attended as a guest. At AEC
headquarters the British were given visitor's badges but were not
required to register at the front desk. They occupied a special
office with a safe for classified documents; the thoughtful Americans even provided a screwdriver with which the British could
set their own combination.[24]

Not surprisingly, the scientists had different interpretations of
what secrets could be made public via the Declassification Guide,
which was itself classified. The discussions, which might provide
clues to research in different areas, tended to be cautious and
opaque, deliberately uninformative. The central issue in all the
discussions was unambiguous, according to an AEC director of
classification: "whether seeking security through secrecy interferes
with security by achievement." The AEC did not request that the
FBI, which by 1947 was in charge of AEC security investigations,
investigate Fuchs or any other British visitor. When Fuchs visited
the Argonne laboratory near Chicago on November 28, he spent
slightly more than an hour discussing neutron spectroscopy instrumentation with fellow scientists, but he did not visit any
restricted area. The next day he had Thanksgiving dinner with

Edward Teller and his wife and Carson Mark, old friends from Los Alamos.[25]

As soon as Fuchs's activities became public in 1950, his 1947 visit to Washington and Chicago became of great interest. It was learned that before the declassification meeting a security officer at Oak Ridge had requested a security check of Fuchs, Peierls, and W. B. Lewis, the director of research at Chalk River, but that nothing had been done about it. Only restricted data already known to the British and Canadians were discussed at the meeting. Robert Bacher, another Los Alamos physicist, wrote that anything discussed would already have been familiar to Fuchs, that the discussions were general and interpretative in nature, and that the information was "negligibly small compared to that which any worker would have assimilated in a short period at Los Alamos."[26]

In February 1950 Lewis Strauss told Hoover that he had recently learned that the British had had a two-room office in the Atomic Energy Commission building for three years after the war. None of the AEC commissioners, claimed Strauss, knew of its existence. British visitors to the office had not even been checked by the FBI. Strauss was understandably flabbergasted.[27]

A year later, in June 1951, Strauss's concerns seemed justified when Donald Maclean fled to the Soviet Union. Maclean, a hard-drinking first secretary at the British Embassy in Washington, had been assigned to the CPC in the late summer of 1945. By late 1947 he was taking minutes of meetings at which information, classification policies, and nuclear raw materials were discussed in great detail. For two years he attended all CPC meetings and in 1947 was given a security pass to the AEC building; he could roam at will unescorted, even after hours.[28] Strauss had learned about Maclean's building pass in the autumn of 1949 and had urged its revocation, though no action was taken. Yet another Soviet spy, again a British citizen, had penetrated the inner recesses of the American nuclear establishment.[29]

■ *Secrecy versus Security*

William S. White of the *New York Times* redefined the security-secrecy debate after Fuchs's arrest. "What is the best security in atomic-hydrogen bomb development? The feeling that the Fuchs case ought now to bring much more secrecy collides frontally with another conviction that it should bring less." Yet as he pointed out, neither the scientists nor the military could fully illustrate their point because the evidence itself was often secret. Hanson Baldwin attacked the "atomic state" where "legislators vote in ignorance and the people accept, passively, decisions made in secret," and he predicted that the Fuchs case would lead to more, not less, secrecy. Columnist Max Lerner also warned about the "religion of secrecy" in which national security was defined by "the double wall of the H-bomb and the G-mind."[30]

British secrecy, after all, which was traditionally severe, had not stopped Fuchs, and American military secrecy during the war had failed to discover him. Henry Smyth, in the *Bulletin of the Atomic Scientists,* agreed that Fuchs was a "Soviet agent" engaged in "treasonable activities" but argued for the "relaxation of excessive security regulations." "There is no one secret," noted Smyth, "which by itself is of overwhelming importance." In 1953 Smyth continued to support "security by achievement" over "security by secrecy" precisely because security had failed in the Fuchs case. Had there been no Fuchs, wrote Smyth, there was "little doubt that the Russians would have made bombs."[31]

But the seeds of the Fuchs case had fallen on fertile soil, and the defenders of secrecy now had their day. Newspaper editorials argued that security was a sham and that it was time for Uncle Sam to "get tough." American democracy must be vigilant regarding the enemies within; scientists would not fear loyalty oaths if they had nothing to hide.[32]

Some congressmen urged that all National Science Foundation fellows be required to obtain security clearances. The House Un-American Activities Committee questioned the political loyalties of scientists in general. Congressman Lawrence K. Smith called for Truman's impeachment. There were rumors of an atomic scientists' plot; Albert Einstein, it was said, had recommended Fuchs for war work. Traitors boring from within were stealing our secrets. Senator Joseph McCarthy claimed to have the names of dozens of communists who had worked in the State Department. The statement by the Soviet news agency, TASS, that "Fuchs is unknown to the Soviet government and no 'agents' of the Soviet

Union had any connection with Fuchs" only confirmed American fears.[33]

Hoover lost no time in urging the elimination of security clearances for foreign nationals and the tightening of security generally. General Groves, who had retired from government service, was called to Washington to testify before the JCAE. Fuchs, Groves told the committee, had been an "important and responsible" member of the British mission to the Manhattan Project, and "like all other members of the British Mission, his responsibility, discretion, and loyalty were vouched for by his government." Groves blamed the British for clearing Fuchs in the first place. "If I had had my way," testified Groves, "I would not have permitted British participation. I would have limited the program to American scientists only."[34]

Senator John W. Bricker claimed that the Fuchs case indicated a "complete breakdown of security" on the part of the British and warned that the era of Anglo-American nuclear information sharing might be over. Bricker demanded the publication of the Quebec Agreement, under which Roosevelt had agreed to accept British security clearances without further vetting. Many now wanted to cut Great Britain off from any information exchange, and Congressman Richard M. Nixon called for a "full congressional investigation."[35]

Eventually the Korean War replaced the Fuchs case in the news, but the secrecy debate went on. In November 1950 AEC chairman Gordon Dean called for less secrecy, arguing that Fuchs was a communist idealist and "you don't usually spot this type in a check." Walter Gellhorn, in his book Security, Loyalty, and Science, noted that Fuchs's scientific information was of value to the USSR only because the Russians were "already capable of exploiting the known facts" regarding an atomic bomb. At any rate, Fuchs was atypical of the scientific community, and the risk of occasional espionage was less dangerous than the risk of excessive secrecy.[36]

Had Fuchs's confessions been released to the public in 1950, they would have shown that he had given the Russians valuable data on the atomic bomb and very little on the hydrogen bomb. But because his confessions remained secret, circulated only in the upper reaches of the American and British governments, the press and the public believed that Fuchs was an "H-bomb spy" who had given Stalin the secret of a new weapon.

■ *Gold and the Rosenbergs*

Within weeks of Fuchs's arrest the FBI learned that in 1942 and 1943 he had met near the town of Banbury with "a woman who has not yet been identified." At their last meeting the woman had specified the arrangements for meeting his contact in New York. By March 17 the FBI knew, without being told by MI5, that Fuchs had named Jurgen Kuczynski and that Kuczynski's sister, Ursula, was a "known Russian espionage agent, having operated in China with Rudolf Hamburger and in Switzerland." They also knew that Ursula's second husband, Len Beurton, was a Soviet agent who had worked with her in Switzerland and that she herself had lived in England since 1941 and was "now in London." The FBI had little interest in the Kuczynskis, for they were British residents. The problem was to establish Fuchs's American connections. Within the FBI "all hell broke loose" because agents Lamphere and Van Loon had failed to run an earlier name check on Fuchs. The hunt for Fuchs's American accomplices thus became especially intense.[37]

On February 6 Senator Styles Bridges told a reporter, "This man must have had contacts in this country and we must follow through to find those contacts, particularly to know if any of them tie into high places." By this time the FBI had already begun the search for Raymond, starting with Kristel and Robert Heineman in Massachusetts. Although the FBI had investigated the Heinemans in 1946, it did not open a formal espionage case file on them until October 1949. During the winter of 1949–50 their telephone was tapped and their mail intercepted in an effort to establish Fuchs's guilt. But until his arrest, the FBI did not interview them, for that might have alerted Fuchs to the net closing around him.[38]

By February 15 the FBI had established that an unknown man had visited the Heineman home three times in 1945, looking for Fuchs. He was said to be about thirty years old, five feet eight inches tall, stocky, slightly bald, and wearing glasses. By March 15 the bureau had learned from Kristel that the man was a chemist and that in February 1945 he had visited the Heinemans and had asked Kristel if she were Fuchs's sister. He had stayed for lunch. On the man's second visit, Fuchs was there; he had spoken privately with Fuchs and had brought candy for the Heineman children. On the third visit, in April, as Kristel recalled, Fuchs was not there; the man had asked when he would return.[39]

Initially the FBI suspected a left-wing chemical engineer from New York named Joseph Arnold Robbins. But Robbins could not have been in Cambridge at the times specified. By mid-March the FBI had narrowed the search to two: a man named Abraham Brothman and Harry Gold, a thirty-nine-year-old pudgy, reticent biochemist at Philadelphia General Hospital. (In 1947 Gold and Elizabeth Bentley, Jacob Golos's secretary, had appeared before a New York grand jury on charges of espionage but had not been indicted for lack of evidence.) On May 9 intense surveillance of Gold began. He had been understandably anxious since Fuchs's arrest, and a nine-hour FBI interview in May increased his anxiety. Although Gold said he had never been west of the Mississippi, on May 22 a search of his apartment turned up a map of the Santa Fe area. When Fuchs finally identified him as his courier, Gold confessed.[40]

On May 23 he was arraigned in federal court in Philadephia and held on $100,000 bail on the charge of espionage. In a complaint filed by the U.S. Commissioner for the Eastern District of New York, Gold was accused of "knowingly and feloniously" conspiring with Fuchs to deliver to the Soviet Union "documents, writings, sketches, notes and information relating to the national defense." Gold claimed that he had only wished to help a wartime ally attain industrial strength.

■ *The FBI and the Fuchs Interview*

On February 12 Cimperman reported to Hoover from London that Fuchs had not revealed to MI5 the names or identities of any of his contacts. Hoover demanded that the FBI be allowed to interview Fuchs, but the British dragged their feet. On March 24

Sillitoe recommended to the Home Office that it grant the FBI permission to do so. A week later Sillitoe reported to Cimperman that the Home Office had refused. He recommended that the State Department make a formal request to the British Foreign Office, which the State Department did. Extensive haggling followed concerning the conditions for the interview. Only on May 5, three months after Fuchs's arrest, did the British Foreign Office inform the State Department that an interview was possible, and by May 7 the final technicalities were worked out. Fuchs agreed to be interviewed with William Skardon present.[41]

Gordon Dean of the AEC reminded Hoover that the commission had a "strong interest" in the interview and provided some specific questions about Fuchs's work on the bomb. The Home Office informed the House of Commons that the "usual practice" would be followed in allowing Fuchs to be interviewed and that a prison officer, as well as Skardon, would be present. The interview was permitted only because of the "exceptional circumstances" of the case. On May 17 State Department officials met with the two FBI agents who would interview Fuchs, Robert Lamphere and Hugh Clegg, and went over the technical questionnaires that had been submitted to the British by the JCAE in March, which Fuchs was expected to answer. By this time the impending interview was public knowledge, and the FBI was armed with seventy-five feet of film taken of Harry Gold in Philadelphia for Fuchs to view. The stage was set for Gold and Fuchs to confirm the crime of the century.[42]

On May 19, 1950, Clegg and Lamphere arrived in London, where there was still widespread objection to foreign police interviewing a British subject. The next day Clegg and Lamphere met with Fuchs for an hour at Wormwood Scrubbs and found him cooperative. They showed him still photographs of Gold, but Fuchs could not conclusively identify him as his courier, Raymond. "I cannot reject them," he said. Under questioning, Fuchs said that Raymond might have been Jewish, a chemical engineer, and a resident of Philadelphia with a wife and children. Clegg and Lamphere decided not to show Fuchs the film of Gold.[43]

On Monday, May 22, Fuchs was interviewed for one hour in the morning and two hours in the afternoon. In a special room with a glass panel in the door were Fuchs, Skardon, Clegg, and Lamphere; a prison official stood guard outside. Fuchs admitted that he and Raymond had first made contact in New York, using a glove and a newspaper (a handball, according to Gold) for identification. Under instructions from his Soviet control in England, Fuchs responded in a "completely absurd manner" to Raymond's first words, to establish his identity. The two men thereafter met a number of times in New York, Cambridge, and Santa Fe, never at the same location twice. Fuchs said he never knew the man's name or identity.[44]

The FBI asked about the technical information disclosed by Fuchs to the Russians. The AEC knew that Fuchs had not provided significant up-to-date information on the hydrogen bomb, but it was interested in the extent of Fuchs's disclosures on plutonium, including its production at Hanford. When the FBI interviewers discussed technical matters with Fuchs on Tuesday, May 23, he admitted that he had given his contact handwritten documents on implosion, the high-explosive lenses (specifying their outer dimensions), and the difficulties of multiple-point detonation around a sphere of plutonium. By June 1945 he had also provided data on the size of the Alamogordo/Nagasaki plutonium bomb, ignition methods, and IBM computer calculations. In September he added information on the Trinity test, initiators, and the bomb core. He could not, he emphasized, give information on uranium separation at Oak Ridge or plutonium production at Hanford.[45]

By May 23 the FBI had elicited a full confession from Gold, excerpts of which were wired to Cimperman in London for assistance in the Fuchs interview. Hoover urged that "efforts should be made to reconcile discrepancies in statements of Fuchs and Gold." The next day the FBI reported to Washington that Fuchs had positively identified the still photographs of Gold as his courier, Raymond, saying "that is my American contact." The agents added that while in the United States Fuchs had apparently furnished no information on the hydrogen bomb, but might have done so after his return to England in June 1946.[46]

On May 26 Fuchs furnished more details of his contacts with Gold. He admitted giving Gold thirteen of his own written papers on gaseous diffusion (in New York), information on how to detonate the plutonium bomb (in Cambridge), and on the problems of spontaneous fission in plutonium. He said he had wanted to help the Soviet Union. He did not accept money, even when it was offered. His contacts with Gold had been prearranged in England by a woman Fuchs identifed only as his "espionage contact at Banbury."[47]

On June 2 Clegg and Lamphere flew home to America while newspaper headlines screamed "ONE HUNDRED RED SPIES NAMED BY FUCHS." Rumors flew that Fuchs had implicated entire networks of Soviet agents in Britain, America, and Canada. He had done no such thing. He had merely said that Harry Gold appeared to be his American contact, and he had detailed the information he had provided on the plutonium bomb. The secrecy surrounding the interview ensured that American opinion would imagine a widening atomic espionage conspiracy, of which the discovery of Gold was only the beginning.[48]

In his two lengthy signed statements to the FBI, on May 22 and July 10, Gold told a remarkable story of Soviet espionage in America and of his role in transferring atomic secrets from Los Alamos to Moscow. He also would ultimately confirm that Klaus Fuchs was not the only Soviet spy operating within the confines of the Manhattan Engineer District. The spy ring of which Gold was a part turned out to include David Greenglass and Julius Rosenberg. The "pattern of infamy" of atomic espionage fit nicely with the widening search by Senator McCarthy and others for evidence of communist subversion in Cold War America.[49]

On November 3, 1950, the FBI effectively closed the Fuchs investigation, noting that twelve full-time and sixty part-time FBI agents had been employed in hunting Fuchs's immediate accomplices in America. The FBI had arrested eight persons as a result, including Gold, Greenglass, and the Rosenbergs, and had identified two Soviet agents, Semyon Semyonov and Anatolii Yakovlev, both of whom had left the country years before. On April 5, 1951, the Rosenbergs were sentenced to death for conspiracy to commit espionage; Gold received a thirty-year prison sentence; Greenglass, fifteen years. The American press noted that Klaus Fuchs was "loafing in prison" under a more lenient British sentence even though he was the "deadliest spy in all history."[50]

American suspicions of lax British security persisted, especially after the defections of Guy Burgess and Donald Maclean in 1951. In July 1953 Strauss suggested that Fuchs be interviewed again, but the FBI was lukewarm. Allen Dulles and the CIA were said to be "continually on the alert for any new information which might be related to the Fuchs case," but none was forthcoming.[51]

The denial of Oppenheimer's AEC security clearance in 1954 brought out the tension between scientifc freedom and national security restrictions. Oppenheimer's early communist connections were said to make him a security risk; he also opposed the hydrogen bomb on both moral and practical grounds. In the course of the Oppenheimer hearings, attempts by William Borden to link Fuchs to Oppenheimer failed for lack of evidence, but not for lack of trying.[52]

Fuchs's release from prison in 1959 brought him back into the news in the United States. Kristel Heineman, who became a naturalized American citizen in 1956, reportedly offered her brother a place to live in Boston. But Fuchs was banned from the United States on thirty-one separate counts under the McCarran Act. Kristel told the *Christian Science Monitor* that "Klaus has never written to me" and "my father has written repeatedly that he is expecting Klaus to live with him . . . We date our lives," she observed, "from 1933," when the family had begun to flee Nazi Germany. But the *New York Times* called Fuchs a "scientist traitor," and David Lawrence of the *New York Herald Tribune* wrote that "Klaus Fuchs betrayed America as well as Britain . . . If anyone deserved to be electrocuted, it was Klaus Fuchs."[53]

In the 1960s attempts persisted to prove that the Rosenbergs had been unjustly convicted and executed. Fuchs, in contrast, was said to have been much more important than Greenglass because he knew much more about the implosion bomb, which was certainly true. In 1966 Morton Sobell, an accomplice of the Rosenbergs, petitioned the U.S. District Court for release from prison, arguing that the "secrecy of the Fuchs confession" prevented his lawyers from showing that Gold was not the courier for both Greenglass and Fuchs or that Greenglass's purloined information was, in contrast to Fuchs's, "valueless." Sobell's petition did not result in the release of Fuchs's confession, but it did elicit testimony from another Manhattan Project veteran, the physicist

Philip Morrison, that "Klaus Fuchs had available to him all of the theoretical and technical information concerning the operation of the test [plutonium] bomb" and that "any information that was sent from Los Alamos by Fuchs to the Soviet Union was very probably correct." Such testimony was intended to show that Fuchs's information was "complete and quantitative," whereas Greenglass's was "worthless." The court, however, was not convinced that Fuchs's importance implied Greenglass's insignificance.[54]

Ronald Radosh and Joyce Milton's book *The Rosenberg File* (1984) helped put to rest the notion that the Rosenbergs were framed or innocent of their crimes. But the idea persisted, even in a 1982 *Washington Post* article, that the FBI should have identified Fuchs earlier because his name had appeared on the Gestapo's suspect list. Physicists who knew Fuchs continue to stress his importance as a scientist and his popularity at Los Alamos, as well as their total ignorance of his political and espionage careers.[55]

Fuchs's imprisonment and the Rosenberg case removed Fuchs from the American political memory. But his case left a lasting imprint on the Cold War and the ongoing debate about whether open science or military secrecy provides the best route to national security.

CHAPTER · 13

The Return Home

Supposition all our lives shall be stuck full of eyes;
For treason is but trusted like the fox.

— *William Shakespeare*

In April 1945 Red Army troops set up a Soviet occupation regime in the eastern part of Germany. Six weeks later an agreement by the Allies provided for joint authority over Berlin, and on July 7 British and American troops entered the city. At the same time Walter Ulbricht and KPD leaders from Moscow flew in to establish a communist government. On July 27, 1945, Jurgen Kuczynski was surprised to find himself listed as finance president of the Soviet zone of Germany, an appointment in absentia, which was not uncommon in those dark and confused days.[1]

Kuczynski found his way home to Berlin in a curious way. When the OSS kidnaped a senior Nazi economist, Rolf Wegenfuehr, from the Soviet zone for interrogation by the U.S. Strategic Bombing Survey, General Zhukov lodged a protest with Eisenhower. Two weeks later Kuczynski brought Wegenfuehr back to the Soviet zone; Kuczynski also wanted to see if his home and library had survived the Allied bombing. When he arrived at party headquarters in Berlin attired in an American army uniform, he was denied entrance, but after telling his story to Ulbricht and Pieck he was invited to return—without the uniform. In November Kuczynski moved to East Germany permanently, but he continued to maintain a residence in West Berlin until the Fuchs case broke in 1950.[2]

The year 1949 saw the establishment of the Federal Republic of Germany (FDR) and the German Democratic Republic (DDR), as well as the formation of NATO in response to Soviet military threats. Wilhelm Pieck became president of the DDR, and the new constitution was passed by the Third German Peoples' Congress on October 7, 1949. At that time the DDR seemed to offer a haven for KPD members who had fled from Hitler and had spent nearly two decades abroad. Although they had been considered valued allies and resources during World War II, German communist refugees were now suspect in England and America as Soviet agents. Like Fuchs, most of them were repelled by the excesses of Stalinism in the Soviet Union: the anti-Semitism, the purge trials, nationalist excesses, and the stifling of independence in Eastern Europe. Many communists turned their backs on their past, but others kept the faith and returned to the new Germany in the east.[3]

Not all of the refugees were welcomed in East Germany. As controls tightened, Ulbricht's Social Unity Party purged anyone suspected of being anti-Soviet or against the party or of spying. Many of those suspected were communists who had spent their exile in England, America, or Mexico rather than in Moscow. In the spring of 1950, as Klaus Fuchs entered a British prison, the Ministry of State Security in East Germany began legal proceedings against more than three thousand political prisoners in the infamous Waldheim Trials. Had Fuchs returned to East Germany in 1949 rather than 1959, he might well have been among them, facing trial for his scientific and intelligence work for Britain and America.[4]

The widely publicized case of KPD leader Gerhard Eisler in 1949 indicated the hardening of Cold War loyalties and emotions. Eisler appeared to have returned home from the West triumphant, despite the machinations of British and American security. But before long he was suspect for having associated with Noel Field, a man who had served both communism and American intelligence. Like Fuchs, Field was a "red pawn" in a larger game of Cold War intelligence.

- *Noel Field and the Rajk Trial*

On May 5, 1949, Field, a forty-five-year-old American diplomat, flew from Paris to Prague and disappeared. A few weeks later he was named in the trial of Alger Hiss, a U.S. State Department official accused of stealing documents in the 1930s. Field's double life as a communist and an OSS agent was as mysterious as his disappearance behind the Iron Curtain and had parallels to the activities and beliefs of both Klaus Fuchs and Jurgen Kuczynski.[5]

Like Fuchs, Field described his existence as a "dual life" of Quaker upbringing, government service, and secret espionage. His father, a biologist and an ardent pacifist, ran Quaker relief efforts in 1918 for war refugees in Switzerland. At fourteen, Noel Field first met Allen Dulles, who was a family friend; their acquaintance was lifelong. In 1926, after graduating from Harvard College, Field joined the State Department and reestablished his contacts with Dulles. The austere, left-wing Field had few friends in those days other than Alger Hiss, another rising diplomat.[6]

In 1935 Field decided to join the American communist party but was dissuaded from joining by two German communists, Hede and Paul Massing, who worked for Gerhard Eisler and the Comintern. They persuaded Field to turn over State Department classified documents to them in the interest of a "higher duty to humanity." Hede Massing continued to run Field in the late 1930s. Field left the State Department in 1936 to work for the League of Nations in Geneva; he spent the next several years helping Republican refugees escape from war-torn Spain. In 1941 he became resident director of the Unitarian Services Committee office in Marseilles. German occupation soon drove him out of France; by November 1942 he was the Unitarian representative in Switzerland, where he once again encountered Dulles, who was wartime station head for the OSS.[7]

During the war Field functioned as both a communist and an American intelligence operative. Refugee work put him in touch with many future communist resistance leaders in Europe, especially those in the notorious French concentration camp of Le Vernet, whose inhabitants included Arthur Koestler, Paul Merker, and Eisler. The OSS recruited Noel Field in 1943 in Switzerland.

Through men like Field and Kuczynski the OSS hoped to establish a network of informants and agents to help defeat Nazi Germany. Field's refugee work was an ideal cover for obtaining intelligence reports and for providing funds for potentially useful communist refugees from Hitler. Field reported to Dulles in Bern, the main Allied intelligence center.[8]

In late 1944 Field proposed to Dulles that KPD refugees in France be trained as agents and parachuted into Nazi Germany in advance of Allied troops to establish contacts and keep the Nazis from sabotaging bridges and factories. The principal organization involved in this was the Comité de L'Allemagne Libre pour l'Oueste (CALPO), one of the many "Free Germany" committees established by Ulbricht from Moscow. For Field and Kuczynski the second agenda was to help establish communist party control. The OSS sent communist agents, often in American army uniform, into Germany, Hungary, Yugoslavia, and Czechoslovakia.[9]

In 1949, after Field lost his job with Unitarian relief and was named in the Hiss investigation, he decided to seek political asylum in the East. In America he was a communist spy; in Eastern Europe he would be portrayed as an agent of the OSS and the CIA. Field soon became a central figure in the tumultuous political purge trials in Eastern Europe. The CIA may well have realized that Field would be arrested and linked with many individuals he had met during the war, who were now in positions of authority in communist governments.[10]

The first sign of trouble for Field was the arrest on June 3 of Hungarian Foreign Minister Laszlo Rajk, a popular leader and a veteran of the Spanish Civil War. Rajk had known Field from his French internment, and Field had helped him return to Hungary during the war as a key anti-Nazi underground leader. In September 1949 Rajk went on trial in Budapest on charges of sedition, treason, and war crimes. Within a few days Field was named as an American spy working for the CIA, a man who "specialized in recruiting spies from among so-called 'left-wing' elements" during World War II. Rajk's connection with Field played a central role in the accusations against him. *Pravda* and *Izvestiia* ran headlines about "Rajk and his accomplices—agents of American intelligence," behind which stood the "Tito clique." On September 24 Rajk was condemned to death for treason, and on October 14 he was executed.[11]

Rajk was not alone. Traicho Kostov in Bulgaria and Koci Xoxe in Albania were accused of similar crimes, based on flimsy or nonexistent evidence. Within a year the East European purges had affected hundreds of thousands of party members and government officials. By 1951 "international networks of Anglo-American espionage" in Hungary, Poland, Czechoslovakia, and Bulgaria had been "unmasked in connection with the well-known Noel Field."[12]

In the DDR thousands of party members were expelled or executed for corruption, Nazi party membership, socialist opposition, or connections with Western intelligence. Anyone associated with Field was particularly suspect. Paul Merker, a Politburo member since 1946, went on trial in August 1950 and was expelled from the SED for his connections with Field at Le Vernet. Merker was also charged with having been a "hostile agent" of the American "financial oligarchy" in Mexico during the war. Eisler and hundreds of others lost their positions because of their ties to the "U.S. master spy."[13]

The purge trials of 1949 and 1950 are essential to understanding how Klaus Fuchs and Jurgen Kuczynski could be communists without being obedient servants of Moscow. Titoism threatened to become the national communist virus that could infect the entire Soviet bloc. As a German communist increasingly dissatisfied with Stalin's policies, Fuchs must have shared the sense of guilt and fear so common in Eastern Europe. As a scientist who had worked with the Allies on secret bomb projects with MI6, he was vulnerable to the charge of being a British or American intelligence agent, however remote the connection with his real research. In 1949 Fuchs could have faced prison or worse in East Germany, as he did in Great Britain.

Jurgen Kuczynski, like Field, was an ex-OSS operative and had served as a go-between for the OSS and exile communist refugees who were sent into Eastern Europe as agents. Shortly after Fuchs's arrest in 1950, Kuczynski also fled from West to East Germany. But Kuczynski was better positioned than Field to avoid trouble.

He was a personal friend of Walter Ulbricht, and since 1945 he had held a number of government positions in the eastern zone. He was president of the Central Financial Administration, professor at Humboldt University, president of the Society for German-Soviet Friendship, and director of the German Economic Institute.[14]

In 1957 Ulbricht criticized Kuczynski for not defending Stalin against Khrushchev's de-Stalinization campaign; after failing to win reelection to the *Volkskammer,* Kuczynski took an extended trip to China. In 1971 East German President Erich Honecker demanded that an article by Kuczynski be withdrawn from publication for being too laudatory of Honecker. But all this lay in the future. In 1950 Kuczynski remained an influential member of the East German government, although threatened by the purges. Under Soviet pressure he was removed as president of the Society for German-Soviet Friendship, probably a Jewish victim of Stalin's anticosmopolitan campaign.[15]

As for Field, five years after he vanished, he was released by the Hungarian police in Budapest, where he sought political asylum. In a 1957 radio broadcast he defended the Soviet crushing of the 1956 Hungarian revolution. Like Fuchs, Field ended as a docile Stalinist in the gray dictatorships of Eastern Europe, his wartime connections with Western intelligence a receding, if troublesome, memory.

As the cases of Noel Field and Klaus Fuchs illustrate, the Allies took security risks during the war that they would not have taken afterward. The war effort made for unlikely bedfellows. British and American intelligence used the expertise of German refugees wherever they could find it; having communist sympathies was, if anything, a guarantee of anti-Nazi sentiment. There was no "positive vetting" or background investigation. If there had been, it is possible that the homosexual cryptographer Alan Turing in Britain would never have been allowed to help break the Ultra code. As it was, the arrest of Fuchs and the disappearance of Burgess and Maclean helped produce the positive vetting system that ultimately drove Turing to suicide in 1954. But from 1939 to 1945 neither sex nor politics was allowed to stand in the way of British national security needs.

■ *Homecoming*

Fuchs's return to Germany in June 1959 was emotional. He was met at Schoenfeld airport in East Berlin by his nephew, Klaus Kittowski, whom he had not seen in years. He then joined his father for a reunion at Emil's weekend cottage at nearby Wandlitz. Fuchs told reporters that he was still a Marxist, intended to become a citizen of the DDR, and held no resentment against the British. "It is such a change," he said, "not only being free, but being in quite a different country. I suppose it will take some time to get used to it." On June 26 he became an East German citizen.[16]

Actually, Fuchs adapted to his new situation quickly. On August 31 he was named deputy director of the Institute for Nuclear Physics at Rossendorf near Dresden; he said he was "pleased to get back to work." Ten days later he married an old friend, Greta Keilson, fifty-four, whom he had met in Paris in 1933 and who served as Wilhelm Pieck's secretary in Moscow. He settled into married life and scientific research under fairly normal conditions for the first time in his life. His communism was never in doubt. In 1961 Fuchs broadcast a statement defending the Soviet resumption of nuclear testing as "necessary" to counter the military efforts of western "warmongers." In August 1986 he made a similar statement and called for a ban on all nuclear tests. His father too became an important supporter of the DDR, holding talks with Ulbricht on party-church relations and urging Protestants to support the regime and its peace movements. Emil died on February 13, 1971, at the age of ninety-seven.

Klaus Fuchs remains cut off from Britain, his home for twenty-five years. He corresponds with very few friends, but he has stayed in touch with Nicholas Kurti of Oxford. During the 1970s he declined to meet his old mentor from Bristol, Nevill Mott, who was visiting the DDR. In his second life Fuchs has been much honored. He remained at Rossendorf until 1974. He was also a professor at the Technische Hochschule, a member of the party's central committee, and in 1972 was named to the Academy of Sciences. For his scientific work he received the National Prize First Class in 1975 and the Karl Marx Order in 1979. In matters of politics he remains an idealist; a visiting western scientist who heard him lecture noted that "his face lit up and he began to talk like a religious revivalist" about the achievements of socialism. As another physicist put it, "I have never before known a person who possesses such a marvelous ability to think in abstract terms who is at the same time so helpless when it comes to either observe or evaluate reality."[17]

Appendixes

The two statements, or confessions, made by Klaus Fuchs to William J. Skardon (January 27, 1950) and Michael Perrin (January 30, 1950) remain classified in Great Britain as official secrets; they have never been released. However, the statements in two memoranda from FBI Director J. Edgar Hoover to Rear Admiral Sidney W. Souers, President Harry S Truman's national security adviser, are probably identical to the original confessions. These memoranda, which are unclassified American documents, are in the President's Secretary's Files, Harry S Truman Presidential Library, Independence, Missouri.

The statements by Harry Gold confirming his espionage connections with Fuchs were made to FBI Special Agents Richard E. Brennan and T. Scott Miller in Philadelphia on May 22 and July 10, 1950. They are in the FBI case file on Klaus Fuchs, Department of Justice, Washington, D.C.

Appendix A

Klaus Fuchs's Confession to William Skardon, January 27, 1950

Rear Admiral Sidney W. Souers   March 6, 1950
Special Consultant to the President   Personal &
Executive Office Building   Confidential
Washington, D.C.   Via Liaison

My dear Admiral:

I believe that the President and you will be interested in the signed statement given by Emil Julius Klaus Fuchs on January 27, 1950. The portions of this statement not read at the public proceedings during the prosecution of Fuchs are still classified Top Secret by the British. The statement follows.

War Office
27th January, 1950

"Statement of Emil Julius Klaus Fuchs, of 17 Hillside, Harwell, Berkshire, who saith:

"I am Deputy Scientific Officer (acting rank) at atomic energy research establishment, Harwell.

"I was born in Rüsselsheim on 29th December, 1911. My father was a parson and I had a very happy childhood. I think that the one thing that mostly stands out is that my father always told us that we had to go our own way, even if he disagreed. He himself had many fights because he did what his conscience decreed, even if these were at variance with accepted convention. For example, he was the first parson to join the Social Democratic Party. I didn't take much interest in politics during my school days except insofar as I was forced into it by the fact that of course all the other pupils knew who my father was, and I think the only political act at school which I ever made was at the celebration of the Weimar Constitution when there was a celebration at school and all the flags of the Weimar Republic had been put up outside, whereas inside large numbers of the pupils appeared with the imperial badge. At that point I took out the badge showing the colors of the Republic, and put it on, and of course it was immediately torn down.

"When I got to the University of Leipzig I joined the S.P.D. and took part in the organization of the students' group of the S.P.D. I found myself soon in opposition to the official policies of the S.P.D., for example on the question of naval rearmament, when the S.P.D. supported the building program of the Panzercreuzer. I did have some discussion with Communists, but I always found that I despised them because it was apparent that they accepted the official policy of their own party even if they did not agree with it. The main point at issue was always the Communist policy proclaiming the united front and at the same time attacking the leaders of the S.P.D. Later I went to Kiel University. It has just occurred to me, though it may not be important, that at Leipzig I was in the Reichsbanner which was a semi-military organization composed of members of the S.P.D. and the Democratic Party. That is a point at which I broke away from my father's philosophy because he is a pacifist. In Kiel I was first still a member of the S.P.D., but the break came when the S.P.D. decided to support Hindenburg as Reich President. Their argument was that if they put up their own candidate it would split the vote and Hitler would be elected. In particular, this would mean that the position of the S.P.D. in Prussia would be lost when they controlled the whole of the police organization. The election was, I think, in 1932. My argument was that we could not stop Hitler by cooperating with other bourgeois parties but that only a united working class could stop him. At this point I decided to oppose the official policies openly, and I offered myself as a speaker in support of the Communist candidate. Shortly after the election of Hindenburg, Papen was made Reich Chancellor, and he dismissed the elected Prussia Government and put in a Reichstaathalter. That evening we all collected spontaneously. I went to the headquarters of the Communist Party because I had in the meantime been expelled from the S.P.D., but I had seen many of my previous friends in the Reichsbanner, and I knew that they were gathering together ready to fight for the Prussian Government, but the Prussian Government yielded. All they did was to appeal to the central Reich Court. At this point the morale of the rank and file of the S.P.D. and the Reichsbanner broke completely and it was evident that there was no force left in those organizations to resist Hitler. I accepted that the Communist Party had been right in fighting against the leaders of the S.P.D. and that I had been wrong in blaming them for it. I had already joined the Communist Party because I felt I had to be in some organization.

"Some time before this I had also joined a student organization which contained members of the S.P.D., as well as members of the Communist Party. This organization was frowned upon by the S.P.D., but they did not take steps against me until I came out openly against the official policy. I was made the Chairman of this organization and we carried on propaganda aimed at those members of the Nazi whom we believed to be sincere. The Nazis had decided to start propaganda against the high fees which students had to pay, and we decided to take them by their word, convinced that we would show them up. I carried on the negotiations with the leaders of the Nazi group at the University, proposing that we should organize a strike of the students. They hedged and after several weeks I decided that the time had come to show that they did not intend to do it. We issued a leaflet, explained that the negotiations had been going on but that the leaders of the Nazis were not in earnest. Our policy did have success because some members of our organization succeeded in making personal contact with some of the sincere Nazis. The Nazi leaders apparently noticed that, because some time later they organized a strike against the Rector of the University. That was after Hitler had been made Reich Chancellor. During that strike they called in the support of the S.A. from the town, who demonstrated in front of the University. In spite of that I went there every day to show that I was not afraid of them. On one of these occasions they tried to kill me and I escaped. The fact that Hindenburg made Hitler Reich Chancellor of course proved to me again that I had been right in opposing the official policy of the S.P.D. After the burning of the Reichstag I had to go underground. I was lucky because on the morning after the burning of the Reichstag I left my home very early to catch a train to Berlin for a conference of our student organization, and that is the only reason why I escaped arrest. I remember clearly when I opened the newspaper in the train I immediately realized the significance and I knew that the underground struggle had started. I took the badge of the hammer and sickle from my lapel which I had carried until that time.

"I was ready to accept the philosophy that the Party is right and that in the coming struggle you could not permit yourself any doubts after the Party had made a decision. At this point I omitted from resolve in my mind a very small difficulty about my conduct of the policy against the Nazis. I received, of course, a great deal of praise at the conference in Berlin which was held illegally, but there rankled in my mind that fact that I had sprung our leaflets on the leaders of the Nazis without warning, without giving them an ultimatum that I would call to the student body lest they made a decision by a certain date. If it had been necessary to do that I would not have worried about it, but there was no need for it. I had violated some standards of decent behavior, but I did not resolve this difficulty and very often this incident did come back to my mind, but I came to accept that in such a struggle things of this kind are prejudices which are weakness and which you must fight against.

"All that followed helped to confirm the ideas I had formed. Not a single party voted against the extraordinary powers which were given to Hitler by the new Reichstag and in the universities there was hardly anybody who stood up for those who were dismissed either on political or racial grounds, and afterwards you found that people whom you normally would have respected because of their decency had no force in themselves to stand up for their own ideals or moral standards.

"I was in the underground until I left Germany. I was sent out by the Party, because they said that I must finish my studies because after the revolution in Germany people would be required with technical knowledge to take part in the building up of the Communist Germany. I went first to France and then to England, where I studied and at the same time I tried to make a serious study of the bases of Marxist philosophy. The idea which gripped me most was the belief that in the past man has been unable to understand his own history and the forces [that] lead to the further development of human society; that now for the first time man understands the historical forces and he is able to control them, and that, therefore, for the first time he will be really free. I carried this idea over into the personal sphere and believed that I could understand myself and that I could make myself into what I believed I should be.

"I accepted for a long time that what you heard about Russia internally could be deliberate lies. I had my doubts for the first time on acts of foreign policies of Russia; the Russo-German pact was difficult to understand, but in the end I did accept that Russia had done it to gain time, that during that time she was expanding her own influence in the Balkans against the influence of Germany. Finally Germany's attack on Russia seemed to confirm that Russia was not shirking and was prepared to carry out a foreign policy with the risk of war with Germany. Russia's attack on Finland was more difficult to understand, but the fact that England and France prepared for an intervention in Finland at the time when they did not appear to be fighting seriously against Germany made it possible to accept the explanation that Russia had to prepare its defenses against possible imperialism powers. In the end I accepted again that my doubts had been wrong and the Party had been right.

"When Germany started the real attack on France I was interned and for a long time I was not allowed any newspapers. We did not know what was going on outside, and I did not see how the British people fought at that time. I felt no bitterness by the internment, because I could understand that it was necessary and that at that time England could not spare good people to look after the internees, but it did deprive me of the chance of learning more about the real character of the British people.

"Shortly after my release I was asked to help Professor Peierls in Birmingham, on some war work. I accepted it and I started work without knowing at first what the work was. I doubt whether it would have made any difference to my subsequent actions if I had known the nature of the work beforehand. When I learned the purpose of the work I decided to inform Russia and I established contact through another member of the Communist Party. Since that time I have had continuous contact with persons who were completely unknown to me, except that I knew that they would hand whatever information I gave them to the Russian authorities. At this time I had complete confidence in Russian policy and I believed that the Western Allies deliberately allowed Russia and Germany to fight each other to the death. I had, therefore, no hesitation in giving all the information I had, even though occasionally I tried to concentrate mainly on giving information about the results of my own work.

"In the course of this work I began naturally to form bonds of personal friendship and I had concerning them my inner thoughts. I used my Marxist philosophy to establish in my mind two separate compartments. One compartment in which I allowed myself to make friendships, to have personal relations, to help people and to be in all personal ways the kind of man I wanted to be and the kind of man which, in personal ways, I had been before with my friends in or near the Communist Party. I could be free and easy and happy with other people without fear of disclosing myself because I knew that the other compartment would step in if I approached the danger point. I could forget the other compartment and still rely on it. It appeared to me at the time that I had become a 'free man' because I had succeeded in the other compartment to establish myself completely independent of the surrounding forces of society. Looking back at it now the best way of expressing it seems to be to call it a controlled schizophrenia.

"In the postwar period I began again to have my doubts about Russian policy. It is impossible to give definite incidents because now the control mechanism acted against me, also keeping away from me facts which I could not look in the face, but they did penetrate and eventually I came to a point where I knew I disapproved of a great many actions of the Russian Government and of the Communist Party, but I still believed that they would build a new world and that one day I would take part in it and that on that day I would also have to stand up and say to them that there are things which they are doing wrong. During this time I was not sure that I could give all the information that I had. However, it became more and more evident that the time when Russia would expand her influence over Europe was far away, and that, therefore, I had to decide for myself whether I could go on for many years to continue handing over information without being sure in my own mind whether I was doing right. I decided that I could not do so. I did not go to one rendezvous because I was ill at the time. I decided not to go to the following one.

"Shortly afterwards my father told me that he might be going into the Eastern Zone of Germany. At that time my own mind was closer to his than it had ever been before, because he also believed that they are at least trying to build a new world. He disapproved of many things and he had always done so, but he knew that when he went there he would say so and he thought that in doing so he might help to make them realize that you cannot build a new world if you destroy some fundamental decencies in personal behavior. I could not bring myself to stop my father from going there. However, it made me face at last some of the facts about myself. I felt that my father's going to the Eastern Zone, that his letters, would touch me somewhere and that I was not sure whether I would not go back. I suppose I did not have the courage to fight it out for myself and my father was going to the Eastern Zone. A few months passed and I became more and more convinced that I had to leave Harwell. I was then confronted with the fact that there was evidence that I had given away information in New York. I was given the chance of admitting it and staying at Harwell, or of clearing out. I was not sure enough of myself to stay at Harwell and, therefore, I denied the allegations and decided that I would have to leave Harwell.

"However, it then began to become clear to me that in leaving Harwell in those circumstances I would do two things. I would deal a grave blow to Harwell, to all the work which I had loved and, furthermore that I would leave suspicions against people whom I loved who were my friends and who believed I was their friend. I had to face the fact that it had been possible for me in one half of my mind to be friendly with people, be close friends and at the same time to deceive them to endanger them. I had to realize that the control mechanism had warned me of danger to myself, but that it had also prevented me from realizing what the combination of the three ideas which had made me what I was, was wrong, in fact that every single one of them was wrong, that there are certain standards of moral behavior which are in you and that you cannot disregard. That in your actions you must be clear in your own mind whether they are right or wrong. That you must be able, before accepting somebody else's authority to state your doubts and to try and resolve them; and I found that at least I myself was made by circumstances.

"I know that I cannot go back on that and I know that all I can do now is to try and repair the damage I had done. The first thing is to make sure that Harwell will suffer as little as possible and that I have to save for my friends as much as possible of that part that was good in my relations with them.

"This thought is at present uppermost in my mind, and I find it difficult to concentrate on any other points. However, I realize that I will have to state the extent of the information that I have given and that I shall have to help as far as my conscience allows me in stopping other people who are still doing what I have done.

"There is nobody I know by name who is concerned with collecting information for the Russian authorities. There are people whom I know by sight whom I trusted with my life and who trusted me with theirs and I do not know that I shall be able to do anything that might in the end give them away. They are not inside of the project, but they are the intermediaries between myself and the Russian Government.

"At first I thought that all I would do would be to inform the Russian authorities that work upon the atom bomb was going on. They wished to have more details and I agreed to supply them. I concentrated at first mainly on the products of my own work, but in particular at Los Alamos I did what I consider to be the worst I have done, namely to give information about the principles of the design of the plutonium bomb. Later on at Harwell I began to sift it, but it is difficult to say exactly when and how I did it because it was a process which went up and down with my inner struggles. The last time I handed over information was in February or March, 1949.

"Before I joined the project most of the British people with whom I had made personal contacts were left wing, and affected, to some degree or other, by the same kind of philosophy. Since coming to Harwell I have met English people of all kinds, and I have come to see in many of them a deep-rooted firmness which enables them to lead a decent way of life. I do not know where this springs from and I don't think they do, but it is there.

"I have read this statement and to the best of my knowledge it is true."
(signed) Klaus Fuchs.

"Statement taken down in writing by me at the permission of Emil Julius Klaus Fuchs at the War Office on January 27, 1950. He read it through, made such alterations as he wished and initialed each and every page."
(signed) W. J. Skardon.

The portion of the statement beginning: "Shortly after my release I was asked to help Professor Peierls in Birmingham on some war work . . ." through the paragraph beginning: "I know that I cannot go back on that and I know that all I can do now is to try and repair the damage I have done . . ." is that portion of the statement from which the prosecutor read or paraphrased certain excerpts during the hearing on February 10, 1950, at the Bow Street Court, London, England.

With expression of my highest esteem and best regards,

Sincerely yours,

J. Edgar Hoover

Appendix B

Klaus Fuchs's Confession to Michael Perrin, January 30, 1950

Rear Admiral Sidney Souers
Special Consultant to the President
Executive Office Building
Washington, D.C.

March 2, 1950
Personal &
Confidential
Via Liaison

My dear Admiral:

It is believed that the President and you will be interested in the substance of a statement made by Emil Julius Klaus Fuchs to Dr. Michael W. Perrin, atomic scientist connected with the British Ministry of Supply, concerning the technical information furnished to the Soviet Government.

The statement of Fuchs to Perrin, which has been classified Top Secret by the British, is as follows:

First Period. From 1942 to December, 1943.

"Fuchs told me that his first contact was early 1942. By this time he had joined Professor Peierls' team at Birmingham University which was working under a contract from the Directorate of Tube Alloys. Fuchs explained that during this first period, he had been at considerable pains to give the agents only the results of work which he himself had done. He was engaged on a study of the basic theory of and the mathematical treatment of problems connected with gaseous diffusion process for separating the uranium isotopes, and using pure uranium 235 and told me that at this time he knew practically nothing about the possibilities of the pile reaction other than what had been published in the scientific literature, and he certainly did not appreciate any possibility of using plutonium as an alternative to U-235 in an atomic bomb. He regarded this part of the atomic energy project as, at the best, a long term possibility for the production of power.

"In accordance with his intention to give only the results of his own work, his main activity with the Russian agent was to hand him copies of all the reports which he wrote while at Birmingham University. These were in the 'M.S.' Series and he usually handed over a spare carbon copy which he had typed. The agent with whom he was in contact clearly understood none of the technical details but, according to Fuchs, was in no way surprised to hear work directed to the production of an atomic bomb, and on one occasion asked Fuchs what he knew about the electro-magnetic method as an alternative means of separating the uranium isotopes. This very much surprised Fuchs who, at the time, knew nothing of any work on this method and had never considered it.

"Apart from the detailed papers of which he was himself the author, Fuchs did tell the agent in general terms that work on the project was being actively prosecuted in the United Kingdom and that a small pilot unit to test out the principal [sic] of the diffusion separation process was being put up at the Ministry of Supply factory 'valley' in North Wales. He said that he gave no details of the design or mechanical construction of the equipment in this pilot plant. He also reported that similar work was being done in the United States and that there was collaboration between the two countries.

"Apart from the question about the electro-magnetic separation process, Fuchs did not remember much about questions put to him and thought that they were very few and were sometimes so garbled as to be almost meaningless.

Second Period. New York. December, 1943, to August, 1944.

"Fuchs was a member of the British Diffusion Mission which went to New York in December 1943, and he stayed on there when the majority came back to the United Kingdom. During this period Fuchs learned a good deal more about the American program and, in particular, that a large production plant for the gaseous diffusion process was being built which would be worked in conjunction with a second large plant using the electro-magnetic process. He knew that both of these plants would be at 'Site X' but he has told me that he did not then know where this was and could not, therefore, report it to the new Russian agent with whom he was in contact in the U.S.A. He did, however, know the general scale of effort of the American program and the approximate timing, and this information was passed over. By now his original intention to pass on only such information as was the result of his own work had been dropped and he did provide some technical information about the American gaseous diffusion plant. He told me that he had given the agent some general information about the membranes and had told him that these would be made of sintered nickel powder, though he did not know any technical details. His main contribution was to pass over copies of all the reports prepared in the New York Office of the British Diffusion Mission. These carried the serial letters 'M.S.N.' and he handed over, usually, the manuscript of each report after it had been typed for duplication.

"During this period Fuchs said that he still had no real knowledge of the pile process, or of the significance of plutonium. He paid one short visit to Montreal and knew that the teams there were engaged on the design and construction of a small, heavy water pile. He took no great interest in this work and imagined it could only be related to the long term possibility of the development of atomic energy as a source of power. As far as he could remember, he did not pass any of this to the Russian agent as he regarded it as of little interest. He told me that during this period he got the impression from the agent that the Russians had a great general interest in the project and that its importance was fully appreciated, but he did not believe that anything very serious was being done by the Russians themselves.

Third Period. Los Alamos. August, 1944, to the Summer of 1946.
"When Fuchs went to Los Alamos he realized for the first time the full nature and magnitude of the American atomic energy program and the importance of plutonium as an alternative to U-235 became clear to him. He also learned then that it was intended to build large plutonium-producing pile as an alternative to the U-235 production plant at Oakridge [*sic*].

"The first contact with the Russian agent after he went to Los Alamos was in February, 1945, when he met him at Boston, Massachusetts. While there Fuchs wrote a report, which he said would have covered several pages, summarizing the whole problem of making an atomic bomb as he then saw it. This report included a statement of the special difficulties that would have to be overcome in making a plutonium bomb. He reported the highly spontaneous fission rate of plutonium and the deduction that a plutonium bomb would have to be detonated by using the implosion method rather than the relatively simple gun method which could be used with U-235. He also reported that the critical mass for plutonium was less than that for U-235 and that about five to fifteen kilograms would be necessary for a bomb. At this time the issue was not clear as to whether uniform compression of the core could be better obtained with a high explosive lens system, or with multipoint detonation over the surface of a uniform sphere of high explosives. He reported the current ideas as to the need for an initiator, though these, at the time, were very vague, and it was thought that a constant neutron source might be sufficient. Finally, when he wrote his report in February, 1945, he referred only to the hollow plutonium core for the atomic bomb as he did not then know anything about the possibility of a solid core.

"He met the Russian agent again in Santa Fe at the end of June, 1945, and this time handed him a detailed report which he had already written in Los Alamos with access to the relevant files so he could be sure that all figures mentioned were correct.

"This second report fully described the plutonium bomb which had, by this time, been designed and was to be tested at 'Trinity.' He provided a sketch of the bomb and its components and gave all the important dimensions. He reported that the bomb would have a solid plutonium core and described the initiator which, he said, would contain about fifty curies of polonium. Full details were given of the tamper, the aluminum shell, and of the high explosive lens system. He told the agent that the two explosives to be used in the system were 'Baratol' and 'Composition B,' though he himself did not know what this really meant in terms of H.E. [High Explosive] Technology.

"The Russian agent was told that the 'Trinity' test was expected to produce an explosion equivalent to about ten kilotons of T.N.T. and was given details of the date and an approximate indication of the site.

"Fuchs told me that, at this time, details of production of pile design, construction and operation were still unknown to him and were, therefore, not passed to the Russian agent. He had several further meetings with him in Santa Fe in the autumn of 1945 and spring of 1946, but could not remember precise dates. During these meetings he gave some information on the delta phase of plutonium and 'probably' made some reference to the use of gallium as an alloying constituent, but he was insistent that he gave no other information on the metallurgy of plutonium and that he did not describe the techniques on its preparation or fabrication.

"During this latter period at Los Alamos, or perhaps soon after he returned to the United Kingdom, Fuchs gave the Russian agent some general information about the possibility of developing a 'mixed' bomb. In particular, he emphasized the advantages of this for the United States because they already had both plutonium production pile and isotope separation plant, and could make use of both materials.

"The Russian agent with whom he was in contact during his whole period in the United States (while at New York and Los Alamos) was rather more capable of understanding the information which he was given than had been the case with his contact in the United Kingdom. Fuchs described him as being perhaps an engineer or chemical engineer. He clearly had no detailed knowledge of nuclear physics or of the sort of mathematics with which Fuchs was competent to deal.

Fourth Period. Harwell. Summer of 1946 to spring of 1949.

"Fuchs explained that during this last period he was having increasing doubts on the wisdom of passing information to the Russians, and he assured me that he did not give them all the information that he could have given and that he did not always answer questions that were put to him. He was, for instance, several times asked for the American rate of production and stockpile of atomic bomb, and about the United Kingdom program. As to the first, he only repeated the information which he had had at the time that he left Los Alamos and said that he knew nothing thereafter. On the United Kingdom program he reported the arguments which had led to the decision to build air-cooled, rather than water-cooled, piles and gave the design figures for the plutonium output from the two Windscale piles that were under construction. Later he told the agent of the plan to build an 'L.S.D.' isotope separation plant in order to economize on raw material.

"While at Harwell Fuchs filled in the picture of the plutonium bomb that he had already given from Los Alamos and provided mathematical details such as those relating to the equation of state, the probability of pre-detonation, and the blast calculations of the Hiroshima and Nagasaki bomb. He was asked some questions about the Bikini test and gave the formula for radiation intensity as a function of distance, but was asked no questions and gave no information about the Eniwetok test. At the end of 1946 or early 1947 he gave the net yield from the referenced formula for the efficiency of an atom bomb explosion. Up to February, 1949, he was several times asked to give the full derivation of this formula, but never provided it.

"During 1947 Fuchs was asked on one occasion by the Russian agent for any information he could give about 'the tritium bomb.' He said that he was very surprised to have the question put in these particular terms and it suggested to him (as had the earlier request for information about the electro-magnetic isotopes separation process) that the Russians were getting information from other sources.

"In reply to the question Fuchs gave the T-D cross-section value before this was declassified, and he also gave all that he knew from his Los Alamos period on the methods for calculating radiation loss and the ideal ignition temperature. He also described the current ideas in Los Alamos when he left on the design and method of operation of a super bomb, mentioning, in particular, the combination fission bomb, the tritium initiating reaction and the final deuterium one.

"Fuchs told me that during 1948 he did not pass to the Russian agent a great deal of information that was then in his possession as a result of his work at Harwell on the design and method of operation of plutonium production pile. He was surprised that very few questions were put to him on this subject, though, during 1948, he was asked how the uranium metal rods were fabricated.

"He did not give this information and was impressed at the time with the peculiarity that this one specific detail had been asked for while there were not questions about the recovery of uranium from its ore, the preparation of pure uranium complements or metals, canning techniques, dimensions of uranium rod or the preparation, purity and dimensions of graphite. He told me that he believed that 'he might have given' the lattice spacing for one particular pile while he was in the United States, but he did not give the lattice formula, nor was he asked for information on how to calculate a pile lattice, and he gave no information on exponential experiments.

"He was never asked anything about Wigner expansion, though he did give, at some period which he could not precisely remember, Los Alamos information on the possibility, which was then being considered, of the release of energy from graphite used as moderator in a pile, and may have mentioned the problem of movement in the graphite as affecting the alignment of cooling tubes.

"Fuchs told me that he was never asked, and never gave 'fundamental nuclear physics data relating to the fission reaction.'

"During this last period Fuchs said that he had given the agent general information on the idea current at Harwell on new types of reactors, including the 'flame trap' design, the 'ball' and 'sandwich' reactors, fast reactor and breeders.

"During the latter part of 1948 he was asked on one occasion for a specific Chalk River report, dealing with neutron distribution in the N.R.X. pile, which he had never seen. He was also told that 'there is a report on mixing devices' and was asked whether he could get it. He had not, at the time, seen this report but identified it at Harwell and provided extracts from it. This information refers to a particular design detail that is relevant only to the Windscale air-cooled production pile.

"He was also asked about the solvent extraction process. He knew hardly anything of this, but was able to get some very limited information from Harwell reports and passed this over, though he believed that this was of no great significance.

"All these questions confirmed his opinion that the Russians had access to information from another source or sources.

"Finally, I discussed with Fuchs the nature of the 'atomic explosion' that had taken place in Russia in the Autumn of 1949. He told me that he would have expected this to be due to a plutonium bomb in the light of all the information he had passed to the Russians. He, personally, believed that this conclusion was confirmed by the measurements on the airborne fission products that had been collected, though he recognized the doubt in this interpretation due to the lack of chemical evidence for the presence of plutonium in the cloud. He said that he was, however, extremely surprised that the Russian explosion had taken place so soon as he had been convinced that the information he had given could not have been applied so quickly and that the Russians would not have the engineering design and construction facilities that would be needed to build large production plants in such a short time.

"I formed the impression that, throughout the interview, Fuchs was genuinely trying to remember and report all the information that he had given to the Russian agents with whom he had been in contact, and that he was not withholding anything. He seemed, on the contrary, to be trying his best to help me to evaluate the present position of atomic energy works in Russia in the light of the information that he had, and had not, passed to them."

This is for your confidential information.
With expressions of my highest esteem and best regards,

Sincerely yours,

J. Edgar Hoover

Appendix C

Harry Gold's Statements to the FBI, May 22 and July 10, 1950

DETAILS: *At Philadelphia, Pa.*   Philadelphia, Penna.
                                                        May 22, 1950

"I, HARRY GOLD, of 6823 Kindred Street, Philadelphia, Pennsylvania, make the following voluntary statement to RICHARD E. BRENNAN and T. SCOTT MILLER, JR., who have identified themselves to me as Special Agents of the Federal Bureau of Investigation, United States Department of Justice. No threats or promises have been made to me, and I realize that any statement I make may be used against me in a court of law. I have been advised that I may secure the services of an attorney.

"In the summer of 1936 I made several inquiries concerning the Communist Party of the United States. At this time I was employed as a chemist by the Pennsylvania Sugar Company, of 1037 North Delaware Avenue, Philadelphia, Pennsylvania.

"In the fall of 1936 I was visited at my home by a man who identified himself as PAUL SMITH. He said that he understood that I was a chemist, and he thought that possibly I might be interested in aiding in the procurement of industrial information for the Soviet Union. This began a period of industrial espionage on my part which lasted until 1943. My association with SMITH was of relatively short duration, during which time I furnished him with some data concerning processes that were being worked on in the laboratory of the Pennsylvania Sugar Company and subsidiaries. This data was as complete and factual as I could make it.

"SMITH, whose name was obviously false, was followed in succession by two men, one of whom identified themselves as FRED, who had a pronounced Russian accent.

"In the early summer of 1938 the possibilities of Pennsylvania Sugar Company had pretty well petered out, and I was several times pressed to try and obtain other sources of information. By this I mean people who could furnish us with technical data. However, in my circle of friends there were none who were even the remotest likely candidate, and so I did nothing. This led to a break of over two years, during which time I attended college in Cincinnati. I graduated in 1940.

"On my return to Philadelphia I was again contacted by the people with whom I had worked before. I was called on the phone in July, 1940, and I went down town to see this man, who turned out to be JACOB GOLOS. He again pressed me to continue the work which I had done previously, and I agreed. However, it was pretty sporadic in nature, and, with the exception of the one contact that he gave me, ABRAHAM BROTHMAN, nothing much came of it. I was supposed to get information of a technical nature from BROTHMAN, but very little came of that, simply because he was extremely unreliable in getting material together. He gave me some data on mixing equipment which was practically all his design, and it seemed to me that practically eveything he gave me at any time was his own invention or design. BROTHMAN kept pressing me on several occasions, and wanted to know about the possibility of his doing consulting work for the Soviet Union on an open basis, as a private individual, and they acting as representatives of their government to this company, and whenever I mentioned it to the people with whom I was in touch they discounted the idea and wouldn't listen to it at all.

"I never told BROTHMAN of my association with the Soviet Union, but I think that he suspected it because of the way that I operated—I introduced myself by another name.

"I knew GOLOS for a very brief time, and he was followed very shortly by a man called SAM about the end of 1940. It was with SAM that my association continued uninterruptedly as a contact. I used to meet SAM almost always in New York. Sometimes, very rarely, he would come to Philadelphia, but usually it was in New York, usually on a street corner that we met. Normally we went for a walk. Sometimes, but rarely, we had something to eat. SAM did not have a Russian accent, but I had an idea he was a Russian.

"Shortly after I met SAM he told me that there was not much purpose to continuing this work in general, and that the best thing I could do would be to forget about it, and this state continued from late 1940 until the fall of 1941, after Russia was attacked by Germany. Then SAM called me up, I met him, and he told me that we had to begin an intensive campaign for obtaining information for the Soviet Union. This happened about a couple of months after Russia was attacked by Germany. At that time I made a half-dozen trips to upper New York state, namely, Syracuse, Rochester, and Buffalo. I was to transmit information—I acted as a go-between.

"What I did on each of these occasions was to obtain information from someone that I didn't know but who was, I'm pretty sure, an American, a native, and I gave it over to SAM, or sometimes not to SAM but to someone who I did not know by name or anything. I just got it and either I received material whose nature I did not know except that they were very bulky packets, and in a matter of hours, or sometimes even minutes, turned it over to a third person, sometimes SAM. There was one man that I saw twice in Rochester, one man that I saw twice in Buffalo, and there were two others that I saw once, and I got the definite impression in each case that they were native Americans. Sometimes I travelled with the information from one city to the adjacent one, that is, say, from Rochester to Buffalo before turning it over.

"In very early 1944 I was told by SAM that I was to undertake an extremely important effort. This was to be work of so critical a nature that I was to think twice and three times before I ever spoke a word concerning it to anyone, or before I made a move, that is before I spoke to anyone concerned in it. He didn't elaborate on what the nature of the work actually was but he gave me the details of an arrangement whereby I met Doctor KLAUS FUCHS. This meeting took place on the east side of New York on a Saturday. As I recall, the arrangements for actual recognition included the fact that I was to carry a pair of gloves in one hand, plus a green-covered book, and Dr. FUCHS was to carry a hand ball in one hand. I cannot recall whether SAM gave me Dr. FUCHS' name, he may have. In any event, we met in, I believe, late February or early March of 1944. I introduced myself to him as RAYMOND. He never used the name. He knew it was a phony. He introduced himself to me as KLAUS FUCHS.

"We went for a brief walk and then took a cab uptown to a restaurant around 3d Avenue in the 50's, where we had dinner, but we did not speak much there. Afterwards we went for a walk, during which we completed arrangements for further meetings. Among these arrangements were:

1. We were to be extremely careful and never meet in a restaurant again.

2. We were only to meet for as brief a period as was necessary to complete whatever we had to do.

3. Each meeting included complete arrangements for further meetings and provisions were made for alternate dates and places, but we were never to meet in the same place twice.

"He told me during the first and second meetings that he was with the British Mission working with the Manhattan Engineer Project. He also explained to me the manpower set-up of the British group as he knew it. He told me that they were working on the separation of isotopes, and it seems to me that there was at least implied the eventual utilization of the energy produced by nuclear fission in the form of a weapon. One thing he told me on many occasions was that they worked in extremely tight compartments, and that one group did not know what the other group was doing. This I can verify by the fact that he told me that he thought that there was possibility of a large-scale installation for isotope separation projected for future development somewhere, he thought, down in Georgia or Alabama. This, of course, later turned out to be Oak Ridge.

"The second meeting with FUCHS consisted of an amplification of our arrangements for meeting and a description by FUCHS of the physical and personnel set-up of the Manhattan Engineer Project. This meeting was in New York.

"During these first two meetings neither Dr. FUCHS nor I made any direct reference to his supplying me with information, but it was more or less mutually understood that he was to supply me with information from the work he was doing.

"The second meeting took place with FUCHS a few weeks following the first one somewhere in Upper Manhattan. Successive meetings took place in a number of widely separated localities, including the Bronx, Brooklyn, Manhattan, and Queens. There were, in all, until the summer of 1944, a total of in the neighborhood of five meetings, on at least two of which occasions I obtained (from Dr. FUCHS) information. This consisted of a number of folded sheets of paper containing (during one brief glance that I took on one occasion) mathematical equations which seemed to concern mathematical derivations. This data I turned over to, I believe, SAM's successor, JOHN.

"I would like to add that SAM was succeeded by a man named JOHN shortly after I met Dr. FUCHS. I do not believe that I ever turned any information over to SAM.

"On the occasions when I turned over information which I had obtained from Dr. FUCHS, the time interval involved was very short; by short I mean a half-hour at the most.

"The exact dates that the information was given to me in New York by Dr. FUCHS I cannot accurately say, except that they were probably between April and June or July of 1944. In August of 1944 Dr. FUCHS failed to show up for his scheduled meeting. This was to be in the vicinity of a movie theater near the Eastern Parkway in Brooklyn. He did not show up for the alternate appointment and I had no means of telling where he had gone, though he had mentioned that he was due to leave for another location. The only information he had was that he thought it was somewhere in Mexico, not New Mexico. JOHN then obtained the information whereby he was once more enabled to get in touch with Dr. FUCHS. He gave me the address of Mrs. HEINEMAN in Cambridge, Massachusetts, who is, I believe, Dr. FUCHS' sister. I went to see her in September of 1944. The family was away on vacation. I did see her the second time that I went to Cambridge, which was in the fall of 1944. I told her that I was a friend of Dr. FUCHS; that I had met him in New York; that I happened to be passing through Boston on business and I just wondered if she knew where KLAUS was. I used here the same name that I had used on meeting KLAUS, which was RAYMOND. She told me that KLAUS was due about Christmas time, was very fond of Mrs. HEINEMAN's children and he had written her that he would be coming home about that time. She did not tell me where he was except that it was somewhere out west. So, I left an envelope containing a name and telephone number in Manhattan. This name I think may have contained the first name 'JEROME' or at least a name with a J was somewhat similar to KAPLUN (phonetic). This is not the name. About all that I can say about it is that it evokes a familiar sound—a familiar memory chord.

"Early in 1945, JOHN got in touch with me and said that we had heard from Dr. FUCHS. I went up to Cambridge and saw KLAUS there. He told me that he was working at a place called Los Alamos in New Mexico, he said some distance from Santa Fe. He also gave me written information at that time and we made an arrangement to meet in June of that year in Santa Fe. This meeting took place in the home of Mrs. HEINEMAN in Cambridge, Massachusetts, but she was not present at the time of our conversation. The whole meeting was of very brief duration. Before I met Dr. FUCHS on this occasion, I was given a sum of approximately $1500, as I recall, to offer to Dr. FUCHS, should he need it. I was told to be very diplomatic about this matter so as not to offend him. He turned it down cold. He turned down cold even my tentative offer, so that when I returned to New York, I gave the money back to JOHN, along with the information which FUCHS had given me at this time.

"During my vacation in June of 1945, I went to Santa Fe via Albuquerque and met Dr. FUCHS there. He gave me another set of data and we agreed to meet again in late September of the same year in Santa Fe. I took this information back with me to New York and gave it to JOHN. Our conversation there was extremely brief and even there, as when he worked in New York, he was dubious about the possibilities for any real and immediate utilization of atomic energy in the form of a weapon. I do not exactly recall the circumstances under which I turned this information over to JOHN in New York. I traveled to Albuquerque, and finally by bus to Santa Fe. My meeting with Dr. FUCHS was on a Saturday afternoon. Then I returned from Santa Fe to Albuquerque by bus on the same day. As I recall, I slept in the hallway of a rooming house where those who were unable to obtain hotel accommodations were bedded. I returned the following day from Albuquerque to Chicago and then via Chicago by plane to either New York or Washington and then by train to Philadelphia. This jumbled up method of travel was necessitated by the traveling conditions at that time.

"Here, I would like to make the following statement: All of the expenses involved in any of the work that I did were paid for by me entirely out of my own funds. Immediately upon my return to New York, I turned over the information which FUCHS had given me, to JOHN. The next meeting with Dr. FUCHS took place in late September 1945. I again met him in Santa Fe, this time on the outskirts. He had a car, a rather dilapidated affair, which he had borrowed, and we conducted all of our conversation in it. He gave me some information again. Also, he told me he had been present at the initial large-scale trial of nuclear fission at Alamogordo in New Mexico, and also described to me the tremendous wonderment that had descended upon even those who had the most intimate knowledge of the potentialities of the weapon—most especially on the occasion of the dropping of the bomb on Hiroshima. It is my best understanding that he was actually present with the group or certainly near the group that set off the trial bomb at Alamogordo.

"Dr. FUCHS told me also at this time that he would probably return to England soon but that by paying a call to his sister I could ascertain just when. This statement may not be completely accurate in this sense, since it also seems to me that he gave a definite time, about Christmas week of 1945 when he expected to again be in Cambridge.

"In early evening I returned by bus to Albuquerque and got an early morning plane from Albuquerque to Kansas City. There, I had to transfer to a train which took me to Chicago and I went from Chicago by way of New York Central to New York. From New York I went to Philadelphia and no more than several days later, turned over the information that Dr. FUCHS had given me to JOHN in New York City. To the best of my recollection, it was out beyond Jackson Heights somewhere in Queens where I turned this information over to JOHN.

"Here again, I would like to repeat what I previously said, that this jumbled up method of travel was necessitated by the lack of facilities at that time and heavy travel at that time and was not intended as a means of throwing anyone off my trail.

"This was the last time that I saw Dr. FUCHS or obtained information from him.

"I made either one or two attempts to see Dr. FUCHS again at the home of his sister. This effort was not successful in that he was still in

New Mexico. After the possible second attempt which was in either late January or early February, 1946, my scheduled appointment to report to JOHN did not take place. This was to be at the Earle Theater in the Bronx, New York. I never saw or heard from JOHN again.

"In summary, to the best of my recollection, Dr. FUCHS gave me information on five occasions. Two times in New York in the Spring and Summer of 1944, one in Cambridge in very early 1945, probably January and twice in Santa Fe, the first time in June, the second time in late September, both 1945. On each occasion I subsequently turned this information over to JOHN. It is possible, although I doubt it, that SAM received from me the first information which I had obtained from Dr. FUCHS.

"During my association with Dr. FUCHS, SAM, and JOHN, I fully realized that the information which Dr. FUCHS was supplying me and which I turned over to SAM or JOHN was for the benefit of the Soviet Union. I also surmised that the information concerned the separation of isotopes and the subsequent nuclear fission to release tremendous amounts of energy even in the form of a weapon.

"I began the work of industrial spying for the Soviet Union in 1936, with the full realization of what I was doing. I thought that I would be helping a nation whose final aims I approved, along the road to industrial strength. Particularly, I was taken with the idea that whatever I did would go to help make living conditions far more advanced along the road as we know them here in the United States. To amplify, I felt that the industrial set up of a Nation which had only very recently begun to get any kind of a basic industry going, was so far inferior to what existed in other countries, that anything that I could do would be helpful.

"Sometimes I was truck by doubts, twofold in nature;

"Number one—Especially early in my association from 1936 to 1938 it seemed that the information I was turning over was exceedingly non-utilitarian but I was always assured that it was well received.

"Second, the one fear that troubled me during the entire time from 1936 on was the possibility that in the event of exposure my family, which had no idea, not even the very slightest, of the work I was engaging in, would be completely and horribly disgraced.

"This affair grew and as I imagine is the case with dealings of such a nature, I got so involved that even had I wanted to, it would have been extremely difficult to get out. However, I would like to qualify this last statement by saying, while on several occasions I did desire to once and for all stop doing this work, that I never once actually suggested it to any of the people with whom I worked. The longest break in all this time was the two year period when I went to school in Cincinnati, 1938 to 1940.

"My reaction to the work that I did with Dr. FUCHS was twofold in nature. On the one hand I felt that as an ally, I was only helping the Soviet Union obtain information that I thought it was entitled to. I was troubled even by this, but I persistently put any thought out of my mind and as I have previously said, I was in so deep that I was, to a certain extent, bewildered and didn't know what to do. Secondly, the realization that I was turning over information to another power concerning a weapon was so frightening that the only thing I could do was to shove it away as far back in my mind as I could and simply not think on the matter at all.

"To amplify somewhat, what I did except during the periods when I actually had to plan to meet Dr. FUCHS or to transmit what he gave me to JOHN, was to simply blot out of my mind as well as I could any thoughts whatever on the subject. I hoped, as many people do, that atomic energy would never again be employed as a weapon.

"I would like to state that so far that I succeed in keeping this whole matter from my thoughts, that some of the feelings I have just stated are more or less recent, in the sense that I have only recently given them complete formulation.

"I would like now to make as absolute a statement as possible concerning the following:

"Neither my mother, father nor brother ever had the slightest inkling that I was ever engaged in any work of such a nature, either industrial espionage or the later affair with Dr. FUCHS. This represented a considerable strain to keep concealing from them over so long a period, but I did succeed by one maneuver or another and as of even this minute, they have not the vaguest idea what went on. The same applies to any people that I have known, and been in intimate contact with, and have worked side by side with, and have been close friends with, over the period of the last 14 years. This particularly applies to people with whom I worked either in industrial laboratories or more recently, in medical research.

"The one possible exception to the above is my former employer and acquaintance, ABRAHAM BROTHMAN, and while I surmised that he suspected that I had given industrial processes to the Soviet Union, still he had not the slightest idea of my work with Dr. FUCHS.

"I read the above typewritten statement consisting of nine pages and have initialed each page and the corrections thereof inasmuch as all my statements therein are true to the best of my knowledge and belief."

/S/ HARRY GOLD
5-22-50
Philadelphia,
Penna.

Witnessed:
T. S. MILLER, JR.   RICHARD E. BRENNAN
Special Agent   Special Agent
FBI, Justice   FBI, Justice
5-22-50, Phila., Pa.

"In addition to the previous nine pages in this statement, I wish to make the following additional statements.

"On my final visit to the HEINEMANS' home in Cambridge, Massachusetts, I very briefly met ROBERT HEINEMAN. This is the only time I ever saw him.

"The entire idea of the underhanded work required in the industrial and subsequent spying was always very repugnant to me. I always considered myself as just a worker in a particular field requiring some degree of technical skill and diligence; and I have been most happy when I was just left alone in the laboratory to work. I always looked forward to the time when such actions as I have described in the body of this statement would no longer be necessary. I even expressed that to the people with whom I was in contact, and they agreed. This is not an attempt to shift any of the blame for my actions away from me."

/S/ HARRY GOLD
5-22-50
Philadelphia,
Penna.

RICHARD E. BRENNAN
Special Agent, FBI, Justice

T. SCOTT MILLER, JR.
FBI, Justice
5-22-50, Phila., Penn.

On July 10, 1950, HARRY GOLD furnished the following supplemental signed statement concerning his meetings with EMIL JULIUS KLAUS FUCHS to SAs T. SCOTT MILLER, JR., and RICHARD E. BRENNAN:

"I, HARRY GOLD, hereby make the following voluntary statement to T. SCOTT MILLER, JR., and RICHARD E. BRENNAN, who have identified themselves to me as Special Agents of the Federal Bureau of Investigation. No threats or promises have been made me, and I realize that I do not have to make any statement, and any statement I do make may be used against me in a Court of Law. I realize that I have a right to counsel.

"I would like to add the following to the statement which I gave the above agents on May 22, 1950. The matter concerns an elaboration on my various meetings with KLAUS FUCHS.

"The first meeting took place in late January or very early February 1944, and was at the Henry Street Settlement on the East side of New York.

"The second meeting, and I had set the place, and the time had been agreed upon mutually by KLAUS and myself, was on the Northwest corner of 59th Street and Lexington Avenue; this was about ten days to two weeks after our initial contact. The corner I have specified has a bank with very tall colonnades, and there is a subway entrance in the bank building itself. I met KLAUS directly under one of the first colonnades, or possibly along 59th Street on the South side of the bank. We walked in the general direction of the Queensboro Bridge, the intention in my mind being that we would walk across the bridge and into Queens itself. However, this bridge was closed to foot traffic during this period, and instead we walked along 1st avenue, North of the bridge. We may have walked as far North as 75th Street, and we may have gone back to 2nd Avenue, and very likely we made at least several passages on the dark deserted streets between 1st Avenue and 2nd, between 55th Street and 70th Street.

"My recollection of the third meeting with KLAUS FUCHS—It occurred in March of 1944. I recall this clearly, it was still quite cold and we both wore overcoats. This took place on Madison Avenue in the 70's, and we immediately turned into one of the dark deserted side streets toward 5th, and the transfer of information took place there. The whole affair took possibly 30 seconds or one minute, and I immediately walked ahead of KLAUS and down 5th Avenue toward 75th Street and 6th Avenue, where approximately 15 minutes later I turned over the information to JOHN. Here again the meeting was one of the briefest possible duration, possibly a minute or so.

"The fourth meeting with KLAUS FUCHS took place in the Bronx of New York, and was in front of a large movie theater on the Grand Concourse near Fordham Road, but not quite that far.

"We went for a walk partly along the Grand Concourse, but usually on the side streets, during which time we discussed the next meeting which was to be at Queens, and at which a second transfer of information was to take place, and the exact details were arranged. After this I took KLAUS to dinner, it was a wet and somewhat chilled night for April, and as I recall, he had a bad cough, and I did not wish to expose him to the elements any more than was necessary. This whole procedure of going to dinner in a restaurant was against anything that we had previously set forth as a matter of technique of meeting, but I felt that the circumstances justified such a deviation from the rules. We had dinner at which we discussed a number of matters, including music and chess. It was also at this dinner that we agreed that should either of us ever be questioned as to how we happened to meet, that the story would be that we had met at one of the New York Philharmonic's concerts sometime in March of 1944, and in Carnegie Hall; the idea was that we had had adjacent seats and had talked together in the lobby during the intermission. Also, there was the idea that at a subsequent time I would go to the files of a New York paper, most likely the *New York Sun*, and I believe I mentioned this paper to KLAUS, and would look up the date of such a concert and would determine what numbers or what musical selections had been on the program. I would then give KLAUS a list of the musical selections so that we would both be familiar with the program were we questioned. The restaurant to which I took KLAUS to dinner was called Rosenhein's—and is adjacent to Alexander's Department Store on Fordham Road and the Grand Concourse. After we had dinner and emerged from Rosenhein's—the weather was still nasty—I recall a cold drizzle was falling, we took a cab and went downtown to the neighborhood of the 80's and Madison Avenue. There is some possibility that it may have been the 90's and Lexington Avenue. We went into a small bar which also contained tables, and sat at one of these tables and had several drinks. We then left the bar and put KLAUS in a cab. I now recall that the reason for KLAUS taking the cab was that he lived on the other side of Manhattan, and direct public transportation through Central Park late at night is very difficult. After KLAUS's cab had departed I waited for a few moments until an empty cab came along, and took this to the Pennsylvania Station and then took the next train to Philadelphia.

"My fifth meeting with KLAUS FUCHS took place in May of 1944, and was in Queens, not too far from Queensboro Plaza. I recall the event clearly because I got lost in the neighborhood of Queens Plaza and had to take a cab for a distance of about a half a mile until I came to the spot I had indicated to KLAUS FUCHS. I was possibly two or three minutes late; he was already there. On this occasion FUCHS gave me the second packet of information, again consisting of some 25 to 40 pages. The total time of the meeting was not over three or four minutes, and after I left him, I walked rapidly further out in Queens, and then took an elevated train some distance further, possibly a ten minute ride. After leaving the elevated I was in the general area where I was to meet JOHN. I still had about five minutes to wait and I recall stopping near a drug store, and taking a glimpse at the information that KLAUS had turned over to me. This was in a very small but distinctive writing; it was in ink, and consisted mainly of mathematical derivations. There was also further along in the report a good deal of descriptive detail. I did not look at the report for much more than two minutes at the most. About five minutes after this I went to the place where I was to meet JOHN, this was somewhere between Woodside and Jackson Heights, and somewhere close to the elevated line which runs out Queens and ends in Flushing; there I turned over the information to JOHN. The total time of transfer was not more than one minute with hardly a word said. The time of the meeting with KLAUS was about 7:00 o'clock in the evening, possibly somewhat earlier. The time of the meeting with JOHN was about 7:30. As I recall, it was dark or certainly very early evening when I met JOHN, but this may have been due to the fact that the entire day was heavily overcast.

"The sixth meeting with KLAUS FUCHS occurred in Brooklyn, and it was somewhere in the area of Boro [Borough?] Hall. This was in June, 1944.

"During this meeting I recall that KLAUS FUCHS told me that there was some possibility that this sister who lived in Cambridge, Massachusetts, he did not give me her name, however, might come to New York. He explained to me that his sister was married and had two children, and that she was having great difficulty with her husband and that she was fully intending to leave her husband and come to New York. Should this occur, KLAUS told me that he would like very much to be able to share an apartment with his sister. I gathered that he and his sister were very close to each other and also the fact that KLAUS was extremely fond of the children. KLAUS told me that he brought up the matter because he first wanted me to inquire of my superior whether such an action would be all right. I said that I would make the inquiry. This conversation took place while we were walking away from Boro Hall and further into Brooklyn. I recall clearly that after this meeting I met JOHN, on the very same evening. The meeting with KLAUS took place at about 8:30 and lasted for possibly half to three quarters of an hour, possibly even an hour, so that I met JOHN sometime about 9:00.

"There may have been during this meeting with JOHN and the just completed one with KLAUS FUCHS, some transfer of information from KLAUS to me and then from myself to JOHN; however, I do not clearly recall such an event. I do not recall much of the subject of my conversation with JOHN, except that he was extremely satisfied with the way that things were going and that he left me after a very brief meeting of possibly five to ten minutes. It is this briefness of the meeting with JOHN that makes me think that there may have been some transfer of information.

"The seventh meeting with KLAUS FUCHS occurred in either very late June, but most likely in early July of 1944. This took place near an art museum in the 80's, and on the West side of 5th Avenue. We went for a long walk, almost entirely in Central Park and in the many winding roads and small paths leading through the park itself. This meeting took at least an hour and a half and was a very leisurely one.

"During this walk KLAUS told me that there was some possibility that later in the year or early the next year that he would be transferred somewhere to the Southwest. He thought that possibly this would be Mexico. He also told me at this time that his brother, GERHARD, was now in Switzerland and was convalescing as a result of having been only recently released from a German concentration camp. I gathered from the conversation that GERHARD was of the same political conviction as KLAUS FUCHS. I also told KLAUS that it would be perfectly all right, should his sister come to New York, for him to take an apartment along with her and the children. Actually, I had not mentioned the matter to JOHN at all, but had taken it upon myself to tell KLAUS that such a proceeding was O.K.

"The eighth meeting was to take place in Brooklyn and was to be in about two weeks, possibly three, after the meeting in Central Park in July; this would place it about the end of July 1944. The meeting was to occur in front of the Bell Cinema, which is just off the Eastern Parkway in Brooklyn and very close to the Brooklyn Museum of Art, only it is on the opposite side of the Parkway from the Museum. This meeting did not take place, nor did a subsequent one which had been scheduled for such an eventuality, on Central Park West, and somewhere about 96th Street and possibly somewhat above 96th.

"On the second occasion I became very worried, particularly since the area is very close to a section of New York where 'muggings' often occur, and also the fact that KLAUS was of slight build and might seem an inviting prey. I would like to emphasize that neither the meeting at the Bell Cinema in Brooklyn, nor the one on Central Park West, about 96th Street, occurred because of the fact that KLAUS FUCHS did not show up—I was there on both occasions.

"When I reported the fact of the second unsuccessful attempt with KLAUS FUCHS to JOHN, we held a very long discussion lasting possibly two hours, in which we speculated upon just what the difficulty might be. Our principal trouble was to decide whether KLAUS, for some reason was unable to keep the meetings, if he was still in New York, or whether he had actually left New York.

"On the occasion of my next meeting with JOHN, which was in, I believe very late August of 1944, the following events occurred:

"This meeting took place on a very early Sunday morning, I would say about 8:30 to 9:00 o'clock, and it occurred in downtown New York, near Washington Square. At this time JOHN told me that he had ascertained the address of KLAUS FUCHS, and that I should, that very morning, make inquiry at that address as to whether KLAUS was there. Toward this end I went some distance up town and in one of the railroad stations I purchased a book called JOSEPH THE PROVIDER which had recently been published and had been written by THOMAS MANN. On the inside cover of this book I printed very legibly the following, 'K. FUCHS, 128 West 77th Street, New York, N.Y.' which address JOHN had given me. It was this book that I took with me to the address given. I recall, about a four-story dwelling, used as an apartment house. This building was on the South side of the street. I looked around outside the building, and down a very short flight of steps, and just to the side of the door leading into the building was an old man whom I took to be a janitor; he was handling some rubbish from the apartment house. I believe that I made an inquiry of him as to whether KLAUS FUCHS lived there, but he appeared somewhat puzzled by my question. I then opened the door and went into the vestibule. There may have been a very short flight of steps leading up to the vestibule. There to my gratification, above the nameplates, I saw one reading, 'Dr. KLAUS FUCHS' though it might have read, 'Dr. K. FUCHS.' I pressed the buzzer, but there was no answer, and finally I opened the door leading from the vestibule into the main hall; this door was unlocked. I went into the main hall, along the first floor, looking for the apartment which as I recall had been given alongside the nameplate as being 1-E or 1-F (there is some possibility that it may have been 1-D). As I walked along the vestibule a door opened, either in the very apartment where KLAUS was supposed to live or possibly in the one alongside it, and an old woman looked out. Also at that time there came behind me the janitor. I asked the woman for the apartment of Dr. FUCHS, and at this time the janitor joined in the conversation. I can not recall clearly whether it was he or she who told me that Dr. FUCHS was no longer there. On further questioning, when I asked how I could get in touch with him they said that they did not think that I could; that he had left town for 'somewhere on a boat.' I then explained to them that I was a friend of Dr. FUCHS and that I had merely wanted to return this book which he had loaned to me. I did not deem it wise to make any further inquiries at 128 West 77th Street, but I do recall the janitor and the woman, who I believe was his wife, talking as I left.

"Later that morning, and somewhere between 10:00 and 11:00 o'clock, possibly closer to 11:00, I met JOHN on Broadway, somewhere around 96th and Broadway, and possibly further up on Broadway and very close to Columbia University. I told JOHN about the results of my investigation and we held a long discussion, principally while walking along Riverside Drive and in the area of the 90's. We talked at great length as to how we might possibly send a letter or communication to the 77th Street address with the hope that it would be forwarded to FUCHS. I believe that our conclusion was that such a procedure might be too risky as it might involve an awkward explanation on KLAUS' part to the authorities, who were very likely censoring all mail. After some further discussion the only conclusion we could come to, and the advice which JOHN gave me, was to 'sit tight.'

"On the occasion of a subsequent meeting in early September of 1944, we again discussed at length the matter of getting in touch with KLAUS FUCHS, and it was there, I believe, that I mentioned the fact that FUCHS had a sister who lived in Boston. Now it may be possible that JOHN himself may have brought up the matter of FUCHS' sister. I believe this latter to be true, since I had not previously mentioned anything about FUCHS' sister to JOHN. In any event, JOHN told me that he thought that there lay our best line of inquiry.

"On the occasion of the next meeting, about the middle of September, JOHN told me with great glee that he had ascertained both the name and the whereabouts of FUCHS' sister. The name that he gave me was that of Mrs. ROBERT HEINEMAN, and the address was merely Cambridge, Massachusetts. I do not recall JOHN having given me the street and number.

"I went by coach on a Sunday in very late September to Boston, Massachusetts. I arrived there very early in the evening and recall looking up the address of ROBERT HEINEMAN in the telephone directory. This was, as I recall, 144 Lakeview Street or Avenue, in Cambridge. I went to this address and the entire street was dark as well as the home where the HEINEMANS lived. However, I knocked at the door and a woman answered. I inquired for Mrs. HEINEMAN and the woman replied that the HEINEMANS were still away on their vacation and were not expected back until sometime in October. I gathered somehow that the woman was a housekeeper of some sort. I believe that the woman wanted me to leave my name and address, but I think that I merely said that I would call again sometime in October and that the matter was not very important. I gave no indication that I was from out of town.

"First I returned from Boston to Philadelphia, and then several days later I met JOHN in New York and told him about the results of my trip. He was highly pleased that we had succeeded in locating Mrs. HEINEMAN, and we agreed that in October I would take another trip to Cambridge.

"This second trip to Cambridge occurred in either very late October or most likely in early November. Upon this occasion I took with me a piece of paper or a card inclosed in an envelope, and on this piece of paper were the following instructions: There was given the name of a man and a phone number. I believe that the first name began with a 'J' and that the last name was something like 'KAPLOUN,' but I am not very certain on this point at all. Also on the piece of paper was the information that KLAUS was to call the phone number given, any time—on any morning between the hours of 8:00 and 8:30, and was to give the following message: Merely to say, 'I have arrived in Cambridge and will be here for —————— many days.' This message was printed by me in engineering lettering, but the details were given to me by JOHN. Also, the message was sealed in the envelope. As I have said, I arrived in Cambridge early on a weekday morning and sometime in early November of 1944. The reason for my making the trip during a weekday, and the reason for arriving in the morning, was the recollection I had of a warning from JOHN that it would be inadvisable to be at the HEINEMAN home while ROBERT HEINEMAN was there. The trip took place as I have indicated, and as it was planned. I arrived in Boston on a weekday morning early in November. I then went directly to Cambridge, and at 144 Lakeview Avenue, walked up to the door and rang the bell. A young woman appeared, somewhere in her very early 30's, and I asked for Mrs. HEINEMAN. She said that she was Mrs. HEINEMAN. I told her that I was a friend of KLAUS FUCHS, and for a moment she seemed somewhat puzzled, and then she said, 'Oh, yes, by any chance did you call sometime in September when we were away?' I said, 'Yes, I am the man.' I entered the house and stayed there for possibly half an hour. I noticed that there were two children there, the oldest one a boy called STEVE, and I recall a very small child, and there is also some possibility of a third child, considerably younger than STEVE, whom I took to be about seven years of age, and this third child was a girl of about four. We spoke for some time about KLAUS, and Mrs. HEINEMAN said that she was very glad that he was now in the United States, since they were very close and KLAUS was very fond of the children. She may, at this time have indicated that at some prior time KLAUS visited Cambridge. I told her that I had met KLAUS in New York, and that we had become very firm friends, and that I just happened to be on business in the Boston area and had thought that I would stop by and inquire for him. Mrs. HEINEMAN told me that KLAUS had been transferred somewhere in the Southwest United States, but that she expected him home about Christmas time, as he usually made a great event of bring[ing] presents for the children. I told her that my plans for the future and my whereabouts were very uncertain, and in that eventuality I would leave a message for KLAUS which would tell him how best to get in touch with me. I then gave her the sealed envelope, and told her should KLAUS arrive, to give it to him.

"I then returned to Philadelphia, and some days subsequent, possibly a week or so later, reported the results of my trip to JOHN. At this time I recall we made an emergency arrangement, whereby JOHN could get in touch with me should this other party, the one with the phone number in Manhattan, advise JOHN that FUCHS was now in Cambridge. This emergency arrangement, which would even at that have involved the passage of several days, was never used, and instead, in the first week in January 1945, JOHN called me shortly before 7:00 A.M., on a weekday morning, just as I was getting ready to leave for work; with some difficulty he described to me the fact that he was in a gasoline station, near what I finally determined to be Oxford Circle section of Philadelphia. JOHN wanted to know if I would come down there an[d] meet him. I did so. It was a very snowy morning, I recall it well, and JOHN was wet. We got in the car again and went down to the terminal in Frankford, where JOHN told me that he had just the previous day received notification that FUCHS was now at Cambridge. He also told me at that time that the reason he had not used the emergency meeting was that he had some other affairs to attend to which would have taken him out of New York, and where he would have been unable to get in touch with me. He then told me that I must, as soon as possible, arrange to go to Cambridge. I did so. I believe that I met JOHN on a Tuesday or Wednesday, and that I arrived in Cambridge on most likely a Friday. I went directly to the HEINEMAN home, this was in the morning, and when I knocked I was admitted by, I believe, a servant girl. KLAUS was there and welcomed me, Mrs. HEINEMAN left after a few minutes and excused herself, saying, 'I have to pick up the children from the school.' KLAUS asked me to go upstairs with him to his room which was the front one looking out on the street, and we sat there for possibly 15 or 20 minutes, during which time the following took place: KLAUS told me that he was located at an atomic energy experimental station which was called Los Alamos and which was located some 30 miles away from Santa Fe, New Mexico. He said that Los Alamos had once been a very exclusive boys' school, and that there was nothing else in that area. The nearest habitation of any kind was Santa Fe. He told me that he was getting along very well there, but that he was strictly limited in regard to being able to leave Los Alamos. He said that it had only been with the greatest difficulty and due to the fact that he had gotten a bit ahead of his work, as regards the rest of the group, that he had been able to wangle time off to come to Cambridge. I had, previously, that is on the occasion of my meeting with JOHN in Philadelphia, been told of an arrangement which involved meeting KLAUS again in Cambridge, should he make another trip. The place of the meeting was to be somewhere in the area of the Charles River. JOHN told me that it would be inadvisable to meet at the HEINEMAN home again and we were only doing so this time because it was the only way I could meet KLAUS without utilizing too lengthy a message or set of instructions. When I mentioned the proposed meeting near the Charles River to KLAUS, he told me that such would be impossible; that he was certain that it would be a very long time, possibly even a year, before he could again leave Los Alamos, and that the next meeting would have to take place in Santa Fe. We discussed this matter at some length. I believe that KLAUS told me that about April he would again have information for me, but I told him that I could not possibly get to Santa Fe in April. We finally set a date which was very early in June, and we also set the exact hour, which as I recall, was 4:00 o'clock in the afternoon of the first Saturday in June. KLAUS showed me a map of Santa Fe, and indicated on it the Castillo Street Bridge over the Rio Santa Fe. He also told me that he would make every effort to keep this appointment.

"To the best of my recollection, I recall that should this scheduled meeting on the first Saturday in June not take place, that there was provision made for an alternate meeting, most likely on the first Saturday in the following month, and at the same time and place.

"KLAUS gave me a quite considerable packet of information, and by this time, I recall, Mrs. HEINEMAN had returned and one of the children peered curiously into the room. Mrs. HEINEMAN called the child back, though possibly it may have been the housekeeper who called the child back. In any event the child was called away. There also occurred the following events:

"As a Christmas present I gave KLAUS a wallet of the very thin dress or opera type. Also, I had been given the sum of $1,500.00 by JOHN with instructions to give it to KLAUS, but that I must proceed very delicately in this last matter so as not to offend him and that under no circumstances must I insist upon or make an issue of this matter. KLAUS did accept the wallet, but looked somewhat bewildered, and when I made some very tentative inquiries concerning whether he needed any money either for himself or possibly for his sister, the reply was so cold and final that I went no further with the matter. It was quite obvious that by even mentioning this I had offended the man. I left shortly thereafter, and returned to New York. There I turned over the information to JOHN and also returned to him the $1.500.00, saying that I had made some tentative inquiry, but that KLAUS FUCHS had responded so violently that I deemed it inadvisable to pursue the subject further. I recall very well that on the occasion of my meeting KLAUS FUCHS at the HEINEMANS' in Cambridge, that there was a heavy snow on the ground. This transfer of the information from me to JOHN was in New York City, but I do not believe it was in Manhattan, and I can not recall the exact borough.

"Just prior to my trip to Santa Fe, and I am referring to the first trip, and in very late May of 1945, on a Saturday afternoon, I met JOHN in a bar near 42nd Street and 3rd Avenue in New York City. I believe it was actually the Southwest corner of 42nd Street at 3rd Avenue. JOHN verified the fact that I was going on the trip and we made arrangements for a meeting in New York on my return from Santa Fe. The actual place of the meeting was to be in Brooklyn.

"I left Philadelphia and went by train to Chicago, just about the end of May. From the Union Station in Chicago, I went to the Dearborn Station, and managed to obtain space (an upper) to Albuquerque, New Mexico. I would like to state here that I had been told by JOHN to use a very circuitous route which involved going around Albuquerque and into Arizona, and then going from Arizona to El Paso, Texas, and then from El Paso to Santa Fe. However, I was extremely short of money, and had to watch what I had very carefully, and such a trip was completely out of the question. Also, there was the matter of time; it was only with the greatest difficulty and only at the last minute that I had been able to arrange to take part of my vacation that early in the year. I recall that the train that I took did not go directly to Albuquerque, but stopped at Clovis, New Mexico; there we took a coach attached to a shunt engine, for a distance of some 25 to 30 miles into Albuquerque. I would also like to add that KLAUS had advised me that getting off at Lamy, New Mexico, some 40 miles from Albuquerque, that I could get direct transportation into Santa Fe, without first going to Albuquerque. This last I had deemed inadvisable, as I thought that the only people going to Santa Fe would be those connected with the atomic energy project and they might wonder who this stranger was in their midst. Very likely, I deemed it certain that most of these people going from Lamy to Santa Fe, would be in uniform. I arrived in Albuquerque in the very early afternoon, just shortly after 12:00 o'clock, and inquired the way to the bus station. I believe that either KLAUS had told me that there was transportation by bus from Albuquerque to Santa Fe, or that I had obtained such information from one of the porters or conductors on the Santa Fe line. I took the bus to Santa Fe, and arrived there about 2:30 in the afternoon. I had considerable time to spare until 4:00, and to avoid drawing attention to myself, I went as any ordinary tourist would, to the rather large historical museum located in Santa Fe. There I inquired about obtaining a map of Santa Fe, and they did give me one which I believe to be identical with the one which KLAUS had shown me in Cambridge, Massachusetts. I wanted such a map because I did not wish to ask the way to the Castillo Street Bridge and have any one in Santa Fe remember such an occurrence. I located the Castillo Street Bridge on the map, and went there promptly at 4:00 o'clock. KLAUS arrived there possibly two or three minutes late, during which two or three minutes I became extremely uneasy, as the area around the Castillo Street Bridge was extremely sparsely settled. He finally came along Alameda Street, a gravel road, and driving a dilapidated old car, a two seater. He parked the car and we went for a walk, during which time the following events took place:

"KLAUS told me that he was getting along very well with his work in Los Alamos, and told me that he did not, however, believe, and that was a reiteration of his statement which he had made several times before, once in Cambridge and at least once or twice in New York, that the atomic energy project would be completed in sufficient time for use in the war against the Japanese.

"He also told me that everyone concerned with this work was working very hard, practically day and night, and that he himself put in an average of from 18 to 20 hours a day. We made arrangements for the next meeting, which KLAUS said should be sometime in August, but I demurred, and we finally set it for the 19th of September 1945.

"The final occurrence was that KLAUS gave me a considerable packet of information. There should be added one more thing, and that is that KLAUS's insistence on a meeting in late August, 1945, may have been due to the fact that he had mentioned that some important development was to take place during August, but he did not indicate what this development was. I left KLAUS and took the first bus from Santa Fe to Albuquerque. I had considerable difficulty that evening in trying to obtain a place to sleep, since I did not intend to leave Albuquerque until the following day, that is Sunday. I believe that in the course of searching for a hotel room, I registered at the Hilton with the understanding that should a room become available they would save it for me. During the evening I made inquiry at practically every other hotel of any size in Albuquerque including one that I recall, the San Francisco. Finally, about 12:00 o'clock at night, the Hilton advised me that there was such a long waiting list ahead of me that they were certain that no room would be available that night. I thereupon wandered through Alburquerque and finally, upon asking a policeman, he directed me to a private home near the main street in Albuquerque, Central Avenue, which had been temporarily converted into a rooming house. The only space that these people had, and I with difficulty talked these people into letting me stay there, was in the hallway on the second floor of this home, where a makeshift screen was put up around a very rickety cot. I spent the night there, and late the following afternoon, about 6:00 o'clock, took the train from Albuquerque to Chicago. Here again I had been unable to make prior reservations, and only obtained my space in the early afternoon of Sunday. When I arrived in Chicago I inquired by telephone at the Airport Terminal and determined that the only space I could get was from Chicago to Washington. Even so, that was cheaper than going by train from Chicago to New York or Philadelphia. Accordingly, I went by plane to Washington, and arrived there about 4:30 or 5:00 in the afternoon, and then took the Pennsylvania Railroad train from Washington to New York. About 9:00 o'clock in the evening and somewhere in the area of Metropolitan Avenue in Brooklyn, and where Metropolitan Avenue approaches Queens, I met JOHN and turned the information over to him, that is, the information I had received from KLAUS FUCHS.

"My last meeting with KLAUS FUCHS occurred as scheduled in Santa Fe on September 19, 1945. Again I had the usual difficulties in preparing for this trip, first the matter of money, and I did a considerable amount of borrowing toward this end, some of it at the very last minute. Also there was the matter of obtaining time off, and again with great difficulty I managed to accomplish this. I took the train from Philadelphia to Chicago and stayed over in Chicago at the Palmer House. In the evening I checked out of the Palmer House and went again to the Dearborn Station, where I had earlier in the day obtained space to Albuquerque. I arrived in Albuquerque early in the week, possibly on a Tuesday or Wednesday, and registered at the Hilton Hotel. I used the name 'HARRY GOLD,' the same which I had used at the Palmer House. From Albuquerque I went to Santa Fe, and very late in the afternoon, about 6:00 o'clock, met KLAUS FUCHS. This meeting was on the outskirts of Santa Fe, and was near a large church.

"For the first time in my association with FUCHS he was late for a meeting which occurred, and by late I mean he was fully twenty or twenty five minutes tardy. He did come along driving from outside of Santa Fe in the direction of the city itself. He explained to me that he was very sorry about not being punctual, but that he had great difficulty, first in obtaining the use of the car, and secondly, in being able to get away from his friends with whom he worked at Los Alamos. He also explained to me that there were some bottles of liquor in the bottom of the car which liquor had been purchased by KLAUS and these friends, in preparation for a party which they were going to have back at Los Alamos that very evening. The purpose of the party was to celebrate the successful use of atomic energy in the form of a weapon. KLAUS also told me, and this occurred while he was driving away from Santa Fe and up into the surrounding hill and desert country, that he himself was rather awestricken by what had occurred, and that, frankly, he had not been too certain that the project might not have been abandoned before it was completed, and that certainly he had grievously underestimated the industrial potential of the United States in being able to complete such a gigantic undertaking. He was also greatly concerned by the terrible destruction which the weapon had wrought. He told me that whereas, before, the townspeople in Santa Fe had regarded them, the people of Los Alamos, as a sort of 'boondoggling' outfit engaged in work which they could not comprehend; that now they were hailed on all sides as conquering heroes, and the townspeople were now very friendly to them. He also told me that the relationship between the British mission and the United States, which once had been extremely cordial and free, had now become somewhat strained, and that there was no longer the free exchange of information between the two groups. He said that certain sections of the project at Los Alamos, which had been freely opened to him now were barred. He further said that he had no idea as to how long he would continue to be at Los Alamos, but that he expected that sometime in the near future, possibly about December of 1945, and possibly sometime early in 1946, that the British would have him return to England where he would again resume work on Atomic Energy, exclusively for them. He told me also that he had been notified by a member of the British Intelligence that they were trying to contact KLAUS's father in Kiel, Germany, though it may be likely that KLAUS actually said they were trying to repatriate his father from Switzerland to Kiel. I believe that KLAUS said his father had for a time lived in Switzerland during the war, taking care of one of his grandchildren who had been orphaned by the death of its parents in a German concentration camp. In any case, KLAUS was concerned because he told me that his father was very old, and was given to talking rather freely about his son's past, meaning KLAUS's activities in the Communist Party in Germany in the years 1932 and 1933. KLAUS told me that as far as he knew the British had no inkling about his past as it related to his Communist activities, and he was anxious that this continue so. He told me that the British intelligence man had also mentioned that it might be possible to bring KLAUS' father to England, and again KLAUS was concerned, lest his father inadvertently let drop some hint as to KLAUS' past. He was also very much concerned about the welfare of the old man, and was in somewhat of a dilemma. I could not give him very much advice, except to tell him to proceed as he thought best, and that possibly he was greatly overestimating the extent to which the old man would talk and also the extent to which the British might be interested in KLAUS' past. I could see that KLAUS was also very much concerned about the welfare and health of his father.

"The following arrangement was made with KLAUS FUCHS for meeting him again should he be transferred to Great Britain. Starting with the first Saturday in a given month, which month was to be determined from inquiry at KLAUS' sister's and the meeting was to take place in England as soon as it could be arranged for someone to meet KLAUS there. To amplify, neither of us had any idea as to how soon we could determine from KLAUS' sister when he would actually leave, or had left for Britain. So that a month after KLAUS' arrival in England, and on the first Saturday, these meetings were to begin. The time was to be 8:00

P.M., and the place was in London at a tube express stop which contained the word 'Crescent,' and may have been something like 'Paddington,' or 'Teddington,' Crescent. The meeting was to be above the tube on the street, and the recognition signal was to be the following:

"In one hand the person meeting KLAUS would have five books bound together by a tight string. These books were to be carried by a couple of fingers hooked under the string. In the other hand the person was to have a book containing the outside jacket of BENNETT CERF's book, popular at that time, and which contained a large collection of anecdotes. The book jacket had, I believe, a yellow and green design on it. I can not recall what KLAUS was to have used for a recognition signal, beyond the fact that the person meeting him would have a complete physical description of KLAUS FUCHS. The other point about this meeting with KLAUS FUCHS was that he mentioned that he had attended the first explosion of the bomb at Alamogordo, New Mexico, and he also mentioned to me that the people back at Los Alamos told him of having seen the flash even though it was raining and the sky was overcast. There was also provided for the contingency should KLAUS be in Cambridge later that year. He said that he hoped in any case to be able to again spend the time around Christmas with the HEINEMAN family in Cambridge, and that the best way of ascertaining his whereabouts was to make an inquiry shortly before that time. This meeting took place as I have said in the hills surrounding Santa Fe and was a fair distance away, because below us I could barely see the lights of Santa Fe in the distance. KLAUS drove me into Santa Fe and just on the outskirts of the central area of the town. The last event that transpired before KLAUS dropped me off in Santa Fe, on the outskirts of the central area of the town, was that KLAUS gave me the packet of information relating to atomic energy. This was in accordance with our procedure, whereby no information was to be passed until such time that we were ready to part. After a period of anxious waiting, about an hour and a half, I finally obtained a bus going back to Albuquerque.

"I spent part of the night in a room at the Hilton Hotel, and very early in the morning, possibly 2:30 A.M., I was informed by the airlines that there was space for me as far as Kansas City. I was picked up by the Airline's limousine, and went to the Albuquerque Airport and from there by plane to Kansas City. At Kansas City I was forced to leave, and from there I took a day coach to Chicago, arriving late in the evening. I just managed to catch a train leaving La Salle Street Station and going to New York. I rode part of the way until the morning in the day coach, and the rest of the way on a Pullman space.

"I went directly from New York home to Philadelphia, and carried on my person the information which KLAUS had given me, for the next few days. Actually there was one meeting with JOHN which did not occur simply because I was far too rushed for time to keep such a meeting. It was all that I could do to accomplish this trip to Santa Fe and back. I did meet JOHN some days later after my return to Philadelphia, and the place was in Queens, New York, and was somewhere between Jackson Heights and Flushing, and also somewhere in the neighborhood of the elevated line that runs through Flushing. There I transferred the information which KLAUS FUCHS had given me to JOHN. Since this last meeting that I had with KLAUS FUCHS, in September of 1945, I have never seen nor heard from him again.

"I would like to set out the conversations I had with KLAUS FUCHS concerning his work for the Manhattan Engineer Project.

"On one occasion, and I believe this to be on the occasion of our fourth meeting, that is, the one where we had dinner at Rosenhein's Restaurant, KLAUS told me that the atomic energy project was being pursued, or was going to be pursued on a very large scale as regards the separation of the necessary isotope of uranium, somewhere in the Southeastern United States, and he thought possibly that the location would be in Georgia or possibly even Alabama. Also on the occasion of our last meeting in New York, this was the seventh meeting and occurred during a walk in Central Park, KLAUS told me that the place where he expected to be transferred was somewhere in the Southwest, and he thought most likely in Mexico, not New Mexico. Further, on the occasion of this meeting in Central Park, KLAUS told me that the Danish Nobel prize winner, NILS [sic] BOHR, was at present in this country under the name of NICHOLAS BAKER. KLAUS said that obviously the pseudonym NICHOLAS BAKER was being used because too many people might recall that NILS BOHR was the discoverer of the commonly accepted BOHR Theory of Atomic Structure, and might relate this fact to the circumstance that some activity regarding atomic energy was going on in the United States. I am certain that I turned the information concerning the separation of the isotopes of uranium by gaseous diffusion in the Southeast United States over to JOHN, as well as the fact that KLAUS was due to be transferred to the Southwestern part of the country, probably Mexico, and also the information that NILS BOHR was in this country under the name NICHOLAS BAKER.

"I would like to add that KLAUS knew of only two methods for the separation of the isotope from uranium, that is methods as were being pursued here in the United States, and that these methods were. (1) The gaseous diffusion process. (2) The electromagnetic separation method.

"I recall that this last information concerning the methods for the separation of isotopes was given to me on the occasion of our second meeting, when we were walking along 1st Avenue in Manhattan. I also recall that at that time I had mentioned to KLAUS the possibility of the use of thermal diffusion as a means of separating isotopes, but that KLAUS had brushed this aside.

"On any occasion when KLAUS gave me verbal information, either separate from, or which he wanted to go along with written information, I made good mental notes of such data and at the first opportunity I put this material in writing, and later handed it over to JOHN. The verbal information which KLAUS gave me was such as the fact concerning NILS BOHR being in the country under the name NICHOLAS BAKER; the information concerning the location of the atomic energy project on a large scale, involving gaseous diffusion in the Southeastern United States; and the information concerning the fact of the location of a large scale experimental station in the Southwestern part of the country, possibly even Mexico, which data I later reduced in writing and turned over to JOHN.

"I recall that on the occasion of the sixth meeting with KLAUS, near Boro Hall in Brooklyn, that JOHN had given me several typewritten pieces of paper about three by nine inches, of irregular size, which had contained a number of questions relating to atomic energy. The phraseology of these questions was extremely poor, and I had great difficulty in making any sense out of them. For example, in place of the word 'installation' the word 'factory' was used; in place of the word 'techniques or methods' the words 'How to make out' were used.

"I believe that the original message was probably more accurately phrased, but that either in coding or in translating, or possibly both, the person who had done such probably had no technical background whatever, possibly being on the level of a clerk, and as such, the message had become badly jumbled. I did make what sense I could out of the message, and on this occasion of this meeting in Brooklyn, began to tell KLAUS about what further information was desired. I did not get very far along this course because KLAUS seemed to take offense at being instructed and said very briefly that he had already covered all of such matters very thoroughly, and would continue to do so.

"I further believe that on the occasion of our first meeting in Santa Fe, New Mexico, early in June, 1945, KLAUS told me that among the data he had given me was a sketch of the atomic bomb itself. I did not, however, inspect this material, so I can not say whether there was any such, but I do recall clearly FUCHS' statement to that effect.

"I would like to add that throughout our entire meetings, the relationship between KLAUS FUCHS and me was that of two firm friends. Further, on the occasion of the last meeting in Santa Fe, KLAUS expressed the hope that sometime in the near future we might be able to meet openly as friends."

/S/ HARRY GOLD

"I have read the above statement consisting of this and 28 typewritten pages, and have signed each page as all statements contained therein are true to the best of my knowledge and belief."

/S/ HARRY GOLD
July 10, 1950
Phila., Penna.

Witnessed:
/s/ T. SCOTT MILLER, JR., Special Agent
FBI, Justice, 7/10/50, Phila., Pa.

/s/ RICHARD E. BRENNAN
Special Agent, FBI, Justice
July 10, 1950, Philadelphia, Pa.

Notes

Archival Abbreviations

CDEA   Records of the Department of External Affairs, Canadian Public Archives, Ottawa

CHAD   Archives of Sir James Chadwick, Churchill College, Cambridge, England

CIA   United States Central Intelligence Agency Archives, Washington, D.C.

CKFT   Archives of Sir John Cockcroft, Churchill College, Cambridge, England

DOE   Energy History Archives and Atomic Energy Commission Records, U.S. Department of Energy, Germantown, Maryland

FBI   Klaus Fuchs case file, Federal Bureau of Investigation, U.S. Department of Justice, Washington, D.C.

HH   Herbert Hoover Presidential Library, West Branch, Iowa

HST   Harry S Truman Presidential Library, Independence, Missouri

JCS   Records of the Joint Chiefs of Staff, 1942–1945, National Archives, Washington, D.C.

LANL   Archives and Records Center, Los Alamos National Laboratory, Los Alamos, New Mexico

LCP   Lord Cherwell Papers, Nuffield College, Oxford, England

MED   Manhattan Engineer District Records, Record Group 77, Modern Military Branch, National Archives, Washington, D.C.

PRO   Public Record Office, London, England

PLP   Princeton University Press Archives, Princeton, New Jersey

RPP   Sir Rudolf Peierls Papers, Bodleian Library, Oxford University, Oxford, England

SPSL   Society for the Preservation of Science and Learning Papers, Bodleian Library, Oxford University, Oxford, England

1. Secrets

1. On the Rosenberg case, see especially Ronald Radosh and Joyce Milton, *The Rosenberg File: A Search for the Truth* (New York: Holt, Rinehart, and Winston, 1983). The case for the Rosenbergs' innocence is made in Walter and Miriam Schneir, *Invitation to an Inquest: Reopening the Rosenberg "Atomic Spy" Case* (New York: Doubleday, 1965.) On the Fuchs case itself, see Rebecca West, *The New Meaning of Treason* (New York: Viking, 1964); Alan Moorehead, *The Traitors* (New York: Harper and Row, 1964); and H. Montgomery Hyde, *The Atom Bomb Spies* (New York: Atheneum, 1980).

2. For recent accounts of British intelligence as related to Soviet espionage, see Andrew Boyle, *The Fourth Man* (New York: Dial, 1979); Nigel West, *MI5* (New York: Stein and Day, 1982), and *The Circus: MI5 Operations 1945–1972* (New York: Stein and Day, 1983); Chapman Pincher, *Their Trade Is Treachery* (New York: Bantam, 1982), and *Too Secret Too Long* (New York: St. Martin's, 1985); William Stephenson, *A Man Called Intrepid* (New York: Holt, Rinehart, & Winston, 1976), and *Intrepid's Last Case* (New York: Villard, 1983). These accounts are journalistic, often based on interviews with former British security officers.

2. Inner Light, Party Line

1. FBI Special Agent Soucy (Boston) to New York and Washington offices, Dec. 14, 1949, FBI. *Christian Science Monitor*, Feb. 6, 1950. *Die Welt*, Feb. 6, 1950.

2. *New York Journal American*, Feb. 8, 1950. *Boston Globe*, Feb. 26, 1950. H. B. Fletcher to Lish Whitson, Feb. 10, 1950, and Fletcher to Ladd, Feb. 11, 1950, FBI.

3. Emil Fuchs, *Mein Leben* (Leipzig: Koehler and Amelung, 1957 and 1959), 1:66. This is the major source for the history of the Fuchs family, together with correspondence found by MI5 and the FBI in the apartments of Klaus Fuchs and Kristel Heineman. On Friedrich Naumann, see Moshe Zimmermann, "A Road Not Taken—Friedrich Naumann's Attempt at a Modern German Nationalism," *Journal of Contemporary History*, 17 (October 1982): 689–708.

4. Gerald Jonas, *On Doing Good* (New York: Scribner's, 1971). Frederick B. Tolles, *The Quakers and the Atlantic Culture* (New York: MacMillan, 1960), 1–20.

5. Fuchs, *Mein Leben*, 2: 146.

6. Leonhard Ragaz, *Von Christus zu Marx—Von Marx zu Christus: Ein Beitrag* (Wernigerode am Harz: Harder Verlag, 1929), 62. James Bentley, *Between Marx and Christ: The Dialogue in German-Speaking Europe 1870–1970* (London: NLB, 1982).

7. Martin McCauley, *Marxism-Leninism in the German Democratic Republic: The Socialist Unity Party (SED)* (New York: Harper and Row, 1979), xii. Richard Crossman, ed., *The God That Failed* (New York: Harper and Row, 1950), 59–61.

8. William S. Allen, *The Nazi Seizure of Power: The Experience of a Single German Town* (Chicago: Quadrangle, 1965), 16. Karl Rohe, *Das Reichsbanner Schwarz Rot Gold* (Düsseldorf: Droste, 1966), 374.

9. Fuchs, *Mein Leben*, 2: 128. Klaus Fuchs's confession, Jan. 27, 1950, to William J. Skardon, 1–3, in memorandum from J. Edgar Hoover to Rear Admiral Sidney W. Souers, Mar. 6, 1950, President's Secretary's Files, HST. See Appendix A.

10. "Trial of Pastor Emil Fuchs," undated manuscript, Quaker Collection, Haverford College, Haverford, Pa.

11. Emil Fuchs, "Elisabeth Fuchs-Kittowski—Painter," undated manuscript, Quaker Collection, Haverford College.

12. Fuchs's confession to Skardon, 4.

13. Alan Moorehead, *The Traitors* (New York: Harper and Row, 1964), 68–69. Babette Gross, *Willi Munzenberg: A Political Biography* (Lansing: Michigan State Universtiy Press, 1974), 211. Director, Friedrich Wilhelms Universität-Berlin to Klaus Fuchs, Oct. 3, 1933, in MI5, "Documents in the Possession of Dr. Klaus Fuchs at the Time of His Arrest on 2nd February 1950," FBI, hereafter cited as Fuchs Documents.

14. John Cimperman (London) to J. Edgar Hoover, June 9, 1950, FBI.

15. Fuchs Documents.

16. On the Heineman family's links to Israel Halperin through Wendell Furry, see Lish Whitson to H. B. Fletcher, Feb. 8, 1950, FBI. See also Gerhard Fuchs to Kristel Heineman, July 24, 1940, FBI.

17. Emil Fuchs to Rufus Jones, June 5, 1936, and Mar. 15, 1937, Quaker Collection, Haverford College.

3. Keep an Eye on Them

1. A. J. Sherman, *Island Refuge: Britain and Refugees from the Third Reich, 1933–1939* (London, 1973), 27–28. *Parliamentary Debates (Hansard): House of Commons Official Report* (London), 274 H.C.Deb., 1597 (hereafter cited as *Hansard*). Memorandum from Home Secretary to Cabinet Committee on Aliens Restrictions, Apr. 6, 1933, CAB 24/239, PRO.

2. John Saxon to the author, Dec. 8, 1985.

3. Alan Moorehead, *The Traitors* (New York: Harper and Row, 1964), 68–69, 134. Mrs. J. A. A. Gunn to Chapman Pincher, Feb. 8, 1983, and Apr. 25, 1983.

4. Nevill Mott to the author, Aug. 14, 1985. Chapman Pincher, *Too Secret Too Long* (New York: St. Martin's, 1984), 87–88.

5. Max Born, *My Life and My Views* (New York: Scribner's, 1968), 284–285. FBI interview with Hans Bethe, Feb. 14–15, 1950, FBI.

6. C. Hartly-Hodder to Klaus Fuchs, Oct. 23, 1934, SPSL. Undersecretary of State to Fuchs, Nov. 26, 1934, SPSL.

7. Moorehead, *Traitors*, 71. Nevill Mott, unpublished autobiography, 42.

8. Mott, autobiography, 43. J. Edgar Hoover to Sidney Souers, June 16, 1950, HST.

9. Babette Gross, *Willi Munzenberg: A Political Biography* (Lansing: Michigan State University Press, 1983), 218, 234–238, 251–256.

10. Ibid., 282–286.

11. Ibid., 292, 304.

12. The most complete source on Jurgen Kuczynski is his *Memoiren* (East Berlin: Aufbau, 1983).

13. Henry Krisch, *German Politics under Soviet Occupation* (New York: Columbia University Press, 1974), 11–13. Kuczynski, *Memoiren*, 264–268.

14. Kuczynski, *Memoiren*, 270–271. Hoover to Souers, Mar. 22, 1950, HST.

15. Kuczynski, *Memoiren*, 283–290.

16. Neal Wood, *Communism and the British Intellectuals* (New York: Columbia University Press, 1959). Kuczynski, *Memoiren*, 340–342.

17. Hugh Thomas, *John Strachey* (London: Eyre-Methuen, 1973), 137. B. Vernon, *Ellen Wilkinson 1891–1947* (London: Croom Helm, 1982), 162–167.

18. Thomas, *Strachey*, 141–143.

19. T. D. Burridge, *British Labour and Hitler's War* (London: Andre Deutsch, 1976), 24, 38–39. Thomas, *Strachey*, 201–225. Bill Jones, *The Russia Complex: The British Labour Party and the Soviet Union* (Manchester: Manchester University Press, 1979), 41–43.

20. Werner Roeder and Herbert A. Strauss, eds., *Biographisches Handbuch der deutschsprachigen Emigration nach 1933/International Biographical Dictionary of Central European Emigrés 1933–1945* (New York: K. G. Saur, 1983), 47, 654. Gross, *Munzenberg*, 316–317.

21. Kuczynski, *Memoiren*, 295–312.

22. Kuczynski, *Memoiren*, 335–340, 346–348, 351.

23. Klaus Fuchs to Academic Assistance Council, Dec. 7, 1934, and Max Born to Esther Simpson, Oct. 27, 1937, SPSL. Born, *My Life*, 284, 288.

24. Esther Simpson to Home Office, Aug. 5, 1938; Home Office to Fuchs, Aug. 17, 1938; Fuchs to Society for the Preservation of Science and Learning, Sept. 15, 1939, SPSL.

25. Fuchs's confession to Skardon, 4, HST.

26. Moorehead, *Traitors*, 76–77. Fuchs's confession to Skardon, 4–5, HST.

4. From Internment to Intelligence

1. Norman Berghahn, *The Refugees from Germany: April 1933 to December 1935* (London: Allen and Unwin, 1936), chap. 5. John Wheeler-Bennett, *John Anderson, Viscount Waverly* (New York: St. Martin's, 1962), 239. *Hansard*, 2410 (Mar. 1, 1940). Gerhard Hirschfeld, ed., *Exile in Great Britain: Refugees from Hitler's Germany* (New York: Humanities, 1984), 77.

2. Fuchs Documents.

3. F. Lafitte, *The Internment of Aliens* (London: Penguin, 1940), 37. Angus Calder, *The People's War: Britain, 1939–1945* (New York: Pantheon, 1969), 130–132. Wheeler-Bennett, *Anderson*, 240–241.

4. Max Born to Esther Simpson, May 22, 1940, SPSL. Born to Klaus Fuchs, June 16, 1940, and Nevill Mott to Fuchs, June 29, 1940, Fuchs Documents.

5. P. Gilman and L. Gilman, *"Collar the Lot!" How Britain Interned and Expelled Its Wartime Refugees* (New York: Quartet, 1980), 237–242.

6. Kristel Heineman to Klaus Fuchs, Aug. 16, 1950, and Jessie Gunn to Fuchs, Aug. 23, 1940, Fuchs Documents.

7. Fuchs's confession to Skardon, 5, HST.

8. On Hans Kahle, see Hugh Thomas, *The Spanish Civil War* (New York: Harper and Row, 1961), 479. J. Cortada, ed., *Historical Dictionary of the Spanish Civil War, 1936–1939* (Westport, Conn.: Greenwood, 1982), 283. C. Baker, ed., *Ernest Hemingway: Selected Letters, 1917–1961* (New York: Scribner's, 1981), 794. A. Krammer, "Germans against Hitler: The Ernst Thaelmann Brigade," *Journal of Contemporary History* (April 1969), 65–84.

9. Jurgen Kuczynski, *Memoiren* (East Berlin: Aufbau, 1983), 355–356, 362–366. D. N. Pritt, *From Right to Left* (London: Lawrence and Wishart, 1965), 231.

10. Lafitte, *Internment*, 71–74. Wheeler-Bennett, *Anderson*, 245. Martin Gilbert, *Winston S. Churchill*, vol. 6: *Finest Hour, 1939–1941* (Boston: Houghton Mifflin, 1983), 586. Report of the War Office conference, June 17, 1940, FO 916/2580 and 916/2530, PRO. Gilman and Gilman, *"Collar the Lot!"* 223–225.

11. Wheeler-Bennett, *Anderson*, 242. Hirschfeld, *Exile*, 174. Lafitte, *Internment*, 74–78. On the movement of internees, see Record Group 24, file HQS, 7236-7-42, microfilm C-5371, CDEA. Klaus Fuchs to Esther Simpson, Jan. 13, 1941, SPSL, Hirschfeld, *Exile*, 78.

12. George Ignatieff to James George, Ottawa, Mar. 2, 1950, CDEA.

13. Daniel Kevles, *The Physicists* (New York: Random House, 1971), 222–235.

14. Leo Szilard, *His Version of the Facts: Selected Recollections and Correspondence* (Cambridge, Mass.: MIT Press, 1972), 16–17. Rutherford's comment was reprinted in *Nature*, Sept. 16, 1933, 432–433.

15. A. D. Beyerchen, *Scientists under Hitler: Politics and the Physics Community in the Third Reich* (New Haven: Yale University Press, 1977), 17–22.

16. Jeremy Bernstein, *Hans Bethe: Prophet of Energy* (New York: Basic Books, 1980), 38–43; Szilard, *Facts*, 2: 14–15.

17. Otto Hahn, *A Scientific Autobiography* (New York: Scribner's, 1966), 187–206. Szilard, *Facts*, 55, 62, 66. Lewis Strauss, *Men and Decisions* (Garden City, N.Y.: Doubleday, 1962), 172.

18. David Irving, *The German Atomic Bomb: The History of Nuclear Research in Nazi Germany* (New York: Simon and Schuster, 1967), 35–37, 52–53.

19. Cited in Ronald Clark, *The Greatest Power on Earth:* (New York: Harper and Row, 1980), 63.

20. Otto Frisch, *How Little I Remember*, 126. Rudolf Peierls, *Bird of Passage: Recollections of a Physicist* (Princeton: Princeton University Press, 1985), 145–149.

21. Margaret Gowing, *Britain and Atomic Energy, 1939–1945* (New York: St. Martin's, 1964), 389–393.

22. Ibid., 65–68, 394–436.

23. Fuchs Documents. Born, *My Life,* 287.

24. Peierls, *Bird of Passage,* 163.

25. Fuchs Documents. Gowing, *Britain and Atomic Energy,* 53–54.

26. Peierls, *Bird of Passage,* 163. Rudolf Peierls to James Chadwick, Oct. 29, 1941, box 19/6, CHAD I.

27. W. J. Reader, *Imperial Chemical Industries: A History* (London: Oxford University Press, 1975), 2: 291–293, 447–448.

28. Ronald Clark, *The Greatest Power on Earth,* 118. Spencer Weart, *Scientists in Power* (Cambridge, Mass.: Harvard University Press, 1979), 167–168, 172.

29. Gowing, *Britain and Atomic Energy,* 65–68, 394–436. Irving, *German Atomic Bomb,* 71.

30. Gowing, *Britain and Atomic Energy,* 394.

31. Ibid., 146.

32. Leslie Groves, *Now It Can Be Told* (New York: Harper and Row, 1962), 125. W. P. Coates and Z. K. Coates, *A History of Anglo-Soviet Relations* (London: Lawrence and Wishart, 1943), 678–681.

33. Gilbert, *Churchill,* vol. 6, 1210–1211. Ronald Clark, *Tizard* (Cambridge: MIT Press, 1965), 346.

34. Gowing, *Britain and Atomic Energy,* 155.

35. Andrew Boyle, *The Fourth Man* (New York: Dial, 1979), 249. Gowing, *Britain and Atomic Energy,* 146. Born letter, Perrin letter, Fuchs Documents.

36. On Lindemann's refugee work, see boxes D1 and D23, LCP. See Lord Cherwell's draft letter to *Daily Telegraph,* Aug. 13, 1939, in Martin Gilbert, *Winston S. Churchill,* vol. 5: *The Prophet of Truth, 1929–1939* (Boston: Houghton Mifflin, 1977), 1586–1587. On R. V. Jones's work, see his *Most Secret War: British Scientific Intelligence, 1939–1945* (London: Hamish Hamilton, 1978). See also box D124, LCP.

37. Ronald Clark, *The Birth of the Bomb* (London: Phoenix House, 1961), 141. Gowing, *Britain and Atomic Energy,* 47, 62, 96. Peierls, *Bird of Passage,* 168. G. P. Thompson to Cherwell, July 4, 1941, box D230 LCP.

38. Peierls to James Chadwick, Sept. 23, 1941, box 19/6, CHAD I. See also Klaus Fuchs and Rudolf Peierls, "Report on German Publications," September 1941, box 19/6, CHAD I. Wallace Akers to Chadwick, Nov. 19, 1941, box 10/48, CHAD IV.

39. Fuchs and Peierls, "Report on Current German Literature," February 1942, box 19/6, CHAD I. Michael Perrin to Chadwick, Mar. 16, 1942, box 28/6, CHAD I. Fuchs, "Review of Recent German Literature," Mar. 28, 1942, box 11/52A, CHAD IV.

40. Perrin to Chadwick, Apr. 16, 1942; Peierls, "Condensed Report on a Visit to U.S.A.," May 1942, both in box 11/52A, CHAD IV.

41. Gowing, *Britain and Atomic Energy,* 161. Jones, *Most Secret War,* 395–396, 595. Fuchs to Cherwell, Sept. 14, 1943, box D 230, LCP.

42. Arnold Kramish, *The Griffin* (Boston: Houghton Mifflin, 1986).

5. The Girl from Banbury

1. J. Edgar Hoover to Sidney Souers, Feb. 21, 1950, HST.

2. Bill Jones, *The Russia Complex: The British Labour Party and the Soviet Union* (Manchester: Manchester University Press, 1977), 74–88. Angus Calder, *The People's War: Britain, 1939–1945* (New York: Pantheon, 1969), 270–273. W. P. Coates and Z. K. Coates, *A History of Anglo-Soviet Relations* (London: Lawrence and Wishart, 1943), 708–709, 721–723.

3. Jurgen Kuczynski, and M. Witt, *The Economics of Barbarism: Hitler's New Economic Order* (New York: International, 1942), 64. Jurgen Kuczynski, *Three Hundred Million Slaves and Serfs: Labor under the Fascist New Economic Order* (New York: International, 1943), 23. Kuczynski's articles appeared in *Freies Deutschland* throughout the war, as did articles by his wife and father; see G. Heinz, *Index des Freien/Neuen Deutschland (Mexico) 1941–1946* (Meissenheim am Glan, 1975).

4. Bodo Scheurig, *Free Germany: The National Committee and the League of German Officers,* trans. H. Arnold (Middletown, Conn.: Wesleyan University Press, 1969), 28, 38, 42. Erich Weinert, *Das Nationalkommittee "Freies Deutschland" 1943–1945* (Berlin: Rutten and Loening, 1957), 27, 78–86.

5. Anthony Glees, *Exile Politics during the Second World War: The German Social Democrats in Britain* (Oxford: Clarendon, 1982), 216–217.

6. R. H. Smith, *OSS: The Secret History of America's First Central Intelligence Agency* (Berkeley: University of California Press, 1972), 335–343, 519. Bradley Smith, *The Shadow Warriors: OSS and the Origins of the CIA* (New York: Basic Books, 1983), 80, 334–336.

7. R. Toledano, *J. Edgar Hoover: The Man in His Time* (New Rochelle, N.Y.: Arlington, 1973), 204–205.

8. Maurice Isserman, *Which Side Were You On? The American Communist Party during the Second World War* (Middletown, Conn.: Wesleyan University Press, 1982), 182–183. Arthur Goldberg to the author, July 15, 1985. Smith, *OSS,* 225. *Office of Strategic Services, London, Special Operations Branch and Secret Intelligence Branch War Diaries,* vol. 1: *Introductory Survey of Established Activities of SI/ETO* (Frederick, Md., University Press of America, microfilm), 28, 34.

9. Joseph Persico, *Piercing the Reich* (New York: Ballantine, 1979), 208–213. Jurgen Kuczynski, *Memoiren* (East Berlin: Aufbau, 1983), 403–404. Chapman Pincher, *Too Secret Too Long* (New York: St. Martin's, 1984), 99. *OSS London,* 1: 107–108, 127; 2: 1.

10. William Stevenson, *Intrepid's Last Case* (New York: Villard, 1983), 184. George W. Ball, *The Past Has Another Pattern* (N.Y.: Norton, 1982), 43–45, 49–50. Kuczynski, *Memoiren,* 401–403. John Kenneth Galbraith to the author, June 29, 1984.

11. Kuczynski, *Memoiren,* 403.

12. E. H. Cookridge, *The Third Man* (New York: Putnam's, 1968), 99–100.

13. "The Housewife Who Spied for Russia," *Times* (London), Jan. 27, 1980, 13. BBC monitor of Soviet television interview of Feb. 9, 1985, SWB SU/

7874/A1/7; Feb. 13, 1985. Pincher, *Too Secret*, 138. Ruth Werner, *Sonjas Rapport* (Berlin: Verlag Neuen Leben, 1977), 333–334.

14. Pincher, *Too Secret*, 9–10. A. S. Blank and J. Maser, *Rote Kapelle Gegen Hitler* (Berlin: Verlag der Nationen, 1979), 344–347.

15. CIA, *The Rote Kapelle: The CIA's History of Soviet Intelligence and Espionage Networks in Western Europe, 1936–1945* (Washington, D.C.: University Press of America, 1979), 175. Pincher, *Too Secret*, 34.

16. H. Hohne, *Codeword Direktor: The Story of the Red Orchestra* (New York: Coward, McCann, and Geoghegan, 1971), 21–23, 109. John Saxon to the author, March 1986.

17. Blank and Maser, *Rote Kapelle*, 344–345. Pincher, *Too Secret*, 55.

18. Blank and Maser, *Rote Kapelle*, 345–346. Pincher, *Too Secret*, 38, 54–55. Werner, *Sonjas Rapport*, 225, 227. Alexander Foote, *Handbook for Spies* (New York: Doubleday, 1949), 10–11.

19. Foote, *Handbook*, 23–27. Werner, *Sonjas Rapport*, 232. Anthony Read and David Fisher, *Operation Lucy* (New York: Coward, McCann, and Geoghegan, 1981), 35–36. Blank and Maser, *Rote Kapelle*, 346–347. Foote, *Handbook*, 40.

20. *Lasting Peace the ILO Way: The Story of the ILO* (Geneva: ILO Press, 1951). David Dallin, *Soviet Espionage* (New Haven: Yale University Press, 1955), 222. Foote, *Handbook*, 263.

21. Charles Whiting, *The Spymasters: The True Story of Anglo-American Intelligence Operations within Nazi Germany 1939–1945* (New York: Dutton, 1976), 81–85. Pierre Accoce and Pierre Quet, *A Man Called Lucy, 1939–1945* (New York: Coward, McCann, 1966), 80. Josef Garlinski, *The Enigma War* (New York: Scribner's, 1980), 109–110.

22. CIA, *Rote Kapelle*, 349–350. Dallin, *Soviet Espionage*, 21, 194–198.

23. Foote, *Handbook*, 45. Pincher, *Too Secret*, 57. Dallin, *Soviet Espionage*, 183. CIA, *Rote Kapelle*, 232. Werner, *Sonjas Rapport*, 277–280. Pincher, *Too Secret*, 60–64.

24. CIA, *Rote Kapelle*, 182. Foote, *Handbook*, 49. Charlotte Haldane, *Truth Will Out* (New York: Vanguard, 1950), 286–287. Dallin, *Soviet Espionage*, 200. Whiting, *Spymasters*, 95. Malcolm Muggeridge, *Chronicles of Wasted Time*, vol. 2: *The Infernal Grove* (New York: Quill, 1982), 189.

25. Anthony Read and David Fisher, *Colonel Z: The Secret Life of a Master of Spies* (New York: Viking, 1985), is the first biography of the mysterious Claude Dansey and his organization.

26. Read and Fisher, *Colonel Z*, 23–25, 246–248. Werner, *Sonjas Rapport*, 231–232. Foote, *Handbook*, 11, 21. Christopher Andrew, *Secret Service: The Making of the British Intelligence Community* (London: Heinemann, 1985), 337–339, 380–382.

27. Dallin, *Soviet Espionage*, 98–207.

28. F. H. Hinsley, *British Intelligence in the Second World War* (New York: Cambridge University Press, 1981), 2: 60. Anthony C. Brown and Charles B. MacDonald, *On a Field of Red: The Communist International and the Coming of World War II* (New York: G. P. Putnam, 1981), 576. Peter Calvocoressi, *Top*

Secret Ultra (New York: Pantheon, 1980), 6, 43. Interview with Gen. Walter Scott cited in Brown, *Field of Red,* 576.

29.Whiting, *Spymasters,* 87–88. Dallin, *Soviet Espionage,* 187, 195. Foote, *Handbook,* 260. Hinsley, *British Intelligence,* 2: 60.

30. Gilbert, *Churchill,* vol. 6, 1200. Whiting, *Spymasters,* 101–103.

31. Muggeridge, *Chronicles,* 187–189. Nigel West, *MI6* (New York: Random House, 1983), 84, 116–118, 223–225. Read and Fisher, *Colonel Z,* 99–103.

32. Pincher, *Too Secret,* 394–396. Boyle, *Fourth Man,* 259–260. Whiting, *Spymasters,* 102.

33. CIA, *Rote Kapelle,* 329–330. Foote, *Handbook,* 229–231, 238–242.

34. Richard Deacon, *"C": A Biography of Sir Maurice Oldfield* (London: MacDonald, 1985), 83–84. Foote, *Handbook,* 51. CIA, *Rote Kapelle,* 165.

35. Foote, *Handbook,* 165, 258–260. Dallin, *Soviet Espionage,* 199, 213, 223.

36. "Housewife Who Spied."

37. Ibid. Pincher, *Too Secret,* 42, 56. Werner, *Sonjas Rapport,* 283–286.

38. "Housewife Who Spied." Blank and Maser, *Rote Kapelle,* 491. Werner, *Sonjas Rapport,* 294–295. Pincher, *Too Secret,* 74.

39. Werner, *Sonjas Rapport,* 305–310. Pincher, *Too Secret,* 94. A. H. Belmont to C. E. Hennrich, Mar. 17, 1950, FBI.

40. Alan Moorehead, *The Traitors* (New York: Harper and Row, 1964), 83–84. Sir Michael Perrin to the author, May 30, 1984.

41. On Kremer, see Hoover to Souers, Mar. 22, 1950, HST.

42. Fuchs's confession to Perrin, 2. See Appendix B.

43. Max Born to Fuchs, Dec. 7, 1941, and July 26, 1942, Fuchs Documents.

44. Werner, *Sonjas Rapport,* 297–298. Pincher, *Too Secret,* 42, 56, 92–93. Chapman Pincher to the author, Mar. 20, 1984. Hoover to Souers, June 16, 1950, HST.

45. Fuchs's confession to Skardon, 4.

46. Nigel West, *The Circus: MI5 Operations, 1945–1972* (New York: Stein and Day, 1983), 29–30. Chapman Pincher, *Their Trade Is Treachery* (London: Sidgwick and Jackson, 1981), 55–56. Read and Fisher, *Operation Lucy,* 216, 220. Werner, *Sonjas Rapport,* 323–324. Deacon, *"C,"* 85.

47. John Saxon to the author, Apr. 3, 1986.

48. Werner, *Sonjas Rapport,* 322–329.

49. Ibid., 329–333. Pincher, *Too Secret,* 138–139.

6. Gold in Manhattan

1. James Conant, Chairman, National Defense Research Council, to Lyman J. Briggs, Chairman, Uranium Section, Aug. 15, 1941; Vannevar Bush to Harold Urey, Dec. 18, 1941, LANL. J Reader, *Imperial Chemical Industries: A History* (Oxford: Oxford University Press, 1975), 2: 287. Martin Sherwin, *A World Destroyed: The Atomic Bomb and the Grand Alliance* (New York: Random House, 1973), 68–69.

2. R. V. Jones, *Most Secret War: British Scientific Intelligence, 1939–1945* (London: Hamish Hamilton, 1978), 474.

3. Sherwin, *World Destroyed,* 78–79. Reader, *Imperial Chemical,* 2: 292. Spencer Weart, *Scientists in Power* (Cambridge, Mass.: Harvard University Press, 1979), 179.

4. Sherwin, *World Destroyed,* 100–101. R. Hewlett and O. E. Anderson, *A History of the United States Atomic Energy Commission,* vol. 1: *The New World, 1939–1946* (University Park: Pennsylvania State University Press, 1962), 268.

5. Ronald Clark, *Tizard* (Cambridge, Mass.: MIT Press, 1965), 346–347. Hewlett and Anderson, *New World,* 268–270. Weart, *Scientists in Power,* 193– 195. U.S. Department of State, *The Conferences at Washington and Quebec,* Foreign Relations of the United States Series (Washington, D.C.: Government Printing Office, 1970), 2–3, 6–7. Volumes in this series are cited hereafter as FRUS, by volume and year. Sherwin, *World Destroyed,* 80–83.

6. David Irving, *The German Atomic Bomb: The History of Nuclear Research in Nazi Germany* (New York: Simon and Schuster, 1967), 180–181. Clark, *Tizard,* 348–349. *Manhattan Project: Official History and Documents* (Washington, D.C.: University Publications of America, 1977), vol. 14, app. A-1. Hereafter cited as *MP.*

7. *Conferences,* FRUS, 630.

8. Ibid., 1117–1118.

9. Wilfrid Eggleston, *Canada's Nuclear Story* (Toronto: Clarke, Irving, 1965), 41–53.

10. FBI interview with Tony Skyrme, Princeton Institute for Advanced Studies, Feb. 20–23, 1950, FBI; memorandum of Charlton C. McSwain (Knoxville), Feb. 15, 1950, p. 6, FBI; Lish Whitson to J. Edgar Hoover, Feb. 9, 1950, with documents on Fuchs's visa request from 1943, FBI.

11. J. Edgar Hoover to Sidney Souers, Feb. 6 and 21, 1950, HST. H. S. Traynor to Leslie Groves, "Visit of British Group," Dec. 8, 1943, DOE. C. A. Rolander to Admiral John Gingrich, AEC Security Division, Jan. 12, 1949, DOE.

12. The work of the British mission after Pearl Harbor is described in McSwain memorandum, FBI; see esp. 6–7. Karl Cohen to Senator Brien McMahon, Mar. 19, 1951, in Congressional Joint Committee on Atomic Energy, *Soviet Atomic Espionage* (Washington, D.C.: Government Printing Office, 1951), 23.

13. McSwain memorandum, 7. John Lansdale to Captain H. K. Calvert, Feb. 4, 1944; Claude C. Peirce, Manhattan Engineer District intelligence officer, to Lt. Col. William B. Parson, Mar. 18, 1944, on "Alien Visitors"; Kenneth D. Nichols to Lansdale, Mar. 21, 1944; War Department circular on "Alien Visitors," Mar. 28, 1944, all in DOE.

14. Sherwin, *World Destroyed,* 103: from Stimson's diary, Sept. 9, 1943.

15. Manhattan Engineer District report to Hoover, Mar. 28, 1944, FBI. JCAE, *Soviet Atomic Espionage,* 23. Hoover to Souers, Feb. 6, 1950, HST. FBI interview with Manson Benedict, Mar. 14, 1950, on Fuchs's knowledge of the Oak Ridge plant, 2, FBI.

16. On Harry Gold, see his confession to FBI agents T. Scott Miller and Richard E. Brennan, May 22 and July 10, 1950, pp. 5, 12, FBI (see Appendix C). See also Hoover to Roscoe Hillenkoetter, CIA, Sept. 13, 1950, FBI.

17. Hoover to Souers, Feb. 6, 1950, HST. FBI interview with Hans Bethe, Feb. 14–15, 1950, FBI. James Chadwick to W. L. Webster, July 24 and Aug. 3, 1944, MED.

18. Rudolf Peierls to Wallace Akers, Aug. 15, 1944, box 3/16, CHAD IV. Memorandum, author's name deleted, to Hoover, Aug. 11, 1944, reporting Fuchs's transfer to Los Alamos, FBI.

19. Gold's confession.

7. Los Alamos

1. Margaret Gowing, *Britain and Atomic Energy, 1939–1945* (New York: St Martin's, 1964), 263–264.

2. FBI interviews with J. Robert Oppenheimer, Mar. 24 and 27, 1950, and with Hans Bethe, Feb. 14–15, 1950, FBI. *Washington Star,* Feb. 5, 1950, A-4. Hans Bethe to the author, Aug. 13, 1985.

3. FBI interviews with Manson Benedict, Mar. 14, 1950, with Stanislas and Françoise Ulam, Mar. 14, 1950, with Tony Skyrme, Feb. 20, 21, 23, 1950, and with Richard Feynman, Feb. 24, 1950, FBI.

4. FBI interview with Victor Weisskopf, Mar. 11, 1950, FBI. Michael Perrin to the author, Aug. 14, 1984.

5. J. Edgar Hoover to Lloyd Wright, chairman, Commission on Government Security, Apr. 5, 1956, FBI.

6. *MP,* vol. 14: secs. 2.10, 6.17, 6.18, app. E.

7. "Report of Foreign Personnel at Project Y," Sept. 6, 1944, LANL. J. Edgar Hoover to Sidney Souers, Feb. 6, 1950, HST. "Report of Foreign Personnel at Project Y," Nov. 3 and Dec. 4, 1944, LANL.

8. "Report of Foreign Personnel at Project Y," Jan. 5 and Feb. 5, 1945, LANL. *Manhattan District History: Project Y, The Los Alamos Project* (Berkeley: University of California Press, 1961), 211–213.

9. Harry Gold's confession to FBI agents Miller and Brennan, FBI.

10. "Report of Foreign Personnel at Project Y," Mar. 3 and June 6, 1945, LANL.

11. Gold's confession.

12. "Report of Foreign Personnel at Project Y," July 5 and Aug. 2, 1945, LANL.

13. "Report of Foreign Personnel at Project Y," Sept. 4, 1945, LANL. *MP Official History,* vol. 14, app. E.

14. Fuchs's confession to Perrin, 5.

15. Gold's confession, 25.

16. Gold's confession.

17. Ralph Carlisle Smith to Capt. T. O. Jones, Sept. 18, 1945, LANL.

18. Leslie Groves, *Now It Can Be Told: The Story of the Manhattan Project* (New York: Harper and Row, 1962), 144–145. David Holloway, "Entering the Nuclear Arms Race: The Soviet Decision to Build the Atomic Bomb, 1939–

1945," Working Paper no. 9, Woodrow Wilson International Center for Scholars, International Security Studies Program (1979), 29–30. David Holloway to the author, June 27, 1984.

19. Ronald Radosh and Joyce Milton, *The Rosenberg File: A Search for the Truth* (New York: Holt, Rinehart, and Winston, 1983), 212.

20. Report of Leo H. Frutkin on David Greenglass, June 23, 1951, FBI.

21. Ibid., 27.

22. Ibid., 27. Radosh and Milton, *Rosenberg File*, 66.

23. Radosh and Milton, *Rosenberg File*, 66.

24. Frutkin Report, 32.

25. Radosh and Milton, *Rosenberg File*, 68–69. Frutkin Report, 7.

26. Radosh and Milton, *Rosenberg File*, 70, 211. Frutkin Report, 33.

27. Radosh and Milton, *Rosenberg File*, 188, 445.

28. FBI interview with Martin Deutsch, Feb. 22, 1950, FBI. FBI interview with anonymous source, reported by Special Agent Soucy (Boston) to the FBI's New York and Washington, D.C., offices, Feb. 16, 1950, FBI.

29. Leo Szilard, *His Version of the Facts: Selected Recollections and Correspondence* (Cambridge, Mass.: MIT Press, 1972), 2: 178.

30. S. Rozental, ed., *Niels Bohr* (Amsterdam: North Holland, 1967), 197, 202–203. Ruth Moore, *Niels Bohr: The Man, His Science, and the World They Changed* (New York: Knopf, 1966), 334–335. David Irving, *The German Atomic Bomb: The History of Nuclear Research in Nazi Germany* (New York: Simon and Schuster, 1967), 192–193.

31. *MP*, reel 2, pt. 4, secs: 13.2 and 13.3. Henry Smyth, "The Smyth Report," *Princeton University Library Chronicle*, 37 (Spring 1976): 176–177. The Feynman draft is attached to Henry Smyth, "Receipt for Classified Material," Dec. 15, 1944, LANL.

32. Henry Smyth to J. Robert Oppenheimer, Apr. 6 and 20, 1945; Oppenheimer to Smyth, Apr. 14, 1945, LANL. *MP*, reel 2, pt. 4, sec. 13.10.

33. Oppenheimer to Groves, July 31, 1945, *MP*, reel 2, pt. 4, secs. 13.9 and 13.10. "Future Release Announcement, Bureau of Public Relations, War Department," Princeton University Press Archives, Princeton, N.J. Henry Smyth, *Atomic Energy for Military Purposes: The Official Report on the Development of the Atomic Bomb under the Auspices of the United States Government, 1940–1945* (Princeton: Princeton University Press, 1945), v, vii, 222. "Memo for Mr. Van Gelder on Smyth's 'Atomic Energy for Military Purposes,'" Nov. 5, 1945, Princeton University Press Archives.

34. "Report of Foreign Personnel at Project Y," Oct. 2, 1945, LANL.

35. Ibid., Dec. 4, 1945. See also Sidney Neuberger to the file, Feb. 3, 1950, LANL.

36. James Chadwick to Norris Bradbury, Jan. 23, 1946; Bradbury to Chadwick, Feb. 5, 1946, LANL.

37. Hans Bethe to Klaus Fuchs, Feb. 11, 1946. "Report of Foreign Personnel at Project Y," Mar. 6, 1946, LANL.

38. Fuchs to Bradbury, Mar. 28, 1946. "Report of Foreign Personnel at Project Y," Mar. 28, 1946, LANL. J. F. Jackson, British Supply Office, to General Leslie Groves, June 28, 1946, MED. FBI interview with Bethe, Feb. 15, 1950, FBI. Hoover to Souers, Feb. 6 and 21, 1950, HST.

39. Lt. Col. Charles H. Banks to Hoover, July 2, 1946; memo, author's name deleted, to Ladd, July 20, 1946, FBI.

40. H. Montgomery Hyde, *The Atom Spies* (New York: Atheneum, 1980), 1–6.

41. Nigel West, *The Circus: MI5 Operations, 1945–1972* (New York: Stein and Day, 1983), 26–27. Hyde, *Atom Spies*, 27. Chapman Pincher, *Too Secret Too Long* (New York: St. Martin's, 1984), 104–106.

42. *The Report of the Royal Commission* (Ottawa: 1946), 638–640, 455–456. Hyde, *Atom Spies*, 26–30, 71.

43. Hyde, *Atom Spies*, 33, 36, 38–39, 41, 56.

44. Ibid., 70–71.

45. Hyde, *Atom Spies*, 76. *Royal Commission*, 85, 132–145, 448–449.

46. Hoover to Roscoe Hillenkoetter, CIA, Feb. 8, 1950, FBI. Lester Pearson's information was reported by the *Ottawa Gazette*, May 1, 1950, CDEA. H. B. Fletcher to Ladd, Feb. 3, 1950, p. 6, FBI. Hoover to Souers, Feb. 6, 1950, HST. The fact that Fuchs's name was in the Halperin address book was reported to the FBI on Mar. 12, 1946, by (name deleted), FBI. J. J. Maxwell of the El Paso FBI office reported that an investigation of Kristel Heineman began in February 1946: report of Dec. 9, 1949, FBI.

8. Harwell

1. John Simpson, *The Independent Nuclear State: The United States, Britain, and the Military Atom* (London: St. Martin's, 1983), 40–41. Kenneth Harris, *Attlee* (New York: Norton, 1983), 277–280. John Cockcroft, "Atomic Energy History," typescript, CKFT. Gregg Herken, *The Winning Weapon: The Atomic Bomb in the Cold War, 1945–1950* (New York: Knopf, 1980), 35–36, 61–66. Dean Acheson, *Present at the Creation: My Years in the State Department* (New York: Norton, 1965), 165. Kenneth O. Morgan, *Labor in Power, 1945–1951* (Oxford: Clarendon Press, 1984), 280–282. Henry Pelling, *The Labour Governments, 1945–1951* (New York: St. Martin's, 1984), 124–126. Simpson, *Nuclear State*, 72–73.

2. John Wheeler-Bennett, *John Anderson, Viscount Waverley* (New York: St. Martin's, 1962), 339. R. N. Rosecrance, *Defence of the Realm: British Strategy in the Nuclear Epoch* (New York: Columbia University Press, 1968), 37.

3. Margaret Gowing, *Independence and Deterrence: Britain and Atomic Energy, 1945–1952* (New York: St. Martin's, 1974), 2: 116–117, 130–132, 212.

4. Harris, *Attlee*, 283–284. Simpson, *Nuclear State*, 43.

5. Simpson, *Nuclear State*, 39. Margaret Gowing, *Britain and Atomic Energy, 1939–1945* (New York: St. Martin's, 1964), 110. James Gormly, "The Washington Declaration and the 'Poor Relation': Anglo-American Diplomacy, 1945–1946," *Diplomatic History*, 8 (Spring 1984): 142–143. Wheeler-Bennett, *Anderson*, 337. Rosecrance, *Defence of the Realm*, 48.

6. Rosecrance, *Defence of the Realm*, 84. E. W. Titterton to Rudolf Peierls, Mar. 11, 1947, box 215, folder C297, RPP. Acheson, *Present at the Creation*, 167.

7. Rosecrance, *Defence of the Realm,* 85. Acheson, *Present at the Creation,* 316. Harris, *Attlee,* 289. Simpson, *Nuclear State,* 79.

8. Cockcroft, "Atomic Energy History," 17–18, CKFT. James Chadwick to Fuchs, Jan. 24, 1946, box 3/15, CHAD IV. George Placzek to Chadwick, Feb. 4, 1946, box 3/15, CHAD IV.

9. H. Montgomery Hyde, *The Atom Bomb Spies* (New York: Atheneum, 1980), 113–114. Harris, *Attlee,* 286–288.

10. Gowing, *Independence and Deterrence,* 2: chap. 16.

11. Simpson, *Nuclear State,* 78. R. Hewlett and F. Duncan, *A History of the United States Atomic Energy Commission,* vol 2: *Atomic Shield, 1947–1952* (University Park: Pennsylvania State University Press, 1969), 286.

12. Report by FBI special agent Brenton S. Gordon on Martin Deutsch, Boston, Feb. 22, 1950, FBI.

13. Hewlett and Duncan, *Atomic Shield,* 286–287. Simpson, *Nuclear State,* 80, 289–293. Cockcroft, "Atomic Energy History," chap. 5. James Tuck to Lord Cherwell, Aug. 27, 1946, box D246, LCP. Peierls to John Awberry, Feb. 15, 1947, box 214, folder C286, RPP.

14. Lewis Strauss to AEC commissioners, July 15, 1948, and W. T. Golden to Lewis Strauss, Sept. 10, 1948, "Security" folder, Strauss Papers, AEC series, box 66, HH.

15. Klaus Fuchs and Rudolf Peierls, "Notes on Declassification of Diffusion Plant Papers," July 2, 1948, box 2/6, CHAD I. C. A. Rolander to file, Feb. 2, 1950, DOE. Oppenheimer described his visit with Fuchs in September 1948 in his FBI interviews, Mar. 24 and 27, 1950, FBI. Peierls to Cockcroft, June 24, 1948, box 205, C66, RPP. Peierls to Geoffrey Taylor, Nov. 19, 1948, box 215, C299, RPP.

16. Hewlett and Duncan, *Atomic Shield,* 296. Acheson, *Present at the Creation,* 314. Simpson, *Nuclear State,* 80–81.

17. Rosecrance, *Defence of the Realm,* 114–115. Simpson, *Nuclear State,* 81.

18. Harris, *Attlee,* 290. Hewlett and Duncan, *Atomic Shield,* 305. Simpson, *Nuclear State,* 81–82.

19. Simpson, *Nuclear State,* 83. Hewlett and Duncan, *Atomic Shield,* 308–311.

20. Bennett Boskey to file, Dec. 28, 1949, DOE. J. J. Maxwell (El Paso) to FBI headquarters, Oct. 20, 1949, FBI. Gowing, *Britain and Atomic Energy,* 123. FRUS, 1949, vol. 1: 499–503, 601.

21. J. Edgar Hoover to Sidney Souers, Mar. 22, 1950, HST. MI5 to Herschel Johnson, U.S. Embassy, London, Dec. 26, 1940. Werner Roeder, *Die deutschen sozialistischen Exilgruppen in Grossbritannien* (Hannover: Verlag F. Lit. u. Zeitgeschehen, 1968), 86.

22. FBI interview with Fuchs, 28, FBI.

23. Fuchs's confession to Perrin, 6, HST.

24. Ibid., 6–7.

25. Fuchs's confession to Skardon, 6–8, HST.

26. Emil Fuchs, *Ruf und Antwort* (Leipzig: Koehler und Amelang, 1964), 128–129, 283. (See also his short autobiography, Quaker Collection, Haverford College, Haverford, Pa.) Emil Fuchs to his children, Dec. 12, 1945, FBI.

27. Klaus Fuchs to J. C. S. Clarke, Minister of Defense, Mar. 11, 1946, Fuchs Documents.

28. Emil Fuchs, *Mein Leben* (Leipzig: Kohler und Amelung, 1957), 2:280.

29. Emil Fuchs to Kristel Heineman, May 21, 1947, FBI.

30. Emil Fuchs, "We Look to England," *The Friend*, Mar. 5, 1948, 197–198.

31. *Die Welt*, Feb. 6, 1950.

9. The Super and the Soviet Code

1. Atomic Energy Act of 1946, reproduced in Robert C. Williams and Philip L. Cantelon, *The American Atom: A Documentary History of Nuclear Policies from the Discovery of Fission to the Present, 1939–1984* (Philadelphia: University of Pennsylvania Press, 1984), 79–92.

2. Karl Compton, "Science and Security," *Bulletin of the Atomic Scientists*, 1948, 373–376; Robert Cushman, "Freedom—Security," ibid., 1949, 69.

3. *New York Times*, May 13, May 26, July 10, 1949.

4. Ibid., Sept. 25, 1949, 8; Oct. 6, 1949, 3; S. K. Allison, "The State of Physics: Or the Perils of Being Important," *Bulletin of the Atomic Scientists*, 1950, 2–4.

5. *New York Times*, Oct. 4, 1949, 4; Oct. 7, 1949; Oct. 13, 1949, 1.

6. "Air Capabilities and Intentions of the USSR in the Post-War Period," J. I. S. 80/3/D Report, Oct. 19, 1945, JCS. The Joint Chiefs of Staff estimate of February 1950 is described in John Simpson, *The Independent Nuclear State: The United States, Britain, and the Military Atom* (London: St. Martin's, 1983), 277–278.

7. Herbert York, *The Advisers: Oppenheimer, Teller, and the Superbomb* (San Francisco: W. H. Freeman, 1976), 20–28. Jeremy Bernstein, *Hans Bethe: Prophet of Energy* (New York: Basic Books, 1980), 47–54.

8. Peter Goodchild, *Robert Oppenheimer: Shatterer of Worlds* (Boston: Houghton Mifflin, 1981), 53. Hans Bethe, "Comments on the History of the H-Bomb," *Los Alamos Science*, Fall 1982, 46. Alice K. Smith and Charles Weiner, eds., *Robert Oppenheimer: Letters and Reminiscences* (Cambridge, Mass.: Harvard University Press, 1980), 228.

9. James Kunetka, *City of Fire: Los Alamos and the Atomic Age, 1943–1945* (Albuquerque: University of New Mexico Press, 1978), 52–53, 76.

10. R. Hewlett and O. E. Anderson, *A History of the United States Atomic Energy Commission*, vol. 1: *The New World* (University Park: Pennsylvania State University Press, 1962), 240. Kunetka, *City of Fire*, 76.

11. Kunetka, *City of Fire*, 115–116. Smith and Weiner, *Oppenheimer*, 294: letter from Oppenheimer to Stimson, Aug. 17, 1945.

12. "Fuchs' Participation in the Thermonuclear Weapons Program at Los Alamos," April 1950, DOE. Draft patent application, Apr. 12, 1944, cited in untitled draft memorandum at Los Alamos, Apr. 25, 1950, LANL. Hans Thirring, *Die Geschichte der Atombombe* (Vienna: Neues Osterreich, 1946).

13. Bernstein, *Bethe*, 46. "Report of Conference on the Super," LA 575, June 12, 1946, LANL.

14. Bernstein, *Bethe*, 47. York, *Advisers*, 26.

15. William Leuchtenberg, *In the Shadow of FDR: From Harry Truman to Ronald Reagan* (Ithaca, N.Y.: Cornell University Press, 1983), 7–40. Acting Secretary of State Webb to American embassies, Sept. 23, 1949, FRUS. Robert J. Donovan, *Tumultuous Years: The Presidency of Harry S Truman, 1949–1953* (New York: Norton, 1982), 84–87.

16. Lewis Strauss, *Men and Decisions* (Garden City, N.Y.: Doubleday, 1962), 216–217. David Rosenberg, "American Atomic Strategy and the H-Bomb Decision," *Journal of American History* (June 1979): 79. William Golden to Lewis Strauss, Sept. 25, 1949, Strauss Papers, file "Golden, Wm. T.," HH. Richard Pfau, *No Sacrifice Too Great: The Life of Lewis L. Strauss* (Charlottesville: University of Virginia Press, 1984).

17. Pfau, *No Sacrifice,* 113. Golden to Strauss, May 22, 1947, "Long Range Detection Committee (Monitoring)," Strauss Papers, HH.

18. John Major, *The Oppenheimer Hearing* (New York: Stein and Day, 1971), 103, 105, 117.

19. J. Robert Oppenheimer, USAEC General Advisory Committee, to David Lilienthal, Atomic Energy Commission, Oct. 30, 1949, DOE. Major, *Oppenheimer Hearing,* 113–116, 119. David Lilienthal, *The Journals of David E. Lilienthal,* vol. 2: *The Atomic Energy Commission Years, 1945–1950* (New York: Harper and Row, 1964), 580–581.

20. Major, *Oppenheimer Hearing,* 125. Lilienthal, *Journals,* 2: 594–596. Lilienthal to AEC commissioners, Nov. 9, 1949, Strauss Papers, file "Lilienthal, David E.," HH.

21. Stuart Symington, Secretary of the Air Force, to Louis Johnson, Secretary of Defense, Nov. 8, 1949, President's Secretary's File, HST. Lilienthal to Harry S Truman, Nov. 9, 1949, FRUS, 1949, vol. 1: 576–585.

22. Truman to Sidney Souers, Nov. 19, 1949, FRUS, 1949, vol. 1: 587–588.

23. Senator Brien McMahon to Truman, Nov. 21, 1949, FRUS, 1949, vol. 1: 588–595. General Omar N. Bradley, Joint Chiefs of Staff, to Johnson, Nov. 23, 1949, FRUS, 1949, vol. 1: 595–596.

24. Strauss to Truman, Nov. 25, 1949, FRUS, 1949, vol. 1: 596–597. Also cited in Strauss, *Men and Decisions,* 219. Paul Nitze, Deputy Director, Policy Planning Staff, U.S. Department of State, to Truman, Dec. 19, 1949, FRUS, 1949, vol. 1: 610–611. Barton Bernstein, "Truman and the H-Bomb," *Bulletin of the Atomic Scientists,* March 1984, 16.

25. Donovan, *Tumultuous Years,* 132, 247.

26. Joint Chiefs of Staff to Johnson, Jan. 13, 1950, FRUS, 1949, vol. 1: 503–512. See also Rosenberg, "American Atomic Strategy," 82.

27. National Security Council subcommittee draft memorandum, Jan. 31, 1950, on the super may be found in Lilienthal, *Journals,* 2: 624; also FRUS, 1949, vol. 1: 517.

28. Lilienthal, *Journals,* 2: 632–633. Rosenberg, "American Atomic Strategy," 62. Bernstein, "Truman," 17.

29. Bernstein, *Bethe,* 94. Major, *Oppenheimer Hearing,* 161.

30. Louis Ridenour, "The Hydrogen Bomb," *Scientific American,* 182 (March 1950): 11–15. Hans Bethe, "The Hydrogen Bomb: II," ibid. (April

1950): 18–23. R. F. Bacher, "The Hydrogen Bomb: III," ibid. (May 1950): 11–15. Ralph Lapp, "The Hydrogen Bomb: IV," ibid. (June 1950): 11–15.

31. Bethe, "Hydrogen Bomb," 48. Bernstein, "Truman," 18.

32. W. B. McCool to file, "Declassification of Thermonuclear Weapons Information," Aug. 9, 1957, DOE. Untitled secret memorandum, Security and Intelligence Division, Atomic Energy Commission, Nov. 1, 1949, DOE.

33. York, *Advisers,* 69. Strauss to Truman, Jan. 31, 1950, and Truman to Strauss, Feb. 7, 1950, HST. Strauss to Truman, "Memorandum for the President," Feb. 1, 1950, HST.

34. J. Edgar Hoover to Tolson, Ladd, and Nichols, 2:05 P.M. and 2:40 P.M., Feb. 1, 1950, FBI.

35. *New York World Telegram and Sun,* Feb. 4, 1950, 1. *Brooklyn Eagle,* Feb. 4, 1950, 1.

36. Bradley Smith, *The Shadow Warriors: O.S.S. and the Origins of the C.I.A.* (New York: Basic Books, 1983), 353–355. For a good and brief introduction to the British decrypting of German "Enigma" messages, code-named "Ultra," see Peter Calvocoressi, *Top Secret Ultra* (New York: Random House, 1980). David Martin, *Wilderness of Mirrors* (New York: Ballantine, 1980), 43.

37. Ronald Radosh and Joyce Milton, *The Rosenberg File: A Search for the Truth* (New York: Holt, Rinehart, and Winston, 1983), 6–9. Nigel West, *The Circus: MI5 Operations, 1945–1972* (New York, Stein and Day, 1983), 31. According to West, the British government had been reading Soviet messages, called "U-traffic," through intercepts since 1945 in a program comparable to the American "Bride" program, but using Australian intercept stations.

38. Memos to FBI Director, Mar. 28 and Aug. 11, 1944, originating source deleted, FBI.

39. Philadelphia FBI office to Director, July 31, 1945, FBI. Memo to FBI Director, Mar. 12, 1946, originating source deleted, FBI. Lt. Col. Charles Banks, War Department, to FBI Director, July 2, 1946, FBI. The story of the captured German reports is reported in a memorandum from J. P. Mohr to Mr. Tolson, FBI, Feb. 12, 1950. Also V. P. Keay to H. B. Fletcher, Feb. 7, 1950, and D. M. Ladd to Director, Feb. 16, 1950, FBI.

40. C. A. Rolander, Jr., to Admiral John Gingrich, Security Division, Atomic Energy Commission, Jan. 12, 1949, DOE. Ralph Carlisle Smith to Carroll L. Wilson, AEC, July 18, 1949, LANL. Also Hans Bethe to Wilson, same date, LANL.

41. See the memorandum of C. A. Rolander, Jr., to the files on "Dr. K. Fuchs," Sept. 19, 1949; Frank Hammack, AEC Security, to the file, Mar. 28, 1950, DOE.

42. Hoover to Souers, Feb. 6, 1950, IIST. Robert Lamphere to the author, Aug. 25, 1985. Security and Intelligence Division, AEC, to Carroll Wilson, Nov. 1, 1949; summary of the meeting (no. 327) of the AEC commissioners, Nov. 2, 1949, DOE. SAC, N.Y., to Director, Sept. 22, 1949; H. B. Fletcher to D. M. Ladd, Sept. 27, 1949; Lish Whitson to H. B. Fletcher, Sept. 26, 1949; J. Jerome Maxwell (El Paso, Texas) to Director, Oct. 20, 1949; Fletcher to Ladd, Oct. 21, 1949; FBI Knoxville Office to Director, Oct. 22, 1949, FBI.

43. H. Montgomery Hyde, *The Atom Bomb Spies* (New York: Atheneum,

1980), 119. Radosh and Milton, *Rosenberg File,* 8–9. Robert Lamphere and Thomas Schachtman, *The FBI-KGB War: A Special Agent's Story* (New York: Random House, 1986), 134–137.

10. Confession and Trial

1. The account here of Fuchs's interrogation by Skardon derives primarily from Matt C. McDade, U. S. Embassy, London, "Report on Bow Street Hearing," Feb. 10, 1950, attached to Atomic Energy Commission Information Memorandum 273/8 (Mar. 8, 1950), 9, DOE; and from Alan Moorehead, *The Traitors* (New York: Harper and Row, 1964), 130–146. See also H. Montgomery Hyde, *The Atom Bomb Spies* (New York: Atheneum, 1980), 125–130.

2. William Skardon's testimony at the hearing, Feb. 10, 1950, p. 8, FBI.

3. Guy Hartcup and T. E. Allibone, *Cockcroft and the Atom* (Bristol: Eng and Hilger, 1984), 148.

4. Moorehead, *The Traitors,* 148–149.

5. Fuchs's confession to Michael Perrin on January 30 is summarized in the memorandum from J. Edgar Hoover to Admiral Sidney Souers, Mar. 2, 1950, HST. See Appendix B.

6. Michael Perrin to the author, May 30 and Aug. 14, 1984.

7. Hyde, *Atom Bomb Spies,* 129–130. On Fuchs's confessions, see also Rebecca West, *The New Meaning of Treason* (New York: Viking, 1964).

8. McDade, "Report," 9.

9. The British press reports are cited in *New York Post,* Feb. 8, 1950; *New York Journal American,* Feb. 11, 1950; *Brooklyn Eagle,* Feb. 10, 1950; *New York Times,* Feb. 11, 1950; *New York World Telegram and Sun,* Feb. 11, 1950.

10. H. B. Fletcher to Hoover, Feb. 9, 1950; A. Rosen to Hoover, Feb. 9, 1950; Hoover to John Cimperman, Feb. 9, 1950, FBI.

11. The transcript of the Bow Street hearing of Feb. 10, 1950, was prepared from notes taken in court by Sergeant H. Holden of Special Branch, Scotland Yard, and given to Cimperman by Commander Burt. Dispatched by Lish Whitson to Hoover, Feb. 13, 1950, FBI.

12. *New York Herald Tribune,* Feb. 11, 1950.

13. *New York Times,* Feb. 12, 1950, 13.

14. Hoover to Cimperman, Feb. 1 and 17, 1950; Fletcher to Ladd, Feb. 17, 1950; J. P. Mohr to Clyde Tolson, Feb. 20, 1950, FBI.

15. McDade, "Report."

16. Bernard O'Donnell, *The Old Bailey and Its Trials* (New York: Macmillan, 1951).

17. The Fuchs indictment terms are discussed in memorandum from A. H. Belmont to D. M. Ladd, Mar. 1, 1950, FBI.

18. *New York Times,* Mar. 2, 1950, 1, 14.

19. Barton L. Ingraham, *Political Crime in Europe: A Comparative Study of France, Germany, and England* (Berkeley: University of California Press, 1979). West, *New Meaning of Treason,* 7.

20. G. Brook-Shepherd, *The Storm Petrels: The Flight of the First Soviet Defectors* (New York: Ballantine, 1977), 155–159, 164–165.

21. William Stevenson, *Intrepid's Last Case* (New York: Villard, 1983), 160–164. Hyde, *Atom Bomb Spies*, 67–68, 71–74. Margaret Gowing, *Independence and Deterrence: Britain and Atomic Energy, 1945–1952* (New York: St. Martin's, 1974), 2: 142.

22. Patrick Devlin, *The Criminal Prosecution in England* (London: Oxford University Press, 1960), 29–35.

23. H. M. Wilson and J. Glickman, *The Problem of Internal Security in Great Britain, 1948–1953* (Garden City, N.Y.: Doubleday, 1954), 77.

24. Leonard Krieger, *The German Idea of Freedom* (Boston: Beacon Press, 1957), 460, 464.

25. Arthur Koestler, in *The God That Failed*, ed. R. H. Crossman (New York: Harper and Row, 1950), 32, 260. Fuchs's confession to Skardon, 4, HST.

26. A. P. French to the author, Aug. 1, 1985, on Fuchs's relationship with Arnold.

27. Rudolf Peierls, *Bird of Passage: Recollections of a Physicist* (Princeton: Princeton University Press, 1985), 223–225.

28. W. A. Brannigan to A. H. Belmont, Apr. 7, 1958; Belmont to W. V. Cleveland, Apr. 3, 1958; Cimperman to Hoover, Nov. 14, 1958, FBI. *Sunday Dispatch*, Apr. 12, 1959, 1.

29. *Daily Mail*, June 24, 1959, 1.

11. A Serious Mistake

1. Kenneth Harris, *Attlee* (New York: Norton, 1958), 442–445.

2. F. Hoyer Millar report, Feb. 8, 1950, FO 371/8161, XCA/5200, AU 1026/2, PRO.

3. Dean Acheson, *Present at the Creation: My Years in the State Department* (New York: Norton, 1969), 321. John Simpson, *The Independent Nuclear State: The United States, Britain, and The Military Atom* (London: St. Martin's, 1983), 84. Margaret Gowing, *Britain and Atomic Energy, 1939–1945* (New York: St. Martin's, 1964), 124. *New York News*, Feb. 10, 1950. AEC commissioners' meetings, nos. 371 and 373, Feb. 14, 1950, DOE. *New York Herald Tribune*, Feb. 28, 1950.

4. AEC commissioners' meetings, no. 379, Mar. 8, 1950, and no. 380, Mar. 14, 1950, DOE.

5. CPC meeting of the American members, Washington, D.C., Apr. 25, 1950, FRUS, 1950, vol. 1: 547–557. See report of AEC Committee of Senior Responsible Reviewers on nuclear espionage by Fuchs, AEC Info memo 273/15, April 1950. On Acheson's meeting with Attlee, see FRUS, 1950, vol. 1: 559–560. Report of the Tripartite Talks on Security Standards, June 19–21, 1950, DOE. Roger Hollis used the phrase "serious mistake."

6. Rudolf Peierls to Chadwick, Nov. 4, 1946, box 223, folder 4, RPP.

7. John Cockcroft, "Atomic Energy History," chap. 5, CKFT. Otto Frisch, *What Little I Remember* (Cambridge: Cambridge University Press, 1979), 200–201. Peierls to Walter Schneir, Feb. 6, 1963, box 197, folder A18, RPP. J. Edgar Hoover to the Attorney General's office, Mar. 10, 1950, FBI. Dee is cited in Guy Hartcup and T. E. Allison, *Cockcroft and the Atom* (Bristol: Eng and Hilger, 1984), 158.

8. Rudolf Peierls, *Bird of Passage: Recollections of a Physicist* (Princeton: Princeton University Press, 1985), 223–225.

9. Peierls to Hans Bethe, Feb. 15, 1950, box 202, folder 17, RPP. Peierls to Nevill Mott, Feb. 16, 1950, box 223, folder 8, RPP.

10. Peierls to Federation of American Scientists, Mar. 1, 1950; G. P. Thompson to Peierls, Mar. 7, 1950, box 223, folder 6, RPP.

11. Lord Cherwell to R. V. Jones, Feb. 2, 1951; Cherwell to H. W. B. Skinner, June 21, 1951, boxes D125 and J117, LCP.

12. George Strauss, "Atomic Energy Programs" (Top Secret), deposit 98, folders 84–86, Attlee Papers, Bodleian Library, Oxford University, Oxford, England.

13. H. Montgomery Hyde, *The Atom Bomb Spies* (New York: Atheneum, 1980), 138–139. *Hansard*, vol. 472, H.C.Deb., 71–72 (Mar. 6, 1950).

14. James Tuck to Cherwell, Mar. 27, 1950, box D246, LCP. Esther Simpson to Peierls, Mar. 27, 1950, box 226, folder 47, RPP. Peierls to Bethe, Mar. 30, 1950, box 202, folder 17, RPP. Peierls to David Brunt, Royal Society, Apr. 24, 1950, box 207, folder C111, RPP.

15. Peierls to *Manchester Guardian,* June 14, 1950, box 223, folder 6, RPP. Peierls, "The Lessons of the Fuchs Case," box 197, folder A16, RPP. Statement, March 1950, British Atomic Energy Scientists' Association; *Bulletin of the Atomic Scientists,* 1950, 185.

16. *New York Times,* Feb. 12, 1950.

17. See Chapman Pincher, *Too Secret Too Long* (New York: St. Martin's, 1984).

18. "Extract from Security Conference Notes Prepared by United Kingdom Representatives Concerning Tripartite Talks on Security Standards at Washington, June 19–21, 1950," DOE.

19. Robert Lamphere to the author, Aug. 25, 1985; see also Robert Lamphere and Thomas Schachtman, *The FBI-KGB War: A Special Agent's Story* (New York: Random House, 1986), 244.

20. Pincher, *Too Secret,* 47–51, 59. S. Cochran, *Big Business in China: Sino-Foreign Rivalry in the Cigarette Industry, 1890–1930* (Cambridge, Mass.: Harvard University Press, 1980).

21. Interview with Sir Michael Perrin, Oxford, Nov. 12, 1985.

22. Nevill Mott, unpublished autobiography, 43. Margaret Gowing, *Independence and Deterrence: Britain and Atomic Energy, 1945–1952* (New York: St. Martin's) 2: 147. Chapman Pincher's article on the "Russian background" of Hollis is in *Daily Express,* June 13, 1985. "T.A. [Tube Alloys] Technical Committee Minutes, May 7, 1942," box 30/3, CHAD I.

23. Pincher, *Too Secret,* 54–55.

24. Alan Moorehead, *Traitors* (New York: Harper and Row, 1964), 128–129. Pincher, *Too Secret,* 57.

25. Pincher, *Too Secret,* 89–92. Nigel West, *The Circus: MI5 Operations, 1945–1972* (New York: Stein and Day, 1983), 142–143. John Saxon to the author, spring 1986.

26. Lish Whitson to Fletcher, Feb. 3, 1950, FBI. Information Office, Department of External Affairs, Ottawa, to Canadian ambassador, Washington, D.C., Feb. 6, 1950, CDEA.

27. *New York News,* Feb. 7, 1950. Canadian ambassador, Washington, to Secretary of State for External Affairs, Ottawa, Feb. 6, 1950, CDEA. James George to George Ignatieff, Mar. 4, 1950, CDEA.

28. Report of the Canadian consul general in New York, Feb. 3, 1950, Record Group 25, B3, vol. 2159, "Espionage. Fuchs, Carl," CDEA.

29. Louis Nichols to Clyde Tolson, Feb. 12, 1950, FBI. *Hansard,* 472: 1545–1546 (Mar. 20, 1950).

30. J. Edgar Hoover to Glen Bethel (Ottawa), Mar. 3, 1950, FBI. D. M. Ladd to Hoover, Mar. 3, 1950, FBI.

31. Bethel to Hoover, Mar. 5, 17, 1950, FBI.

32. *New York Times,* Apr. 6, 1950; *Ottawa Evening Journal,* Apr. 6, 1950; *Montreal Gazette,* Apr. 7, 1950. The fact that Canada had turned over the Halperin address book in 1946 was confirmed by the Information Division of the Department of External Affairs, Apr. 6, 1950, CDEA. *Ottawa Gazette,* May 1, 1950. *Hansard,* 475: 567–568 (May 11, 1950).

33. B. Page, D. Leitsch, and P. Knightley, *The Philby Conspiracy* (New York: Doubleday, 1968), 40–52, 58–61. P. Seale and M. McConville, *Philby: The Long Road to Moscow* (London: Hamilton, 1973), 31–53. E. H. Cookridge, *The Third Man* (New York: G. P. Putnam, 1968), 22–23, 35–36.

34. Malcolm Muggeridge, *Chronicles of Wasted Time,* vol. 2: *The Infernal Grove* (New York: Quill, 1982), 124–125. Hugh Trevor-Roper, *The Philby Affair* (London: William Kimber, 1968), 37.

35. Seale and McConville, *Philby,* 127, 134–135. Cookridge, *Third Man,* 100–101. Trevor-Roper, *Philby Affair,* 73–77.

36. Page et al., *Philby Conspiracy,* 167. Cookridge, *Third Man,* 101. Muggeridge, *Chronicles,* 243. Trevor-Roper, *Philby Affair,* 41.

37. Kim Philby, *My Silent War* (New York: Grove Press, 1968), 186. Seale and McConville, *Philby,* 203–204. Pincher, *Too Secret,* 140. When the British government informed the U. S. Department of State of Philby's appointment on Oct. 21, it reported that he was born in India in 1912, was educated at Cambridge, worked as a *Times* correspondent from 1936 to 1940, and was "attached to a department of the Foreign Office [MI6] 1941–1947." State Department Record Group 59, 701.411/10-2149; National Archives, Washington, D.C. See also Andrew Boyle, *The Fourth Man* (New York: Dial, 1979), 347, and Page et al., *Philby Conspiracy,* 196–197.

38. David Martin, *Wilderness of Mirrors* (New York: Ballantine, 1980), 47, 59. Robert Lamphere to the author, Aug. 13, 1985. D. Sutherland, *The Great Betrayal* (London: Penguin, 1980), 88. Philby, *My Silent War,* 188–202, 223–225. Hyde, *Atom Bomb Spies,* 132.

39. Douglas Hyde is quoted in Boyle, *Fourth Man,* 244–245.

40. John Saxon to the author, March 1986.

12. Science, Secrecy, and Security

1. John Major, *The Oppenheimer Hearing* (New York: Stein and Day, 1971), 307 n. 93. Herbert York, *The Advisers: Oppenheimer, Teller and the Superbomb* (San Francisco: Freeman, 1976), 69. McGeorge Bundy, "The Missed Chance to Stop the H-Bomb," *New York Review of Books,* May 13, 1982, 13–

82. The case that the real decision on the hydrogen bomb was made only on March 10, not January 31, is made by Werner R. Schilling, "The H-Bomb Decision: How to Decide without Actually Choosing," *Political Science Quarterly*, 76 (1961): 24–46.

2. David Lilienthal, *The Journals of David Lilienthal*, vol. 2: *The Atomic Energy Commission Years, 1945–1950* (New York: Harper and Row, 1964), 634.

3. D. H. Ladd to J. Edgar Hoover, Feb. 2, 1950, FBI. Hoover to John Cimperman, Feb. 2, 1950, FBI.

4. Ladd to Hoover, Feb. 3, 1950, FBI.

5. Ibid. Hoover to Sidney Souers, Feb. 6, 1950, HST.

6. *New York Times*, Feb. 5, 1950, 1. *New York Daily Mirror*, Feb. 7 and 10, 1950. *New York Times*, Feb. 4, 1950, 1; *Washington Times-Herald*, Feb. 4, 1950, 1; *Boston Post*, Feb. 4, 1950, 1. *New York Times*, Feb. 6, 1950, 1.

7. *New York Post*, Feb. 10, 1950. *New York Journal American*, Feb. 7, 1950. *Brooklyn Eagle*, Feb. 6, 1950. *New York Post and Home News*, Feb. 7, 1950. *New York Daily Mirror*, Feb. 7 and 10, 1950, 1. *New York Herald Tribune*, Feb. 11, 1950, 1, 4.

8. Lilienthal, *Journals*, 2: 635. H. B. Fletcher to Ladd, Feb. 2, 1950, FBI. The decision not to mention Fuchs's connection with the super was made at AEC meeting no. 364, Feb. 3, 1950, DOE.

9. Lilienthal to Hoover, Feb. 9, 1950, DOE. C. A. Rolander to the file, Feb. 10, 1950, DOE. AEC meeting no. 371, Feb. 14, 1950, DOE. Sumner Pike to Dean Acheson, Feb. 15, 1950, DOE.

10. Lilienthal, *Journals*, 2: 634. Hoover to Tolson, Ladd, and Nichols, 11:02 A.M., 11:35 A.M., and 5:06 P.M., Feb. 2, 1950, FBI. Fletcher to V. P. Keay, Feb. 16, 1950, FBI. Sumner Pike to Russell, Apr. 14, 1950, DOE. Pike to AEC commissioners and general manager, May 4, 1950, DOE.

11. AEC Info Memo 271/6, "Letter to Director of FBI Regarding Dr. K. Fuchs," Feb. 28, 1950, DOE. "Fuchs' Participation in the Thermonuclear Weapons Program at Los Alamos," April 1950, DOE. Report of the Committee of Senior Responsible Reviewers, Los Alamos, to the Atomic Energy Commission, April 1950, DOE. Norris K. Bradbury to Carroll Wilson, Mar. 11, 1950, DOE.

12. Hoover to Souers, Mar. 2, 1950, HST.

13. *New York Journal American*, Feb. 5, 1950, 1. Hoover to Tolson, Ladd, and Nichols, 3:36 P.M., Mar. 10, 1950, FBI. Brien McMahon to Pike, Mar. 17, 1950, DOE.

14. Minutes of meeting, State-Defense Policy Review Group, Feb. 27, 1950, FRUS, 1949, vol. 1: 173.

15. Willard Libby to J. G. Beckerley, Mar. 23, 1950, DOE.

16. AEC meeting no. 385, Mar. 20, 1950, DOE. *New York Times*, *New York Journal American*, *New York Daily Mirror*, and *Brooklyn Eagle*, all Mar. 12, 1950. J. G. Beckerley to Carroll Wilson, Mar. 29, 1950, DOE.

17. Major General Kenneth D. Nichols and Brigadier General Herbert B. Loper, "A Basis for Estimating Maximum Soviet Capabilities for Atomic Warfare," forwarded by Robert LeBaron, chairman, Military Liaison Committee to the AEC, to Secretary of Defense Johnson, Feb. 20, 1950, HST.

18. Louis Johnson to Harry S Truman, Feb. 24, 1950, FRUS, 1950, vol. 1, 538–539.

19. Special committee of the National Security Council to Harry S Truman, Mar. 9, 1950, FRUS, 1950, vol. 1: 541–542. Rosenberg, "American Strategy," 85. Sumner Pike to AEC commissioners and general manager, May 4, 1950, DOE. AEC meeting no. 378, Mar. 7, 1950, DOE. AEC Info Memo 273/9, Mar. 9, 1950, and 273/10, Mar. 10, 1950, DOE.

20. S. A. Blumberg, *Energy and Conflict: The Life and Times of Edward Teller* (New York: G. P. Putnam, 1976), 253. R. Hewlett and O. E. Anderson, *A History of the United States Atomic Energy Commission,* vol. 1: *The New World, 1939–1946* (University Park: Pennsylvania State University Press, 1962), 440.

21. Sumner Pike to AEC commissioners and general manager, May 4, 1950, DOE.

22. AEC meeting no. 416, June 1, 1950, DOE. Pike to McMahon, June 12, 1950, DOE. Hoover to Souers, June 16, 1950, HST. R. W. Cook, Manager, Oak Ridge Operations Office, AEC, to Walter J. Williams, Director of Production, AEC, July 12, 1950, DOE.

23. York, *Advisers,* 79.

24. AEC press release on "Dr. Karl Fuchs," Feb. 2, 1950, DOE. On the declassification meetings of Nov. 14–16, 1947, see C. A. Rolander to file, Feb. 2, 1950, and H. A. Fidler to B. F. Laplante, Nov. 12, 1947, DOE.

25. Margaret Gowing, *Britain and Atomic Energy, 1939–1945* (New York: St Martin's, 1964), 121–123. Minutes of July 15, 1949, meeting, Hickenlooper Papers, Joint Committee on Atomic Energy, "Foreign Exchange Information" folder, HH. On Fuchs's visit to Argonne in 1947, see Hoover to Lloyd Wright, Apr. 5, 1956, and Hoover to Souers, Feb. 6, 1950, FBI. W. H. Zinn to D. Saxe, Manager, AEC Chicago Operations Office, Feb. 3, 1950, DOE.

26. Contrary to the FBI claims, a security check of the British delegates was requested by Mr. Keller of Oak Ridge Security; see D. Dean to T. O. Jones, Aug. 6, 1947, DOE. Also R. F. Bacher to McMahon, Feb. 11, 1950, LANL.

27. Hoover to D. M. Ladd, Feb. 2, 1950, FBI.

28. Minutes of the Combined Policy Committee meeting, Feb. 3 and Dec. 10, 1947, DOE. Andrew Boyle, *The Fourth Man* (New York: Dial, 1979), 295.

29. William Borden to McMahon, June 7, 1951, Records of the Joint Committee on Atomic Energy 1946–1977, Record Group 128, box 316, National Archives. Strauss to Hoover, Jan. 2, 1953, Lewis Strauss Papers, AEC "Security" file, HH.

30. *New York Times,* Feb. 12, 1950. *New York Times,* Feb. 6, 1950, 1. *New York Post,* Feb. 7, 1950.

31. *New York Post,* Feb. 16, 1950. *Bulletin of the Atomic Scientists,* 1950, 68, 94, 180–184. Henry Smyth, "Analysis of Secrecy," AEC 111/25, June 17, 1953, Strauss Papers, HH.

32. *Buffalo Evening News, Houston Post, Indianapolis Times,* and *Nashville Tennessean,* all Feb. 6, 1950.

33. Lawrence K. Smith, *Congressional Record,* Feb. 9, 1950, Appendix, A995. *New York Journal American,* Feb. 12–16, 1950. *Congressional Record,* Feb. 27, 1950, Appendix, A1439. *New York Times,* Mar. 2 and 8, 1950.

34. *New York Times,* Feb. 5, 1950, 1. *New York World Telegram and Sun,* Feb. 4, 1950, 1. *Boston Herald,* Feb. 5, 1950, 1.

35. *New York Post,* Feb. 10, 1950, 1. *New York Journal American,* Feb. 7, 1950.

36. *New York Times,* Nov. 21, 1950. Walter Gellhorn, *Security, Loyalty, and Science* (Ithaca: Cornell University Press, 1950).

37. Hoover to Souers, Feb. 21, 1950, HST. Robert Lamphere and Thomas Schachtman, *The FBI-KGB War: A Special Agent's Story* (New York: Random House, 1986), 134.

38. *New York World Telegram Sun* and *New York Journal American,* Feb. 6, 1950.

39. Hoover to Cimperman, Mar. 15, 1950, FBI.

40. Ronald Radosh and Joyce Milton, *The Rosenberg File; A Search for the Truth* (New York: Holt, Rinehart, and Winston, 1983), 37–39.

41. Cimperman to Hoover, Feb. 12, 1950, FBI. Attorney General to Secretary of State, Apr. 3, 1950, HST. G. W. Perkins, Assistant Secretary of State, to Attorney General, Apr. 14, 1950, and Hoover to Attorney General, Mar. 31, 1950, FBI. Ladd to Hoover, Apr. 28, 1950, FBI. Hoover to Cimperman, May 2, 1950, FBI. Records of the U.S. State Department, 5/AE/57D688, box 18. *New York Daily Telegraph,* May 8, 1950.

42. Atomic Energy Commission Info Memo no. 405, May 11, 1950, DOE. *Hansard,* 89–90 (May 11, 1950). Cimperman to Hoover, May 12, 1950, FBI. Belmont to Ladd, May 18, 1950, FBI.

43. U. S. Embassy, London, to Department of State, May 24, 1950, FBI. Telegram, Clegg to Hoover, May 20, 1950, FBI.

44. Clegg to Hoover, May 22, 1950, FBI.

45. Hoover to Cimperman, May 22, 1950, FBI. Clegg to Hoover, May 23, 1950, FBI.

46. Hoover to Cimperman, May 23, 1950, FBI. Cimperman to Hoover, May 24, 1950, FBI. C. L. Marshall, AEC Deputy Director of Classification, to file, July 18, 1950, DOE.

47. Cimperman to Hoover, May 26, 1950, FBI.

48. *New York World Telegram and Sun* and *New York Mirror,* May 29, 1950.

49. Gold's confession consists of two signed statements to FBI agents T. Scott Miller and Richard E. Brennan, in Philadelphia, May 22 and July 10, 1950, FBI. Department of Justice press release, May 23, 1950, FBI. *New York Times,* May 24, 1950, 1, 21. *New York Mirror,* June 12, 1950.

50. Ladd to Hoover, Feb. 15, 1950, FBI. "Memorandum for ASAC W. M. Whelan," Nov. 3, 1950, FBI. Belmont to Ladd, Feb. 28, 1951, FBI. Belmont and Ladd, "Report on Soviet Atomic Espionage of JCAE," Mar. 22, 1951, FBI. *New York World Telegram and Sun,* Apr. 6, 1951. *New York Mirror,* Apr. 9, 1951.

51. Belmont to Ladd, June 2, 1952, FBI. Belmont to Ladd, July 17, 1953, FBI. Strauss to Hoover, July 15, 1953, FBI.

52. *In the Matter of J. Robert Oppenheimer* (Washington, D.C.: Govern-

ment Printing Office, 1954), 802. See Bryan Laplante to Lewis Strauss, Apr. 9, 1953, Strauss Papers, AEC box 57, HH.

53. SAC Boston to Director, June 8, 1959, FBI. *Christian Science Monitor,* May 11, 1959, 1. *New York Times,* June 24, 1959, 5.

54. *U.S. District Court, Southern District of N.Y., Morton Sobell, Petitioner, against the U.S.A., respondent, 66 civ. 1328,* Aug. 22, 1966, 38, 64, and addendum.

55. T. O'Toole, "Spy's Presence Went Unheeded," *Washington Post,* Aug. 29, 1982. Hans Bethe to the author, Aug. 13, 1985.

13. The Return Home

1. Henry Krisch, *German Politics under Soviet Occupation* (New York: Columbia University Press, 1979), 25.

2. John Kenneth Galbraith, *A Life in Our Times: Memoirs* (Boston: Houghton Mifflin, 1981), 222–223. Jurgen Kuczynski, *Memoiren* (Berlin: Aufbau Verlag, 1983), 416.

3. Richard Mayne, *Postwar: The Dawn of Today's Europe* (New York: Schocken, 1983), 150–151. Martin McCauley, *Marxism-Leninism in the German Democratic Republic: The Socialist Unity Party (SED)* (New York: Harper and Row, 1979), 59.

4. Mayne, *Postwar,* 147–151. McCauley, *Marxism-Leninism,* 63–65. See also Robert J. Donovan, *Tumultuous Years: The Presidency of Harry S Truman, 1949–1953* (New York: Norton, 1982), 50–51. David Childs, *The German Democratic Republic: Moscow's German Ally* (London: Allen and Unwin, 1983), 23–25.

5. Flora Lewis, *Red Pawn: The Story of Noel Field* (New York: Doubleday, 1965), 197. Stewart Steven, *Operation Splinter Factor* (Philadelphia: Lippincott, 1974), 107. Allen Weinstein, *Perjury: The Hiss-Chambers Case* (New York: Knopf, 1978), 455.

6. Weinstein, *Perjury,* 199. Steven, *Splinter Factor,* 72–80.

7. Leonard Mosely, *Dulles: A Biography of Eleanor, Allen and John Foster Dulles and Their Family Network* (New York: Dial, 1978), 48–49, 147–148.

8. Weinstein, *Perjury,* 199. Arthur Koestler, *Scum of the Earth* (1941; reprint, London: Hutchinson, 1968), 7–12. M. Marrus and R. Paxton, *Vichy France and the Jews* (New York: Schocken, 1983), 174–175. Steven, *Splinter Factor,* 80–84. R. H. Smith, *OSS: The Secret History of America's First Central Intelligence Agency* (Berkeley: University of California Press, 1972), 205–212.

9. Mosely, *Dulles,* 171–172. Steven, *Splinter Factor,* 84–86. Smith, *OSS,* 227–228.

10. Steven, *Splinter Factor,* 87–99.

11. Mosely, *Dulles,* 275–277. Steven, *Splinter Factor,* 124–130, 132–141. Lewis, *Red Pawn,* 205–215. Harrison Salisbury, *Moscow Journal* (Chicago: University of Chicago Press, 1961), 61.

12. D. Kartun, *Tito's Plot against Europe: The Story of the Rajk Conspiracy* (New York: International Publishers, 1950), 19–21.

13. Childs, *German Democratic Republic*, 25–27. McCauley, *Marxism-Leninism*, 65–67, 239. Lewis, *Red Pawn*, 225.

14. McCauley, *Marxism-Leninism*, 99–100, 116.

15. Ibid., 182. Jurgen Kuczynski, *Dialog mit Meinem Urenkel: Neunzehn Briefe und Ein Tagebuch* (Berlin: Aufbau Verlag, 1982), 51.

16. *New York Times*, June 25, 1959, 4. *New York Times*, Sept. 1, 1959.

17. Nevill Mott to the author, Aug. 14, 1985. D. L. Kettenacker to the author, Aug. 28, 1984. R. Landshoff to Carson Mark, Mar. 21, 1962, DOE.

Selected Bibliography

Archives

Bodleian Library, Oxford University, Oxford, England
    Clement Attlee Papers
    Rudolf Peierls Papers
    Society for the Protection of Science and Learning Papers
Canadian Public Archives, Ottawa, Canada
    Records of the Department of External Affairs, Record Group 25, B3, vol.
    2159, 1950, file "Espionage: Fuchs, Carl"
Churchill College Archives, Cambridge University, Cambridge, England
    Archives of Sir James Chadwick
    Archives of Sir John Cockcroft
Haverford College Library, Haverford, Pennsylvania
    Quaker Collection
Herbert Hoover Presidential Library, West Branch, Iowa
    Bourke B. Hickenlooper Papers
    Lewis L. Strauss Papers
Los Alamos National Laboratory Archives, Los Alamos, New Mexico
Nuffield College Archives, Oxford University, Oxford, England
    Lord Cherwell (F. A. Lindemann) Papers
Princeton University Press Archives, Princeton, New Jersey
    Documents related to *Smyth Report*
Public Record Office, London, England
    Documents pertaining to internment of aliens
Society of Friends, Wallingford, Pennsylvania
    Pendle Hill Archives
Harry S Truman Presidential Library, Independence, Missouri
    President's Secretary's Files
    National Security Council—Atomic—Russia File
U. S. Central Intelligence Agency Archives, Washington, D.C.
U. S. Department of Energy, Germantown, Maryland

Energy History Archives
Atomic Energy Commission Records
U.S. Department of Justice, Federal Bureau of Investigation, Washington, D.C.
  "Foocase" file on the Klaus Fuchs case of atomic espionage (approximately
  4500 pages)
MI5 Records. "Documents in the Possession of Dr. Klaus Fuchs at the Time of
  His Arrest on 2nd February 1950"
U.S. Department of State
  Documents pertaining to Klaus Fuchs, including, "Report on the Bow Street
  Hearing, February 10, 1950"
U.S. National Archives, Washington, D.C.
  Record Group 77, Records of the Office of the Chief of Engineers, Manhattan
  Engineer District: MED 201, "Fuchs, K., Dr."
  Records of the Joint Chiefs of Staff, 1942–1945

Primary Sources

Acheson, Dean. *Present at the Creation: My Years in the State Department*.
New York: Norton, 1969.

Ball, George W. *The Past Has Another Pattern*. New York: Norton, 1982.

Bethe, Hans. "Comments on the History of the H-bomb." *Los Alamos Science*,
Fall 1982, 43–53.

Born, Max. *My Life and My Views*. New York: Scribner's, 1968.

Brown, A. C., ed. *The Secret War Report of the OSS*. New York: Berkeley,
1976.

Burke, Michael. *Outrageous Good Fortune*. Boston: Little, Brown, 1984.

Cadogan, Alexander. *The Diaries of Sir Alexander Cadogan, 1938–1945*. London: Cassell, 1971.

Calvocoressi, Peter. *Top Secret Ultra*. New York: Pantheon, 1980.

Catchpool, Corder. *On Two Fronts: Letters of a Conscientious Objector*. New
York: Garland, 1972.

Cockburn, Claud. *I, Claud*. London: Penguin, 1962.

Foote, Alexander. *Handbook for Spies*. Garden City, N.Y.: Doubleday, 1949.

French, Naomi Livsay. "Recollections of Klaus Fuchs." Unpublished manuscript,
1985.

Frisch, Otto. *What Little I Remember*. Cambridge: Cambridge University Press,
1979.

Fuchs, Emil. *Die Kraft des Sozialismus*. Rudolfstadt, 1925.

———— *Predigten eines Religiosen Sozialisten*. Gotha: Klotz, 1928.

———— *Von Naumann zu den Religiosen Sozialisten: 1894–1929*. Mannheim,
1929.

———— *Eisenach: Arbeitslosigkeit*. Zurich, 1930.

———— *Die Botschaft der Inneren Lichtes*. Bad Pyrmont: Quaker-Verlag, 1939.

———— *Leonhard Ragaz—Prophet Unserer Zeit*. Oberursel: Kompass Verlag,
1947.

———— *Christentum und Sozialismus*. Offenbach: Bollwerk, 1948.

———— *Marxismus und Christentum*. Leipzig: Kohler und Amelung, 1952.

———— *Christliche und Marxistliche Ethik*. Leipzig: Kohler und Amelung, 1956–1959.

———— *Mein Leben*. 2 volumes. Leipzig: Kohler und Amelung, 1957, 1959.

———— *Christliche Glaube*. Halle, 1958, 1960.

———— *Jesus und Wir*. Bad Pyrmont, 1960.

———— *Der Ruf Jesus Christi*. Hamburg, 1961.

———— *Die Christenheit am Scheideweg*. Berlin: Union Verlag, 1963.

———— *Ruf und Antwort*. Leipzig: Kohler und Amelung, 1964.

Galbraith, John Kenneth. *A Life in Our Times: Memoirs*. Boston: Houghton Mifflin, 1982.

Groves, Leslie M. *Now It Can Be Told: The Story of the Manhattan Project*. New York: Harper and Row, 1962.

Haldane, Charlotte. *Truth Will Out*. New York: Vanguard, 1950.

In the Matter of J. Robert Oppenheimer: Transcript and Hearing before Personnel Security Board and Texts and Principal Documents and Letters. Washington, D.C.: Government Printing Office, 1954.

Joint Committee on Atomic Energy, U.S. Congress. *Soviet Atomic Espionage*. Washington, D.C.: Government Printing Office, 1951.

Kahle, Hans. *Know Your Enemy: Aspects of the German Army's Strategy and Morale*. London: ING, 1943.

———— *Under Stalin's Command*. London, Caledonian Press for the Russia Today Society, 1943.

———— *They Plotted against Hitler*. London: ING, 1944.

———— *Stalin and the Soldier*. London: Russia Today Society, 1948.

Koestler, Arthur. *Scum of the Earth*. 1941. Reprint. London: Hutchinson, 1968.

Krivitsky, Walter. *In Stalin's Secret Service*. New York: Harper and Row, 1939.

Kuczynski, Jurgen. *Hitler and the Empire*. London: Lawrence and Wishart, 1936.

———— *New Fashions in Wage Theory*. London: Lawrence and Wishart, 1937.

———— *Labour Conditions in Western Europe*. London: Lawrence and Wishart, 1937.

———— *Hunger and Work*. London: Lawrence and Wishart, 1938.

———— *Labour's Economic Position*. London: Lawrence and Wishart, 1939.

———— *The Conditions of the Workers in Great Britain, Germany, and the Soviet Union, 1932–1938*. London: Gollancz, 1939.

———— *Freedom Calling!* London: Muller, 1939.

———— *Allies inside Europe*. London: Free Germany League of Culture, 1942.

———— *The Economics of Barbarism*. London: Muller, 1942.

———— *Three Hundred Million Slaves and Serfs*. London: ING, 1942.

———— *British Workers in the War*. N.Y.: International, 1943.

———— *Germany under Fascism*. London: Muller, 1944.

———— *Dialog mit Meinem Urenkel: Neunzehn Briefe und Ein Tagebuch*. Berlin: Aufbau Verlag, 1983.

———— *Memoiren. Die Erziehung des Jurgen Kuczynskis zum Kommunisten und Wissenschaftler*. Berlin: Aufbau Verlag, 1983.

Kuczynski, Robert Rene. *Deutschland und Frankreich*. Berlin: Prager, 1925.

—— *American Loans to Germany*. New York: Macmillan, 1927.

—— *The Balance of Births and Deaths*. New York: Macmillan, 1928.

—— *Birth Registration and Birth Statistics in Canada*. Washington, D.C.: Brookings Institution, 1930.

—— *The Measurement of Population Growth*. London: Sidgwick and Jackson, 1935.

—— *Population Movements*. Oxford: Clarendon, 1936.

—— *Colonial Populations*. London: Oxford University Press, 1937.

—— *The Cameroons and Togoland*. London: Oxford University Press, 1939.

—— *The New Population Statistics*. Cambridge: Cambridge University Press, 1942.

—— *Demographic Survey of the British Colonial Empire*. London: Oxford University Press, 1948.

Lamphere, Robert, and Thomas Schachtman. *The FBI-KGB War: A Special Agent's Story*. New York: Random House, 1986.

Lilienthal, David E. *The Journals of David E. Lilienthal*. Volume 2: *The Atomic Energy Commission Years, 1945–1950*. New York: Harper and Row, 1964.

The Manhattan Project: Official History and Documents. Washington, D.C.: University Publications of America, 1977.

Mott, Nevill. "Autobiography." Unpublished manuscript, n.d.

Muggeridge, Malcolm. *Chronicles of Wasted Time*. Volume 2: *The Infernal Grove*. New York: Quill, 1982.

Nielsen, F. W. *Emigrant für Deutschland*. Darmstadt, 1977.

Office of Strategic Services, *London Special Operations Branch and Secret Intelligence Branch War Diaries*. Frederick, Md.: University Press of America. Microfilm, eight reels.

Parliamentary Debates (Hansard): House of Commons Official Report. London: HM Stationery Office, 1949–1951.

Peierls, Rudolf. *Bird of Passage: Recollections of a Physicist*. Princeton: Princeton University Press, 1985.

Philby, Kim. *My Silent War*. New York: Grove Press, 1968.

Pritt, D. N. *From Right to Left*. London: Lawrence and Wishart, 1965.

Rees, Gorony. *A Chapter of Accidents*. London: Chatto and Windus, 1972.

The Report of the Royal Commission Appointed under Order in Council P.C. 411 of February 5, 1946. Ottawa, 1946.

Roeder, Werner, and Herbert Strauss, eds. *Biographisches Handbuch der deutschsprachigen Emigration nach 1933/International Biographical Dictionary of Central European Emigrés, 1933–1945*. New York: K. G. Saur, 1983.

Smith, Alice K., and Charles Weiner. *Robert Oppenheimer: Letters and Recollections*. Cambridge, Mass.: Harvard University Press, 1980.

Smyth, Henry. *Atomic Energy for Military Purposes: The Official Report of the Development of the Atomic Bomb under the Auspices of the United States Government, 1940–1945*. Princeton: Princeton University Press, 1945.

Strauss, Lewis, L. *Men and Decisions*. Garden City, N.Y.: Doubleday, 1962.

Szilard, Leo. *His Version of the Facts: Selected Recollections and Correspon-*

dence. Edited by S. Weart and G. Szilard. Cambridge, Mass.: MIT Press, 1972.

Truman, Harry S. *Memoirs*. Volume 2: *Years of Trial and Hope*. Garden City, N.Y.: Doubleday, 1956.

Ulam, Stanislas. *Adventures of a Mathematician*. New York: Charles Scribner, 1976.

United States Department of State, Foreign Relations of the United States Series (Washington, D.C.: Government Printing Office, 1949–).

Werner, Ruth [Ursula Kuczynski]. *Sonjas Rapport*. Berlin: Verlag Neues Lebens, 1977.

—— *Olga Benario. Die Geschichte eines tapferen Lebens*. Berlin: Verlag Neues Lebens, 1962.

—— *Uber Hundert Berge. Roman*. Berlin: Verlag Neues Lebens, 1965.

—— *Immer Unterwegs*. Berlin: 1956.

—— *Ein Ungewöhnliches Mädchen*. Berlin: Verlag Neues Lebens, 1958.

Williams, Robert C., and Philip L. Cantelon, eds. *The American Atom: A Documentary History of Nuclear Policies from the Discovery of Fission to the Present, 1939–1984*. Philadelphia: University of Pennsylvania Press, 1984.

Secondary Sources

Accoce, Pierre, and Pierre Quet. *A Man Called Lucy, 1939–1945*. New York: Coward McCann, 1966.

Andrew, Christopher. "F. H. Hinsley and the Cambridge Moles: Two Patterns of Intelligence Recruitment." In *Diplomacy and Intelligence during the Second World War*, edited by Richard Langhorne. Cambridge: Cambridge University Press, 1985.

—— *Secret Service: The Making of the British Intelligence Community*. London: Heinemann, 1985.

—— and David Dilks, eds. *The Missing Dimension: Governments and Intelligence Communities in the Twentieth Century*. New York: Macmillan, 1984.

Badash, Lawrence. *Kapitsa, Rutherford, and the Kremlin*. New Haven: Yale University Press, 1985.

Bentley, James. *Between Marx and Christ. The Dialogue in German-Speaking Europe, 1870–1970*. London: NLB, 1982.

Bentwich, Norman. *The Refugees from Germany, April 1933 to December 1935*. London: Allen and Unwin, 1936.

Berggren, Erik. *The Psychology of Confession*. Leiden: Brill, 1975.

Berghahn, Marian. *German-Jewish Refugees in England: The Ambiguities of Assimilation*. London: St. Martin's, 1984.

Bernstein, Barton J. "Truman and the H-Bomb," *Bulletin of the Atomic Scientists*, March 1984: 11–18.

Bernstein, Jeremy. *Hans Bethe, Prophet of Energy*. New York: Basic Books, 1980.

Beyerchen, A. D. *Scientists under Hitler: Politics and the Physics Community in the Third Reich*. London: Yale University Press, 1977.

Blank, A. S., and J. Maser. *Rote Kapelle gegen Hitler.* Berlin: Verlag der Nationen, 1979.

Blumberg, S. A. *Energy and Conflict: The Life and Times of Edward Teller.* New York: G. P. Putnam, 1976.

Boveri, Margaret. *Treason in the Twentieth Century.* Translated by Jonathan Steinberg. New York: G. P. Putnam, 1963.

Boyle, Andrew. *The Fourth Man.* New York: Dial, 1979.

Brook-Shepherd, G. *The Storm Petrels: The Flight of the First Soviet Defectors.* New York: Ballantine, 1977.

Brown, A. C., and C. B. MacDonald. *On a Field of Red: The Communist International and the Coming of World War II.* New York: G. P. Putnam, 1981.

Burridge, T. D. *British Labour and Hitler's War.* London: Andre Deutsch, 1976.

Butler, E. *Mason-Mac. The Life of Lt. Gen. Sir Noel Mason-MacFarlane.* London: 1972.

Buxton, Dorothy. *The Challenge of Bolshevism: A New Social Ideal.* London: Allen and Unwin, 1928.

Calder, Angus. *The People's War: Britain, 1939–1945.* New York: Pantheon, 1969.

Central Intelligence Agency. *The Rote Kapelle. The Central Intelligence Agency's History of Soviet Intelligence and Espionage Networks in Western Europe, 1936–1945.* Washington, D.C.: University Press of America, 1979.

Childs, David. *The GDR: Moscow's German Ally.* London: Allen and Unwin, 1983.

Clark, R. W. *The Greatest Power on Earth: The International Race for Nuclear Supremacy from the Earliest Theory to Three Mile Island.* New York: Harper and Row, 1980.

——— *Sir Edward Appleton.* Oxford: Pergamon Press, 1972.

——— *Tizard.* Cambridge, Mass.: MIT Press, 1965.

Coates, W. P., and Z. K. Coates. *A History of Anglo-Soviet Relations.* London: Lawrence and Wishart, 1943.

Constantinides, George C. *Intelligence and Espionage: An Analytical Bibliography.* Boulder, Colo.: Westview, 1983.

Cookridge, E. H. *The Third Man.* New York: G. P. Putnam, 1968.

Crossman, R. H., ed. *The God That Failed.* New York: Harper and Row, 1950.

Dallin, David. *Soviet Espionage.* New Haven: Yale University Press, 1955.

Deacon, Richard. *C: A Biography of Sir Maurice Oldfield.* London: Macdonald, 1985.

De Silva, Peer. *Sub Rosa. The Central Intelligence Agency and the Uses of Intelligence.* New York: 1978.

Donovan, Robert J. *Tumultuous Years: The Presidency of Harry S Truman, 1949–1953.* New York: Norton, 1982.

Du Cann, Charles, *English Treason Trials.* London: Frederick Miller, 1964.

Duhnke, Horst. *Die K.P.D. von 1933 bis 1945.* Cologne: Kiepenheuer and Witsch, 1972.

Eggleston, Wilfrid. *Canada's Nuclear Story.* Toronto: Clarke, Irwin, 1965.

Feingold, Henry L. *The Politics of Rescue: The Roosevelt Administration and the Holocaust, 1938–1945.* New Brunswick, N.J.: Rutgers University Press, 1970.

Fisher, John. *Burgess and Maclean: A New Look at the Foreign Office Spies.* London: Robert Hale, 1977.

Foot, Michael. *Aneurin Bevan: A Biography.* Volume 1: *1897–1945.* London: Macgibbon and Kee, 1962.

Fowkes, Ben. *Communism in Germany under the Weimar Republic.* New York: St. Martin's, 1984.

Garlinski, Josef. *The Enigma War.* Scribner's, 1980.

Gellhorn, Walter. *Security, Loyalty, and Science.* Ithaca, N.Y.: Cornell University Press, 1950.

Gilbert, Martin. *Winston S. Churchill.* Volume 6: *Finest Hour, 1939–1941.* Boston: Houghton Mifflin, 1983.

Gillman, P., and L. Gillman. *"Collar the Lot!" How Britain Interned and Expelled Its Wartime Refugees.* New York: Quartet, 1980.

Glees, Anthony. *Exile Politics during the Second World War: The German Social Democrats in Britain.* Oxford: Clarendon Press, 1982.

Gormly, James L. "The Washington Declaration and the 'Poor Relation': Anglo-American Atomic Diplomacy, 1945–1946." *Diplomatic History,* 8 (Spring 1984): 125–143.

Gorodetsky, Gabriel. *Stafford Cripps' Mission to Moscow, 1940–1942.* Cambridge: Cambridge University Press, 1985.

Gowing, Margaret. *Britain and Atomic Energy, 1939–1945.* New York: St. Martin's, 1964.

—— *Independence and Deterrence: Britain and Atomic Energy, 1945–1952.* Volume 1: *Policy Making.* Volume 2: *Policy Execution.* New York: St. Martin's, 1974.

Gramont, Sanche de. *The Secret War: The Story of International Espionage since World War II.* New York: G. P. Putnam, 1962.

Gross, Babette. *Willi Munzenberg: A Political Biography.* Lansing, Michigan State University Press, 1974.

Grossman, Kurt R. *Emigration: Geschichte der Hitler Fluchtlinge, 1933–1945.* Frankfurt am Main: Europaische Verlagsanstalt, 1969.

Gruber, Helmut. "Willi Munzenberg's German Communist Empire, 1921–1933." *Journal of Modern History,* 38 (September 1966): 278–297.

Hauck, H. "Sir Stafford Cripps as British Ambassador in Moscow, May 1940–June 1941." *English Historical Review,* 94 (1979): 48–70; 97 (1982): 332–344.

Harper, Alan D. *The Politics of Loyalty: The White House and the Communist Issue, 1946–1952.* Westport, Conn., 1969.

Harris, Kenneth. *Attlee.* New York: Norton, 1983.

Hartcup, Guy, and T. E. Allibone. *Cockcroft and the Atom.* Bristol: Eng and Hilger, 1984.

Hawker, Pat. "Clandestine Radio: The Early Years." *Wireless World,* January 1982: 34–38; February 1982: 81–83.

Herbig, J. *Kettenreaktion: Das Drama der Atomphysiker.* Munich: Carl Hanser Verlag, 1976.

Herken, Gregg. *The Winning Weapon: The Atomic Bomb in the Cold War, 1945–1950.* New York: Knopf, 1980.

Hewlett, R., and O. E. Anderson. *A History of the United States Atomic Energy Commission,* Volume 1: *The New World, 1939–1946.* University Park: Pennsylvania State University Press, 1962.

Hewlett, R., and F. Duncan. *A History of the United States Atomic Energy Commission.* Volume 2: *Atomic Shield, 1947–1952.* University Park: Pennsylvania State University Press, 1969.

Hinsley, F. H. *British Intelligence in the Second World War.* 3 volumes. New York: Cambridge University Press, 1979–1984.

Hirschfeld, Gerhard, ed. *Exile in Great Britain: Refugees from Hitler's Germany.* New York: Humanities Press, 1984.

Hodges, Sheila. *Victor Gollancz.* London: Gollancz, 1978.

——— *Gollancz: The Story of a Publishing House, 1928–1978.* London: Victor Hull, 1978.

Hohne, H. *Codeword, Direktor: The Story of the Red Orchestra.* New York: Coward, McCann, Geohagen, 1971.

Holloway, David. "Entering the Nuclear Arms Race: The Soviet Decision to Build the Atomic Bomb, 1939–1945." Working Paper no. 9, Woodrow Wilson International Center for Scholars International Security Program. Washington, D.C.: 1979.

Hyde, H. Montgomery. *The Atom Bomb Spies.* New York: Atheneum, 1980.

Hynes, Samuel. *The Auden Generation: Literature and Politics in England in the 1930s.* London: Bodley Head, 1976.

Ingraham, Barton L. *Political Crime in Europe: A Comparative Study of France, Germany, and England.* Berkeley: University of California Press, 1979.

Irving, David. *The German Atomic Bomb: The History of Nuclear Research in Nazi Germany.* New York: Simon and Schuster, 1967.

Isserman, Maurice. *Which Side Were You On? The American Communist Party during the Second World War.* Middletown: Wesleyan University Press, 1982.

Jaeger, Hans. "Refugee Internment in Britain, 1939–1940," *Wiener Library Bulletin,* 9 (September–December 1955).

Jones, Bill. *The Russia Complex: The British Labour Party and the Soviet Union.* Manchester: Manchester University Press, 1977.

Jones, R. V. *Most Secret War: British Scientific Intelligence, 1939–1945.* London: Hamish Hamilton, 1978.

Jones, Vincent C. *Manhattan: The Army and the Atomic Bomb.* Washington, D.C.: Center of Military History, 1985.

Kevles, Daniel, *The Physicists.* New York: Random House, 1971.

Kramish, Arnold. *Atomic Energy in the Soviet Union.* Stanford: Stanford University Press, 1959.

——— *The Griffin.* Boston: Houghton Mifflin, 1986.

Krisch, Henry. *German Politics under Soviet Occupation.* New York: Columbia University Press, 1979.

Kunetka, James. *City of Fire: Los Alamos and the Atomic Age, 1943–1945.* Albuquerque: University of New Mexico Press, 1978.

Kurz, Hans Rudolph. *Nachrichtenzentrum Schweiz.* Frauenfeld: Verlag Huber, 1972.

Lafitte, F. *The Internment of Aliens*. London: Penguin, 1940.

Langhorne, Richard, ed. *Diplomacy and Intelligence during the Second World War*. Cambridge: Cambridge University Press, 1985.

Lewis, Flora. *Red Pawn: The Story of Noel Field*. New York: Doubleday, 1965.

Lewis, John. *The Left Book Club: An Historical Record*. London: Gollancz, 1970.

Lidz, Theodore. *The Origin and Treatment of Schizophrenic Disorders*. New York: Basic Books, 1973.

Macnab, F. A. *Estrangement and Relationship: Experience with Schizophrenics*. Bloomington: Indiana University Press, 1966.

Major, John. *The Oppenheimer Hearing*. New York: Stein and Day, 1971.

Manhattan District History: Project Y, The Los Alamos Project, Berkeley: University of California Press, 1961.

Martin, David. *Wilderness of Mirrors*. New York: Ballantine, 1980.

Matthias, E., and A. J. Nichols, eds. *German Democracy and the Triumph of Hitler*. London, 1971.

Mayer, S. L., and W. J. Koenig. *The Two World Wars: A Guide to Manuscript Collections in the United Kingdom*. London: Bowker, 1976.

Mayne, Richard. *Postwar: The Dawn of Today's Europe*. New York: Schocken, 1983.

McCauley, Martin. *Marxism-Leninism in the German Democratic Republic: The Socialist Unity Party (SED)*. New York: Harper & Row, 1979.

McKay, Alwyn. *The Making of the Atomic Age*. New York: Oxford University Press, 1984.

Merson, A. *Communist Resistance in Nazi Germany*. New York: Humanities Press, 1984.

Montagu, Ewen. *Beyond Top Secret Ultra*. New York: Coward, McCann, Geoghegan, 1978.

Moore, Ruth. *Niels Bohr: The Man, His Science, and the World They Changed*. New York: Knopf, 1966.

Moorehead, Alan. *The Traitors*. New York: Harper and Row, 1964.

Morgan, Kenneth. *Labour in Power, 1945–1951*. Oxford: Clarendon Press, 1984.

Mosely, Leonard. *Dulles: A Biography of Eleanor, Allen, and John Foster and the Family Network*. New York: Dial, 1978.

Northedge, F. S., and A. Wells. *Britain and Soviet Communism: The Impact of a Revolution*. London: Macmillan, 1982.

Page, B., D. Leitsch, and P. Knightly. *The Philby Conspiracy*. New York: Doubleday, 1968.

Pelling, Henry. *The Labour Governments, 1945–1951*. New York: St. Martin's, 1984.

Peretz, M. F. "That Was the War: Enemy Alien," *New Yorker*, Aug. 12, 1985.

Persico, Joseph. *Piercing the Reich: The Penetration of Nazi Germany by American Secret Agents during World War II*. New York: Ballantine, 1979.

Pfau, Richard. *No Sacrifice Too Great: The Life of Lewis Strauss*. Charlottesville: University of Virginia Press, 1984.

Pimlott, Ben. *Labour and the Left in the 1930s*. Cambridge: Cambridge University Press, 1977.

Pincher, Chapman. *Inside Story.* London, 1978.
—— *Their Trade Is Treachery.* London: Sidgwick and Jackson, 1981.
—— *Too Secret Too Long.* New York: St. Martin's, 1984.
Radosh, Ronald, and Joyce Milton. *The Rosenberg File: A Search for the Truth.* New York: Holt, Rinehart, and Winston, 1983.
Read, Anthony, and David Fisher. *Operation Lucy.* New York: Coward, McCann, and Geoghegan, 1981.
—— *Colonel Z: The Secret Life of a Master of Spies.* New York: Viking, 1985.
Reader, W. J. *Imperial Chemical Industries: A History.* 2 volumes. London: Oxford University Press, 1975.
Roeder, Werner. *Die Deutschen Sozialistischen Exilgruppen in Grossbritannien 1940–1945.* Bonn: Verlag Neue Gesellschaft, 1973.
Rogge, John. *Why Men Confess.* New York: Thomas Nelson, 1959.
Rosecrance, R. N. *Defence of the Realm: British Strategy in the Nuclear Epoch.* New York: Columbia University Press, 1968.
Rosenberg, David. "American Atomic Strategy and the H-Bomb Decision," *Journal of American History,* 66 (June 1979): 62–86.
Rositzke, Harry. *The Central Intelligence Agency's Secret Operations.* New York: Crowell, 1977.
Rozental, S., ed. *Niels Bohr.* Amsterdam: North Holland, 1967.
Sanford, Gregory. *From Hitler to Ulbricht: The Communist Reconstruction of East Germany, 1945–1946.* Princeton: Princeton University Press, 1983.
Schafer, Stephen. *The Political Criminal: The Problem of Morality and Crime.* New York: Free Press, 1974.
Scheurig, Bodo. *Free Germany: The National Committee and the League of German Officers.* Translated by Herbert Arnold. Middletown, Conn.: Wesleyan University Press, 1969.
Seale, P., and M. McConville. *Philby: The Long Road to Moscow.* London: Hamish Hamilton, 1973.
Sherman, A. J. *Island Refuge: Britain and Refugees from the Third Reich, 1933–1939.* Berkeley: University of California Press, 1973.
Sherwin, Martin J. *A World Destroyed: The Atomic Bomb and the Grand Alliance.* New York: Random House, 1973.
Simpson, John. *The Independent Nuclear State: The United States, Britain, and the Military Atom.* London: St. Martin's, 1983.
Smith, Bradley. *The Shadow Warriors: O.S.S. and the Origins of the C.I.A.* New York: Basic, 1983.
Smith, R. H. *OSS: The Secret History of America's First Central Intelligence Agency.* Berkeley: University of California Press, 1972.
Stafford, David. *Britain and European Resistance, 1940–1945.* New York: Macmillan, 1980.
Stephan, M. *Die Deutsche Exilliteratur, 1933–1945: Eine Einführung.* Munich: Beck, 1979.
Steven, Stewart. *Operation Splinter Factor.* Philadelphia: Lippincott, 1974.
Stevens, Austin. *The Dispossessed: German Refugees in Britain.* London, 1975.
Stevenson, William. *A Man Called Intrepid.* New York: Holt, Rinehart, and Winston, 1976.

———— *Intrepid's Last Case*. New York: Villard, 1983.

Thomas, Hugh. *John Strachey*. London: Eyre Methuen, 1973.

Tolles, Frederick B. *The Quakers and the Atlantic Culture*. New York: Macmillan, 1960.

Trevor-Roper, Hugh. *The Philby Affair: Espionage, Treason and Secret Services*. London: William Kimber, 1968.

Weart, Spencer. *Scientists in Power*. Cambridge, Mass.: Harvard University Press, 1979.

Weinert, Erich. *Das Nationalkomitee "Freies Deutschland," 1943–1945*. Berlin: Rutten und Loening, 1957.

Weinstein, Allen. *Perjury: The Hiss-Chambers Case*. New York: Knopf, 1978.

West, Nigel. *MI5: The True Story of the Most Secret Counterespionage Organization in the World*. New York: Stein and Day, 1982.

———— *The Circus: MI5 Operations, 1945–1972*. New York: Stein and Day, 1983.

———— *MI6: British Secret Intelligence Operations, 1909–1945*. New York: Random House, 1983.

West, Rebecca. *The New Meaning of Treason*. New York: Viking, 1964.

Wheeler-Bennett, John. *John Anderson, Viscount Waverly*. New York: St. Martin's, 1962.

Whiting, Charles. *The Spymasters: The True Story of Anglo-American Intelligence Operations within Nazi Germany, 1939–1945*. New York: Dutton, 1976.

Wilson, H. M., and J. Glickman. *The Problem of Internal Security in Great Britain, 1948–1953*. Garden City, N.Y.: Doubleday, 1954.

Wyman, David. *Paper Walls: America and the Refugee Crisis, 1938–1941*. Amherst: University of Massachusetts Press, 1968.

York, Herbert. *The Advisers: Oppenheimer, Teller, and the Superbomb*. San Francisco: W. H. Freeman, 1976.

Index